The Idea of
Civil Society

The Idea of
Civil Society

ADAM B. SELIGMAN

THE FREE PRESS
A Division of Macmillan, Inc.
NEW YORK
Maxwell Macmillan Canada
TORONTO
Maxwell Macmillan International
NEW YORK   OXFORD   SINGAPORE   SYDNEY

The Free Press
A Division of Macmillan, Inc.
866 Third Avenue, New York, N.Y. 10022

Maxwell Macmillan Canada, Inc.
1200 Eglinton Avenue East
Suite 200
Don Mills, Ontario M3C 3N1

Macmillan, Inc. is part of the Maxwell Communication
Group of Companies.

Printed in the United States of America

printing number

1 2 3 4 5 6 7 8 9 10

Library of Congress Cataloging-in-Publication Data

Seligman, A.
    The idea of civil society/Adam B. Seligman.
       p.   cm.
    Includes bibliographical references and index.
    ISBN 0–02–928315–9
    1. Civil society. I. Title.
JC336.S38   1992
306.2—dc20   92–19591
                                  CIP

A Klee painting named "Angelus Novus" showes an angel looking as though he is about to move away from something he is fixedly contemplating. His eyes are staring, his mouth is open, his wings are spread. This is how one pictures the angel of history. His face is turned toward the past.

—Walter Benjamin
Theses on the Philosophy of History

Contents

Preface and
Acknowledgments

∾

The idea of civil society has had a long history in the traditions of Western political thought. Its roots go back to Christian natural law speculation, while its early modern articulation in the Scottish Enlightenment has provided the inspiration to more contemporary arguments for its recovery. Resurrected in the 1970s, in the struggles between the Polish Workers' Movement and the State appartus, the concept has, in recent years, been central to political debates in both Eastern and Western Europe as well as in the United States.

In this contemporary "revival" of the idea of civil society, the concept has come to mean different things to different people. Different thinkers have stressed different aspects of the concept as well as different historical sources and traditions as relevant to its contemporary usage. The resulting picture is one of great ambiguity and not a little confusion as the idea of civil society has come to mean one set of principles and practices to thinkers working in the liberal tradition of politics and another to their more conservative critics. Similarly, and perhaps even more importantly, the idea of civil society resonates very differently in the

ix

streets of Bucharest, Budapest, Vilna, or Prague than in Oxford, Princeton, Chicago, or Toronto.

Despite these differing theoretical perspectives and political agendas, what nevertheless makes the idea of civil society so attractive to so many social thinkers is its assumed synthesis of private and public "good" and of individual and social desiderata. The idea of civil society thus embodies for many an ethical ideal of the social order, one that, if not overcomes, at least harmonizes, the conflicting demands of individual interest and social good.

As it is this vision that, I believe, stands at the core of most contemporary attempts to resurrect the idea of civil society, it is this that will form the focus of the following analysis. By properly identifying both the historical and what may be termed philosophical conditions that made this vision possible in the past we may, I hope, arrive at a more coherent understanding of its relevance to contemporary political life, in both the West and the East.

In organizing this inquiry along these lines, the work of many thinkers—however important to the idea of civil society in general—has not been dealt with. Notable perhaps in their absence are Bernard Constant, Lorenz Von Stein, and Antonio Gramsci—all of whom made significant contributions to the idea of civil society in the nineteenth and beginning of the twentieth centuries. Constant's comparison of liberty and civic virtue in ancient and modern societies, Von Stein's attempt to unite legal science with state administration in a philosophical theory of *Verwaltungslehre*, and Gramsci's analysis of the primacy of civil society in opposition to the State as locus for revolutionary praxis, all had direct bearing on the civil society debate. The absence of these and other thinkers from the present work is thus to be understood not in terms of their insignificance for the historical development of any idea of civil society but in terms of the volume's defining and rather circumscribed problematique focused on the ethical component of the idea of civil society.

In some cases, the concerns of these and other thinkers were deemed tangential to or repetitive of our main line of argument while others led us too far afield of the ethical component of civil society per se and more toward a theory of the State. This is true

x

of the work of Lorenz Von Stein. Indeed, this last aspect of the civil society debate, centering more fully on the State/Civil Society dichotomy is much more salient among continental thinkers than Anglo-American ones. Though our own inquiry is oriented more to the tradition emanating from the Scottish Enlightenment than later continental thought (with a few important exceptions) the very reasons for this distinction are, it is hoped, made clear. Ultimately, the various traditions dealing with the idea of civil society are of different relative emphases, to be explained, in part, by the historical conditions pertaining in different countries and periods during the eighteenth, nineteenth and indeed twentieth centuries. My own belief is that the constitutive core of the civil society debate is however strikingly similar and adequately examined through the approach adopted here—the ultimate wisdom of which must be left with the reader to decide.

This book was written in Budapest. It was conceived in Los Angeles (at the gentle prodding of Peter Dougherty of The Free Press) and owes much (perhaps too much) to many years spent in Jerusalem—in practical and theoretical engagement with the constitutive issues of citizenship and so of civil society. In developing my own ideas on the theme of civil society I have incurred immense debts to people in all three cities. To list all those whose thoughts, insights, and actions have contributed to my own ideas would be daunting. However, I would like to thank Marie Heller, Dénes Némedi, and György Csepeli at the Institute of Sociology, Eötvös Loránd University, Budapest, for reading and commenting on various chapters and, together with members of the Sociology of Law Department, for sharing their thoughts and feelings during this period of transition with me.

My own ideas on civil society were further developed during long discussions with Jeffrey Alexander, Ivan Szelényi, Shaul Friedlander, and Amos Funkenstein during the time I spent in Los Angeles. Perhaps, however, they owe most to the hard course in civic education that any resident of Israel must pass, almost every day with each morning's headlines. Here I would especially like to thank Sholomo Fischer, Avishai Ehrlich, Menucha Orushkies, Omar Elhaija, and Uri Ram as only a few among many who contributed to any sense I eventually made of these "headlines." Years of professional association with Erik Cohen, Nachman Ben

Yehuda, and most especially with S.N. Eisenstadt, whose provocative criticism, lucid insights, and standards of intellectual rigor pursued me to both Los Angeles and Budapest, formed, in no small measure, any understanding I may have of the constitutive issues of modern politics and society. The intellectual debt I owe to the latter—notwithstanding our deep disagreements on the idea of civil society—is beyond recompense.

I would also like to thank the Rothchild Foundation for enabling me to participate in the stimulating intellectual environment of UCLA during the 1988–89 academic year and the Fulbright Foundation for enabling me to spend the past two years in Budapest during this critical period of political and social change and transformation.

Finally, and most important, without the love, trust, and hope of my family, of Rahel Wasserfall, and of Sarah Ana Seligman the ideas set forth here would never have been put to paper. Responsibility for all errors and misinterpretations must, nevertheless, remain mine alone.

Introduction

❧

I

However modern (or even postmodern) we take our-selves to be, our sustaining beliefs—in the "Rights of Man," the equality of citizens, the integrity of the person, and freedom of belief—are as old as the revolutions of the eighteenth century. They are rooted in a world that identified the workings of Reason with those of the good life and saw (at least since Immanuel Kant) in the "troika" of Reason, Equality, and the Public Realm the ultimate touchstone of moral beliefs.

We, however, live amid the debris of Reason. The "rights of Reason," as final arbitrators of ethical and moral dilemmas, have in this century increasingly been questioned, most recently by a plethora of postmodern philosophies. This very questioning of first principles brings in its wake a host of additional questions, and those questions define the classical and recently resurrected debates about what constitutes civil society. Thus, the perduring question of how individual interests can be pursued in the social arena and, similarly, the social good in individual or private life is once again a subject of public debate across the political spectrum, not only in the United States but, significantly, in Eastern and East-Central Europe as well. What is ultimately at stake in this question is, of course, the proper mode of constituting society itself, whether in terms of private individuals or of a shared public sphere.

The debate about the direction of civil society has its roots in the historical traditions of Western political theory and social philosophy but ironically now finds itself at center stage in the writings of contemporary observers. Intellectuals of stature such as Charles Taylor, Edward Shils, Michael Waltzer, and Daniel Bell have all been among the contributors to this renaissance.[1] For Daniel Bell the concept of civil society is crucial in understanding the issue of American exceptionalism. In a recent issue of *The Public Interest* he noted that "the demand for a return to civil society is the demand for a return to a manageable scale of social life," one which "emphasizes voluntary association, churches and communities, arguing that decisions should be made locally and should not be controlled by the state and its bureaucracies."[2] Similarly, Charles Taylor posits the idea of civil society as part of any continuing struggle for freedom in the modern world. For Michael Waltzer it points to an achieved synthesis of different values in the search for the "good life."

Broadly stated, the continuing debate over the changing institutional politics of Western democracies (including the very existence of a "public sphere"), as well as the reorganization of the European Economic Community, the revolutions in Eastern Europe in 1989, and the rising tide of national consciousness there, have all led to a renewed interest in civil society.

Thus, for example, Vladimir Tismaneanu has argued that the emergence of civil society through such organizations as Solidarity in Poland, Charter 77 in Czechoslovakia, and the Hungarian National Forum have undermined the authority of the State in Eastern Europe.[3] John Keane has called for a reexamination of Thatcherite policies of privatizing long-established British public service institutions such as broadcasting in the name of a free press "which is held accountable to [its] citizens who work and consume, live and love within an independent, self-organizing civil society."[4] *New Republic* journalist Mickey Kaus has called for an expansion of civil society in America through policies that "induce rich and poor actually to rub shoulders as equals" in improved public schools, communal day care centers, mandatory

2

national service, and other institutions of citizenship. Finally, Anna Quindlen has put the best label on these and other issues by giving her *New York Times* column the name and theme of "Public and Private." In short, this notion of civil society would seem to be one whose time has come again.

This treatise on the idea of civil society will explain this concept, whose importance as a means for understanding contemporary political and social life is increasingly being embraced by thinkers across the political spectrum. As mentioned above, recent writings of both a popular and theoretical nature on the contemporary politics of Europe (East and West) as well as the United States have been returning to this classical concept in an attempt to explain phenomena as diverse as the revolutions of 1989 in Eastern Europe and the nature of "postmodern" society in the industrialized countries of Europe and the United States at the close of the twentieth century.

The very idea of civil society touches on and embraces the major themes of the Western political tradition. Originally posited in the eighteenth century as referring to a realm of social mutuality, in the nineteenth century it was used to characterize that aspect of social existence which existed beyond the realm of the State. It points, in its different articulations, to those elements of both community and individualism that have served to define political thought for the past two hundred years. For civil society is, at the same time, that realm of "natural affections and sociability" recognized by Adam Smith as well as that arena where man "acts as a private individual, regards other men as means, degrades himself into a means and becomes a plaything of alien powers," in Marx's famous characterization of market relations.[5] It is the realm of "rights" but also of property, of civility but also of economic exploitation. It rests on the legally free individual, but also on the community of free individuals. Apart from the State, it is nevertheless regulated by law. A public realm, yet one constituted by private individuals.

Given these very different resonances, it is no wonder that contemporary uses of the term tend to be broad and often lack analytic rigor. The works of writers as diverse as Ferguson and Marx, Hegel and Adam Smith, Tocqueville and Gramsci are all invoked in the contemporary "rediscovery" of civil society.[6] Adding to this confusion is the strange and somewhat asymptotic development of the term itself in the twentieth century. For though ignored for decades by mainstream West European and North American writing on social philosophy and political theory, the idea of civil society continued (and continues) to be hotly debated among intellectuals on the left and critics of both the former state-socialist regimes of Eastern Europe and of postindustrial Western societies. Indeed, it is to a large extent only in the wake of the recent transformations of East European politics and society that the idea of civil society has once again gained currency among wider sectors of the academic, professional, and reading public.

Given this state of affairs, and especially the current renaissance of a 250-year-old concept long relegated to disuse, it would seem imperative to clarify and to present a clear exposition of the developing idea of civil society, its historical antecedents, the social context of its emergence and transformation (in the eighteenth and nineteenth centuries), and its continuing relevance to the problems and crises of modern existence (in both the West and the formerly communist East European societies). It is precisely this set of themes that the present volume on the idea of civil society will address. Moreover, I wish to stress here at the outset that the focus of this essay will be on the concept of civil society as a concept and not as an existing social or historical reality. For before we can fruitfully make use of this notion as either a descriptive or (as Clifford Geertz would remind us) a prescriptive model of (or for) social reality, we must clarify just what intellectual baggage we carry with us on the *portmanteau* of civil society. Consequently, this short inquiry will be devoted in the main to an exploration of those ideational positions which were central to the original articulation of the idea of civil society and without which any attempt to resurrect this concept must remain meaningless. This intervention in the current debates around civil society thus aims at clearing the necessary ground upon which any contemporary usage of the idea of civil society must be based. As an essay in the sociology of knowledge it hopes to clarify certain intellectual positions, to bring others, less immediately manifest, to light, and, in so doing, perhaps to make the current "idols of the marketplace" somewhat less attractive.

4

II

The concept of civil society as a collective entity existing independently from the State has, as noted, been critical to the history of Western political thought. In its different interpretations it has been central to the development of both the liberal-parliamentary tradition and the socialist, Marxian one. And although the concept of civil society was defined differently by the different theorists of the French, Scottish, and German Enlightenments, what was common to all attempts to articulate a notion of civil society was the problematic relation between the private and the public, the individual and the social, public ethics and individual interests, individual passions and public concerns.

It was this problem, or set of problems, that stood at the heart of the classical eighteenth- and nineteenth-century attempt to expound a theory of society, and it is this set of problems which continues to define the most salient issues of political and social life today. For if the sense of a shared public is constitutive of civil society, so is the very existence of the private. It is after all the very existence of a free and equal citizenry—of that autonomous, agentic individual—of the private subject that makes civil society possible at all. For civil society is, most essentially, that realm where the concrete person—that particular individual, subject to his or her own wants, caprices, and physical necessities—seeks the attainment of these "selfish" aims. It is that arena where the "burgher" as private person seeks to fulfill his or her own interests. Civil society is thus that arena where—in Hegelian terms—free, self-determining individuality sets forth its claims for satisfaction of its wants and personal autonomy.

The public space of interaction in civil society is thus a public space only insofar as it is distinguished from those social actors who enter it as private individuals. Where there is no private sphere, there is, concomitantly, no public one: both must exist in dialectic unity for sense to be made of either one.

It is precisely this dialectic and tension between public and private, as constitutive of civil society, that I will develop in the following essay. This work will focus on precisely that definition of the individual—as moral agent and as subject without whom no cogent theory of civil society is possible. This inquiry into the constitutive individual or private aspect of civil society must, of necessity, be historical in nature. For the differentiation of civic selfhood from communal or collective attributes was a process that, in Western Europe, took place over hundreds of years. It owed much to the religious doctrines of sectarian or ascetic Puritanism, from which the notions of the individual as possessing metaphysical and moral value emerged. That selfhood, which, as both Marcell Mauss and Max Weber realized, was validated in the *Déclaration des Droits de l'homme et du citoyen*—stemmed, ultimately, from a religious paradigm whose roots were firmly tied to Reformation religion.[7] Civil society, as originally articulated in the Scottish Enlightenment, thus owed—as we shall come to see—as much to Revelation as to Reason. And it is to relevation as well as to reason that we must turn to understand not only the original coherence and clarity of the idea of civil society but also the severe problems inherent to any contemporary attempt to rescue the notion of civil society and to use it as a model for social organization. As I hope to show, it was precisely these two sources—reason and revelation—and a unique, fragile and historically contingent balance between them that infused the original notion of civil society with its overwhelming saliency, but which today can no longer provide the ground for contemporary arguments for civil society.

In this context, contemporary Eastern Europe presents an interesting example of the problems incumbent on any contemporary usage of the term civil society. For while in Western Europe and in America many scholars are lamenting "The Fall of Public Man" and the dissolution of the ties of civil society (a fear already present in Tocqueville), in Eastern Europe an attempt appears to be under way to reconstitute civil society, and with it an autonomous public domain.[8] Given the current interest in and concern over the "crises of postindustrial (or 'postmodern') societies," the events in Eastern Europe are thus of great significance. On the one hand, Eastern Europe would seem to be almost a latter-day "laboratory" of the Scottish Enlightenment and of the passions, interests, and concerns that defined political thought at the onset of the modern era. Significantly, the current social and political changes in Eastern Europe would seem to present a unique historical reenactment of the development of an autonomous, self-

6

regulating domain independent of the State. At present, in Hungary, Poland, Czechoslovakia, and other East-Central European countries, the nature of the relationship between civil society and the State is being rethought and is undergoing the most radical transformations.

Whereas the Western tradition of parliamentary, liberal democracy has always maintained the primacy and autonomy of civil society in its relation with the State, East (and East-Central) European countries have been characterized by a subsuming of the interests of civil society to those of the State. This tradition is currently being transformed in the most fundamental manner. The drafting of new Constitutions, the growth of free political parties, and the development of market economies have all led East European politicians, intellectuals, and indeed citizens to rethink the very constitutive premises of social and political organization. What is being forged in contemporary Eastern Europe, according to some observers, is nothing less than an experiment in civil society as a collective entity free of State regulation.

Yet, on closer scrutiny, there are serious problems with this vision of Eastern Europe as the Scottish Enlightenment *revividus*. One has only to look at contemporary Hungary to see the markedly *Realpolitik* character of the use of civil society in today's Eastern Europe. A banner for the opposition between 1987 and 1989, the term became, with the fall of the communist regime, a legitimizing device for the new government. The quest for the realization of civil society was, it was argued, fulfilled with an elected Parliament and the Antal government of the Hungarian Democratic Forum. Civil society was realized in—the new State apparatus.

This what may seem at first sight a cynical use of the idea of civil society has deep roots in the concept's very emergence in Eastern Europe. For it was after all in Poland in the late 1970s that the idea of civil society reemerged and became an important part of political discourse. But to understand the saliency of this idea in Poland we must also recall the tragic history of that country. Divided between Prussia, Austria, and Russia in 1772, 1793, and 1795, its revolutions of the nineteenth century crushed by Czarist Russia, enjoying a brief period of independence (as an authoritarian and militant State under Pilsudski) in the interwar years and then under the domination of Germany from 1939 and of the Soviet Union from 1945, Poland never had an autonomous State in modern times. The idea of civil society thus provided the only ideological alternative to foreign domination. Here too we see—as will be dealt with at greater length in the following chapters—the *Realpolitik* nature of civil society in Eastern Europe and its lack of that transcendental (what I earlier referred to somewhat meta-phorically as revelatory) dimension, which was critical to the eighteenth-century idea of civil society. Thus, for all its popularity as a theme of international conferences, journal articles, and tele-vision debates in Eastern Europe, the concept is, metaphorically speaking, truncated, lacking that one important aspect of its ear-lier incarnation and hence, in today's East European political de-bates of logistical and tactical and not of substantive value.[9]

A similar dynamic, as well as lacunae in the necessary precon-ditions for civil society, can be found in the West European and North American contexts, where the idea of civil society is also being "rediscovered." Indeed the current transformations in East-ern Europe are themselves matched by a concomitant restructur-ing of political action and thought in the West European and North Atlantic countries, particularly the United States. The United States, which, in contrast to both Eastern and Western Europe, always lacked a coherent concept of the State, has tradi-tionally been presented as a model of civil society. Yet in the closing decades of the twentieth century the adequacy of this model is increasingly being questioned.

Any reading, however cursory, of the newspapers brings one face to face with those issues of individual rights and entitle-ments, public regulation and private liberties which stand at the core of civil society. Whether in the ethical dilemmas arising from biotechnology (IVF-GIFT of donated ova, surrogate motherhood, or artificial insemination), religious beliefs that stand in conflict with modern medical practice (as the tragic case of the Christian Science couple in Boston), the debates over corporate ownership and worker participation, or the legislation of antidrug laws—all are contemporary issues that question the existing synthesis of boundaries between the public and the private, the limits placed on individual liberties, and essentially the proper conceptualization of the social good and its relation to individual rights, responsibilities, and freedoms.

In fact, the increasingly problematized relation of the individual to the social whole can be noted in the subtle shift of social protest and its slogans from "All power to the people" (of the 1960s) to "the personal is political" (of the 1970s and 1980s). Flying in the face of traditional politics (of both liberal and socialist intervention), this attitude has been increasingly prominent in institutional politics of the 1980s. It has been manifest in such phenomena as the growth of new political movements oriented to demands not hitherto considered political in nature; in the practice of such movements involving noninstitutional and nonconventional means of political participation and in fact in a protracted struggle in different institutional realms (health care, welfare, and educational entitlements and the definition of the "domain" of women in society) over the very definition of the boundaries of public and private, and indeed of the person *per se*.[10] The common thread running throughout all these different themes is, however, a concern to reassert (and often redefine) a sphere of civil society (or civil life) beyond the State and yet transcending purely individual existence.

In some cases the (often problematic) relation of contemporary politics to the classical conceptualizations of civil society is more or less consciously realized. The Women's Movement provides what is perhaps the best example of a contemporary political movement that consciously sets out to revise the tenets of Western political theory. The writings of Carole Pateman on "The Fraternal Social Contract" provide a clear illustration of just such a principled challenge to the constitutive (and, as she would claim, gender-based) categories of Western political thought.[11] In other cases the bearing of classical political theory on contemporary politics is less clear to social actors and activists (as for instance in the cases of the "Animal Rights Movement" and the ecology movement, which can be seen as imbuing natural phenomena—the oceans, whales, trees, etc.—with "rights" and thus bestowing upon them the status of citizens).[12] In all cases, however, a proper appreciation of the underlying issues can be achieved only in terms of their relation to the concept of civil society as both a historical and an analytical tool for political analysis.

III

In the following, I hope to provide just such a context for understanding contemporary issues by stressing both the historical development and the continuing importance of the idea of civil society as part of our conceptual apparatus. The volume is organized both thematically and chronologically. It begins by tracing the development of the concept of civil society from its origins, rooted in natural law theory, through its increasing sophistication as an independent entity, autonomous of and sometimes in conflict with the State. The first chapter is devoted to writings of the classical tradition, emphasizing the roots of the concept in certain aspects of medieval Christian thought. The history of the idea of civil society from John Locke through the thought of the Scottish Enlightenment and to Karl Marx is analyzed in light of both the analytic contributions of and the contradictions inherent in the idea of civil society in the eighteenth and nineteenth centuries.

The aim of this analysis is to arrive at the core component of the classical idea of civil society as an ethical vision of social life. By so doing we shall be in a better position to assess the continuing importance of this idea in nineteenth-century theories of democracy, citizenship, and participatory politics and, more importantly, to view what aspects of the classical vision can or cannot be incorporated (or extended) into the more contemporary pursuit of civil society.

Thus while historical progression of the concept traces the early modern articulation of civil society from the mid-eighteenth to the mid-nineteenth century, its more concrete or political embodiment diverged radically in the following era. For following this period the concept developed along two antithetical lines. One—what may be called the post-Hegelian or Marxist tradition—stressed the contradictions inherent in civil society and their resolution in the political realm of the State. It is this tradition which influenced and in a sense defined the history of socialist thought until today and which is being radically rethought in contemporary Eastern Europe.

The second tradition, which may be broadly termed Anglo-American in origin, was rooted in the thought of the Scottish

Enlightenment and continues to define more liberal positions on the nature of society, the individual, and the State. This tradition posits society as a self-regulating realm, the ultimate repository of individual rights and liberties, and a body that must be protected against incursions of the State. It was, not surprisingly, this tradition that profoundly influenced the sociological tradition itself, mainly through the epistemological assumptions incorporated in Durkheim's writings. As we shall see, current attempts to redefine the relevance of civil society within this sociological tradition cannot bypass Durkheim's legacy, and with it certain assumptions on the nature of the individual and society that are, however, increasingly problematic.

These two traditions, drawing on different assumptions about the nature of man and of society, have in recent years been the subject of renewed scholarly interest among those concerned with the sources of the European and trans-Atlantic political tradition. Rooted on the one hand in a dual vision of both the ascendancy of Reason (or, at very least, reason) and the autonomy (if not, *pace* Durkheim, sacrality) of the individual conscience both traditions carried with them a further set of defining characteristics as well. In the second chapter we shall therefore analyze not only the grounding of both traditions in the ideas of reason and of the individual but also the unique manner in which these united, in the eighteenth century, with certain assumptions about the existence of a transcendental sphere in and through which the belief in both Reason and the individual was legitimized.

It was, as we shall see, on the twin pillars of "Reason" and "Revelation" that the unique balance between public and private, universal and particular interests that defined civil society was maintained. In this context, we stress the importance of the Reformation and the cultural assumptions of ascetic Protestantism in the construction of the idea of civil society, especially in that one society which has been presented (rightly or wrongly) as a model for modernity: the United States.

The first chapter can thus be read as a more or less straightforward history of ideas—albeit from a specific perspective, i.e., that which sees civil society as a mode of overcoming and synthesizing the emergent contradictions between public and private existence in the eighteenth and nineteenth centuries. The second chapter is much more along the lines of a historical sociology. It attempts to uncover those historical and what we may term, following Max Weber, ideational conditions or "world images" which made the positing of this synthesis possible.[13] It was, as we come to see, no mere coincidence that the United States was posited, in the eighteenth century and for many today as well, as the paradigm or model for civil society. The particular terms of defining individual and social existence in the United States are presented as both a model for the European idea of civil society and as the result of a unique historical configuration.

Chapter 3 explores how the eighteenth-century idea of civil society was transformed in the nineteenth-century debates over citizenship. The ideas and practices of citizenship are presented as the concrete venues through which the rather amorphous and labile ideas of the eighteenth century were institutionalized within the organizational and administrative frameworks of the nation-state. In this context a peculiar "paradox" of institutionalization is noted—that every extension of citizenship (whether in the franchise in the nineteenth century or in more contemporary ideas of entitlements) also undermines that very mutuality and communality upon which citizenship and civil society are based. These developments are placed in the context of classical (sociological) and more contemporary debates over "modernity" and the changing definitions of public and private spheres therein. The concept of civil society in its different interpretations is seen to be central in all attempts to analyze the predominant features of the modern world order and its changing nature in the late twentieth century. An abiding contradiction is seen to exist, however, between the premises of the different postmodern philosophies and other critics of "modernity" and those of the civil society tradition rooted in a belief in the transcendence of Reason. This contradiction is analyzed in terms of the collapse of that synthesis between the public and the private which was central to the idea of civil society and which, though no longer tenable, continues to make the idea of civil society so attractive to social theorists and activists at the end of the twentieth century.

Chapter 3 thus continues the theoretically informed historical and sociological approach developed in Chapter 2, but brings the analysis forward into the nineteenth and twentieth centuries and

12

those problems attendant upon the definition and practice of citizenship in the modern world.

Chapter 4 approaches somewhat the same terrain, but from a very different perspective. The nineteenth-century idea of citizenship as an institutional form of social relations is presented in a comparative historical and contemporary perspective. The different resonances of civil society as citizenship in the West and in East-Central Europe are compared and contrasted in terms of the very different historical development of the respective societies. These differences are studied most especially in relation to the problem of national unity and ethnic fragmentation and the effect of these on any meaningful concept of civil society in contemporary East-Central Europe.

Further contrasts with Israel are briefly noted to highlight what is the central and organizing theme of this chapter, the relation between the terms of trust in society and the possible existence of a civil society. Ultimately, it is argued that the problems of civil society—in the West as in East-Central Europe—are, in essence, the problems of constituting trust in society. Moreover, the contrasting definitions and criteria of trust in the West and the East (along universal, general, or circumscribed, particular lines) goes a long way in explaining the very different sets of problems faced by the different societies in revitalizing any idea of civil society. It is, finally, the intractable difficulties in theorizing any concrete and meaningful criteria of trust in modern, rationalized, and highly differentiated societies that make all contemporary (Western) attempts to reconstitute civil society as idea, or, more pointedly, as ideal, so difficult. In East-Central Europe, a different and perhaps more formidable set of obstacles is seen to hold, as the historical conditions of nation-formation together with the social dislocation caused by the transition to privatization and a market economy all contribute to a continued circumscription of the terms of trust in society. These are analyzed in term of the resurgence of national identities and, in certain contexts, of a renewed role of religion and of the Church as a political actor.

In concluding, some of the more contemporary theoretical (and practical) positions on the idea of civil society in the West and in East-Central Europe are addressed. An important distinction is drawn between the political, social-scientific, and normative uses of the concept as well *as* of its different resonances in different societies. These distinctions, and with them the very different strands that make up the contemporary idea of civil society, are very much our shared heritage—to make of them what we will.

CHAPTER 1

The Modern Idea of Civil Society

I

Much like today, the emergence of the idea of civil society in the later seventeenth and eighteenth centuries was the result of a crisis in social order and a breakdown of existing paradigms of the idea of order. The general crises of the seventeenth century—the commercialization of land, labor, and capital; the growth of market economies; the age of discoveries; and the English and later North American and continental revolutions—all brought into question the existing models of social order and of authority. Whereas traditionally the foundation or matrix of social order was seen to reside in some entity external to the social world—God, King, or even the givenness of traditional norms and behavior itself—those principles of order became increasingly questioned by the end of the seventeenth century. By the eighteenth century, people began increasingly to turn inward, to the workings of society itself, to explain the existence of the social order. The execution and more importantly, the trial of Charles I in 1649 (which put the King firmly under the laws of the Realm),

15

the incipient market economy, the Physiocratic doctrine of the economic as a self-regulating realm, the discovery of diverse traditions and models of organizing social life in non-European lands, as well as the later eighteenth-century image of a clockmaker God, all brought into question the idea of the source of social order as external to society.

The image of civil society as a model for conceiving the workings of society and of social order emerged from within this major and radical reorientation of European social thought in the seventeenth and eighteenth centuries. In terms of political theory proper, this was evident in a renewed and salient concern for theorizing the idea of the "contract" as the basis of political authority and social order.[1] The break with past traditions and customs—as the binding forces of society—engendered the search for new principles of moral unity within (and earlier, with Grotius for example, between) societies. The obligations implied by contract and the necessary and complementary idea of the agentic and autonomous individual upon which the contract rested were both formidable concepts in the seventeenth- and eighteenth-century search for a new model of the social order.

Not surprisingly, this search for new models of social order was characterized by both a reworking of existing intellectual traditions and a search for new ground. In this chapter we shall thus trace the emergence, or perhaps more properly the reemergence, of the early modern idea of civil society in the thought of John Locke, the Scottish Enlightenment, and the writings of Immanuel Kant, G. W. F. Hegel, and Karl Marx. This is admittedly but one strand of the modern conception of civil society, but an important one, which reveals some of its most salient components, especially in terms of the idea of civil society as a moral or ethical vision or representation of social life.[2] In beginning our analysis of civil society with these thinkers we wish to set out the parameters of the classical concept in order, in the following chapters, to view their role in influencing later political and social theory as well as institutional practice.

Just as many contemporary eighteenth-century thinkers are not mentioned (Montesquieu and Rousseau, for example), so too the entire range of medieval political traditions that influenced early modern thought is not fully explored. Many aspects of Western

16

political theory, such as the doctrine of corporations or of representative institutions, or Marsilius of Padua's (d. after 1342) distinction between the *universitas civium* (the people) and the *pars principans* (the ruler), which relegated sovereignty to the former alone, played a role in the development of the civil society tradition.[3] Some of these will be addressed in different contexts and some not at all. Here we shall be concerned with only a single central aspect of earlier political theory: the natural law tradition. For the medieval and early modern tradition of natural law speculation was one of the most important components of the existing political and philosophical traditions that served as a fulcrum for the idea of civil society in the eighteenth and nineteenth centuries.

II

The idea of a universal law of nature arising both from a natural (or, later in Christianity, a Godly) providence and from the workings of right reason in the human soul emerged first among the Stoic school of philosophers with the breakdown of the Greek city-state.[4] The destruction of the polis and with it of the intimate bonds between the individual and the community led to an incipient atomistic conception of individual existence whose interaction had now to be conceived in terms of some universally valid rule of justice.[5] A new framework—normative as well as descriptive—for positing the social order had to be conceived. Stoic philosophy, especially that of the later Stoa—of oneness with the moral perfection of the natural order—emerged as one of the most important visions for the later development of European political theory.[6] Perhaps the most articulate vision of this law was offered by Cicero, who affirmed:

> There is in fact a true law—namely right reason—which is in accordance with nature, applies to all men and is unchangeable and eternal. By its commands it summons men to the performance of their duties; by its prohibitions it restrains men from doing wrong. Its commands and prohibitions always influence good men but are without effect upon the bad. To invalidate this law by human

17

legislation is never morally right, nor is it permissible ever to restrict its operation, and to annul it wholly is impossible.[7]

A set of fundamental or ultimate principles of justice—rooted in the cosmic order itself—is thus seen to stand at the basis of all enacted, positive law. It was this idea of ultimate, axiomatic principles of justice and morality, as the foundation of law, that was to play a crucial role in all further attempts to develop the natural law tradition from John of Salisbury in the twelfth century, St. Thomas Aquinas in the thirteenth, and Nicolas of Cusa in the fifteenth, through the *Vindiciae Contra Tyrannos* in the sixteenth century, to the writing of Hugo Grotius in the seventeenth.

The incorporation of natural law theory by the Church Fathers however, profoundly mediated certain of its fundamental premises in line with the new civilizational vision of Christianity, which emerged in late antiquity. Although in its particulars, as well in its general contours, the Christian vision of natural law shared much with its Stoic predecessors, there was a marked change in the fundamental status of natural law relative to the new salvational doctrines of Christianity.[8] The most significant change in the original natural law doctrine that occurred with its incorporation into Christianity was its "denaturalization."[9] The sources of natural law were no longer seen to be immanent in the workings of the world, but the subject of divine will.[10] While the original natural law doctrine saw it emanating equally from the natural order of things and from man's own reason (indeed as expressing, among the Stoics, the ideal unity of both), in its Christian articulation natural law was subordinated to the transcendental dictates of the divine order. As the ninth-century Benedictine Radbertus discerned, "the laws of God do not depend on the nature of things, but the laws about the nature of things flow from the laws of God."[11] And although a rooting of natural law in Divine Providence existed among such thinkers as Cicero, the radically transcendent and revelatory components of the Christian vision brought a new hierarchical understanding to the relations between the transcendent sources of natural law and natural law itself. The social implications of this distinction were felt in the continuing relative indifference of the Church to the existing institutions of the Empire.

18

In the middle ages, however, the Thomistic ethic, modifying Stoic and Patristic principles, posited a much stronger relation between the existent institutions of the State and the dictates of Natural Law.[12] There was in the thought of St. Thomas Aquinas a rapprochement between the institutions of society, of private property, slavery, the patriarchal family—all conceived in terms of natural law—and those of Christian morality that was not present in early Church thought.[13] Indeed, in the thought of Aquinas, the State and its political institutions were posited as the natural expression (and indeed the embodiment) of the human moral order.

This was the great genius of the Thomistic ethic, which in one and the same stroke both absolutized the long-standing contradiction in Christian civilization between nature and grace and posited the means for their reconciliation though a combination of Aristotelian ideas of reason and neo-Platonic mysticism.[14] On the one hand, the integrated ethic of the Thomistic system posited reason and natural law as essential steps toward the realization of the Christian moral vision. On the other, it maintained their subordinate position to the sacramental, ecclesiastical, and miraculous realm of divine grace. In the Thomistic system, the divine law did not contradict or annul the law of nature (or the existing political order) but came to supplement it. Consequently, the ends and purposes of the Political Order—of the State—were firmly tied to those of the divine law, of furthering the moral ends of Christianity.

The late sixteenth and early seventeenth centuries saw a revival of natural law theory that took place within the context of the great continental debates over the constitution of sovereignty in the State—in the ruler or the people—over the divine right of Kings and the right of resistance, all of which were formulated in response to the dual challenges of the Reformation and the rise of absolutist political centers. In the preceding period, the articulation of legal doctrines by such legal-humanists as Bartolus, Alciato, and Salamonio tended to ignore the relevance of natural law theory and to base a theory of rights on *ius gentium* or positive law.[15] Relegating the *ius naturale* to the "presocial" stage of human existence (that common to all animals), the legal-humanists stressed the importance of *ius gentium* as the basis of the (contractual) mutual obligations that constitute civil society. Within this tradition the right of resistance to an unjust ruler was formulated in terms of the contractual elements (and, in the case of just resistance, their abrogation), which stood at the core of social life.

The issues of sovereignty and of resistance to royal rule dramatically changed, however, with the emergence of both absolutist political centers and Reformation religion. The problem of legitimizing (or condemning) resistance to an un-Christian ruler formed the basis of both Huguenot and English Calvinist political theory as well as of the Thomistic revival of the Counter-Reformation. In the case of the former, who were in fact influenced by humanist perspectives, the natural law tradition was fundamentally transformed. In the thought of such reformers as George Buchanan (1506–82) in England and Johannes Althusius (1557–1638), natural law theory developed along markedly political grounds, based on rights and hence emancipated from the constraints of theology and jurisprudence.[16] This interpretation was, in a sense, a continuation of that humanist perspective which stressed enacted, positive law over natural law. (Indeed early Huguenot reformers such as Beza, who had studied in the institute of Alciato, and Morney did not make use of natural law in their defense of resistance to unjust rulers).[17] The "rationalization" of natural law, on the principles of right reason, contract, and individual consent, was in turn developed more methodically by Hugo Grotius, the "founder" of modern natural law theory.[18]

With Grotius there is almost a return to pre-Christian notions of natural law, that is to say, to the idea of natural law as founded on reason and not on revelation. Abjuring theological speculation and the concomitant validation of natural law in terms of either scripture or the authority of the Church, Grotius based the primacy of natural law upon rational axioms—akin to mathematical propositions that could be intuited by everyone (significantly by both Catholics and Protestants). While in the early seventeenth century—and De juri belli ai pacis was first published in 1625—it was still inconceivable to posit the sources of natural law without reference to God, the relation between the principles of natural law and God's will are, in Grotius, very different from those of medieval political theory.

20

> The law of nature is a dictate of right reason, which points out that
> an act, according as it is or is not in conformity with rational na-
> ture, has in it a quality of moral baseness or moral necessity; and
> that, in consequence, such an act is either forbidden or enjoined by
> the author of nature, God.[19]

Godly consent to the dictates of natural law and right reason is, in
the above, a derivative principle and not a constitutive one. This
is made very clear further along, where Grotius posits: "Just as
even God, then, cannot cause that two times two should not
make four, so he cannot cause that which is intrinsically evil be
not evil."[20] We are then, with Hugo Grotius, at the dawn of a new
era in the conceptualization of the natural law tradition where the
relations between worldly-human reason and Godly will as the
sources of the moral order begin a major reorientation.

The tradition of natural law provided as it were the bases for
the development of that strand of social thought we identify with
the idea of civil society. Its continuing relevance was felt in the
eighteenth century, not only in the arguments for independence
from the English crown advanced by the thirteen colonies, but—
and closer to our concerns—as one of the fundamental intellectual
traditions taught in Scottish universities at that time.[21] The traditions of moral philosophy that we associate with the Scottish
Enlightenment and out of which the modern idea of civil society
emerged were steeped in natural law speculation and in the writings of Cicero, Grotius, Puffendorf, and Barberyrac.

Its importance in terms of the "transcendent" rooting of natural
rights was, however, no less salient in the thought of John Locke
(if not more so), without whom no appreciation of the modern
idea of civil society can proceed. Locke, who is often seen—quite
possibly mistakenly—as one of the most important precursors of
modern individualism and so of a "liberal" reading of civil society, was himself in debt to the theorists of natural law for providing the necessary "transcendental" preconditions of his theory
of civil society.[22] And if by the eighteenth century the transcendent aspects of the Lockean vision were already being replaced by
the ideas of moral sentiments and natural sympathy as the source
of the moral order, it is nevertheless with John Locke that we

21

must begin our understanding of the modern concept of civil society.

Locke is, in this context, very much a transitional figure, building on the tradition of individual rights (so central to the civil society tradition) through a "liberal" reading of Hugo Grotius and other medieval political theorists, but, as John Dunn pointedly reminded us, rooting these rights in a religious vision.[23] For Locke, in the *Second Treatise of Government*, civil society is of course still coterminous with the political realm *in toto*, and there does not yet exist that latter differentiation of civil society from the State which we find in the thought of Immanuel Kant as well as later in nineteenth-century writings. Civil society is the realm of political association instituted among men when they take leave of the "state of nature" and enter into a commonwealth.[24] Political or civil society is, for John Locke, the arena where the "inconveniences" and insufficiencies of the state of nature are rectified through the mutuality of contract and consent.[25] Civil society, in this reading, thus completes the "perfect freedom" and the "rights and privileges [enjoyed by men under] the law of nature."[26] It is but a more perfect form through which the freedom, equality, and independence of nature can be realized.

Without entering too much into an analysis of the *Second Treatise of Government*, what is of central importance to our argument is the ontological status of the rights and privileges that Locke posits at the basis of civil society. These of course draw on the traditions of natural law, but also on a specific Christian, if not Calvinist, reading of man's relation with God. The normative status of civil or political society for Locke turns on the state of nature, that "state all men are naturally in, and that is a state of perfect freedom to order their actions and dispose of their possessions and persons as they think fit within the bounds of the law of nature, without asking leave, or depending upon the will of any other man."[27] This state of liberty (though "not of license"), however, is itself rooted in a theological matrix—rooted, in fact, in the medieval Christian tradition of right reason and Christian Revelation. Moreover, as Locke makes clear, the very limits on liberty (as for instance in the prohibitions on suicide or self-enslavement) as well as the sources of this liberty are rooted in a certain set of theological presuppositions:

22

> The state of nature has a law of nature to govern it, which obliges every one and reason, which is that law, teaches all mankind who will but consult it, that being all equal and independent, no one ought to harm another in his life, health, liberty or possessions. For men being all the workmanship of one omnipotent and infinitely wise Maker—all servants of one sovereign Master, sent into the world by His order, and about His business—they are His property, whose workmanship they are, made to last during His, not one another's pleasure, and being furnished with like faculties, sharing all in one community of nature, there cannot be supposed any such subordination among us, that may authorize us to destroy one another, as if we were made for one another's uses, as the inferior ranks of creatures are for ours.[28]

The equality reigning among us, as the rights to property and autonomy are not rooted in a psychological, historical, or logical *a priori* but in a Christian, and more particularly Calvinist, vision of a community of individuals under God's dominion. It is precisely this theological grounding of Locke's state of nature that explains such seeming inconsistencies as the existence of private property therein. The state of nature is not to be understood as a "primitive" idyll, existent before the advent of civilization, but as a jural condition cutting through real or rather historically existent differences of property and status. In John Dunn's words, "men confront each other in their shared status as creatures of God without intrinsic authority over each other and without the right to restrict the (natural) law-abiding behavior of others."[29] The normative status of equality granted to individuals in society rests on their individual responsibility to God, which is what gives validity to the metahistorical reality of Locke's state of nature.

This understanding of the state of nature is also central to any appreciation of Locke's vision of the exercise of authority in society. There is for Locke no worldly authority that is intrinsically legitimate. All authority in this world is derived ultimately from God. Men in civil society abjure that "executive authority," "quitted this natural power [and] resigned it up into the hands of the community," from which political authority is derived.[30] The different structures of political authority found in the world are all derived from the individual's own executive and legislative authority in the state of nature, which individuals hold in their

23

"capacity of agents of God."[31] The very limitations on a ruler's powers were, for Locke, based on the assumption that "nobody can transfer to another more power than he has in himself; and nobody has an absolute arbirtrary power over himself, or over any other to destroy his own life, or take away the life or property of another."[32] This is simply because absolute and arbitrary power are only the province of God from which man's power derives in circumstances that

> . . . must be conformable to the law of nature, i.e. to the will of God, of which that is a declaration, and the fundamental law of nature being the preservation of mankind, no human sanction can be good or valid against it.[33]

As can be seen, Locke was not positing a historical reality of equality and freedom as the bases of civil society but a theological axiom whose ontological status was not given to empirical evidence or questioning.[34] He posits in its stead an ethical and inherently Christian ideal which need not bear any relation to the given historical reality (and inequality) of seventeenth-century English society, or indeed of any other society. Locke's concern (on the substantive and not the polemical level) was to find a point beyond the status and property differences in society, beyond what John Dunn termed "the tangle of seventeenth century social deference" where the moral integrity and autonomy of the individual (male) social actor could be validated, and so serve as the basis for a vision of social order.[35] This ground was to be found only in a set of theological principles which were in fact a natural theology of a uniquely Calvinist variant.

The individual is, as quoted above, God's workmanship, even His property. Man's existence is still rooted in what Charles Taylor termed, in a different context, an "ontic-logics."[36] That is to say, in a cosmic scheme were the existence of man's calling as well as his reason are validated in terms of a specific soteriology. What is Calvinist in this reading is precisely the validation of this-worldly affairs and of the reason that governs them, in transcendent terms. Whereas the original Calvinist emphasis on calling referred to daily affairs—of matrimony and vocation—Locke's emphasis is on the more specifically political aspects of this ethic.

24

Nevertheless, it follows the intense Calvinist emphasis on a unity of this-worldly and other-worldly spheres—on, in other words, an exaltation of worldly affairs in terms of a cosmic and perforce, in Christianity, salvational scheme.

We may add that if that Calvinist community of saints was no longer a viable social model by the end of the seventeenth century, a community of individualized moral agents pursuing the social good in conformity to the "will of God" definitely was, at least in John Locke's vision of civil society. In a later chapter we shall view just how central this internalization of the salvational doctrine of ascetic Protestantism was to the origin and development of the civil society tradition in the United States. Now, however, we must turn to the further development of this idea in the Scottish Enlightenment.

III

If with John Locke the supporting struts of civil society are those of an unproblematic and rationalized theology where God's will and right reason still work in coordinate state (resonant of the Calvinist unity of nature and grace), by the mid-eighteenth century the conjectural basis of the social order had become more problematic. In the writings of Francis Hutcheson, Adam Ferguson, and Adam Smith, there is a new appreciation of the problematic existence of individuals in society that was absent from the thought of Locke. To a great extent the developing idea of civil society is—within the Scottish Enlightenment—an attempt to find, or rather posit, a synthesis between a number of developing oppositions that were increasingly being felt in social life. These oppositions, between the individual and the social, the private and the public, egoism and altruism, as well as between a life governed by reason and one governed by the passions, have in fact become constitutive of our existence in the modern world.

Not surprisingly the attempt to return to the eighteenth-century idea of civil society is today an attempt to readmit that synthesis of private and public, individual and social, egoistic and altruistic sources of action that such an ideal represents. For various reasons, which I will attempt to develop in the course of this essay,

The Idea of Civil Society

Or- that synthesis.

? the eighteenth-century idea of civil society is, however, no longer a tenable option. The reasoning behind this position is less an extreme misanthropy on my part and more a consideration of the loss of that ground upon which the idea of civil society was constituted in the eighteenth century. In John Locke, this ground was a jural condition governed by Godly dictates. In the eighteenth century it was the very labile but nonetheless salient concept of moral affections and natural sympathy. It was, I would like to maintain, through this notion that the thinkers of the Scottish Enlightenment found that synthesis between opposing principles that allowed them to posit the idea of civil society as an ethically obtainable ideal.

Prior to any synthesis, however, lies the very awareness of conflict. And, to be sure, the developing economy of market relations in the eighteenth century problematized social existence in new ways. The freeing of labor and of capital developed together with a new awareness of individuals acting out their private interests in the public realm. By the middle of the eighteenth century it became increasingly difficult to square the traditional image of the individual as bounded by and validated within the network of social relations with that of the autonomous social actor pursuing his (not yet her) individual interests in the public realm. The very grounding of new forms of social action and motivation based on self-interest (indeed, on the very concept of the self) made it imperative to posit a new moral order that would accommodate and in a sense "hold" the development of interpersonal relations based not on a shared vision of cosmic order but on the principle of rational self-interest.

The first expression of this need and the problems it implied in any attempt to "think" society as something over and above its individual parts can be found in the central and growing realization that man is motivated by two divergent and contradictory principles—altruism and egoism. Alasdair MacIntyre has claimed that following Malebranche, Shaftesbury (who was Locke's pupil) was the first of the moral philosophers to have understood this, defining contradiction in human nature and motivation.[37] Its appreciation, however, played a salient role for all the thinkers of the Scottish Enlightenment and continued to the end of the nineteenth century, were we can find it, redefined in more sociolog-

26

ical and what was then assumed to be scientific principles by Emile Durkheim. It was, moreover, the cognizance of this distinction and the need to overcome it, to posit some unitary framework for ethical action (that could no longer by based on Godly dictates), that led eighteenth-century thinkers to the idea of moral affections and natural sympathy, which in turn served as the basis for the idea of civil society.

Moral sentiment by which "men are united by instinct, that they act in society from affections of kindness and friendship" was, for the thinkers of the Scottish Enlightenment, an axiomatic property of human mind.[38] On the epistemological level it is an attempt to ground the existence of the social order in an intimately human propensity of innate mutuality. With society no longer conceived in the hierarchic and holistic terms of medieval orders but of discrete individuals, a new bond between its particulars must be found. This takes the form, with Adam Smith, for example, of *The Theory of Moral Sentiments*, which argues that the moral basis of individual existence is the need for recognition and consideration on the part of others. "To be observed, to be attended to, to be taken notice of with sympathy, complacency and approbation" are for Smith the driving force of "all the toil and bustle of the world . . . the end of avarice and ambition, of the pursuit of wealth."[39] Thus, as is tellingly pointed out by A. O. Hirschman, economic activity itself is rooted, in *The Theory of Moral Sentiments*, in the noneconomic needs for sympathy and appreciation.[40] It is for Adam Smith our interest in "being the object of attention and approbation" that leads to the complex of activity that defines economic life.[41] What is central to this perspective is the idea of the arena of exchange (which is that of civil society) as rooted in a sphere of values predicated on the mutuality of individual recognition. This stress on mutuality and recognition runs through all the writings of the Scottish Enlightenment on civil society and serves to underpin that "propensity to exchange" which is at the heart of market transactions.

Along this same line of thought we can find Adam Ferguson asserting:

> The mighty advantages of property and fortune, when stripped of
> the recommendations they derive from vanity, or the more serious

regards to independence and power, only mean a provision that is made for animal enjoyment; and if our solicitude on this subject were removed, not only the toils of the mechanic, but the studies of the learned, would cease; every department of public business would become unnecessary; every senate-house would be shut up and every palace deserted.[42]

Vanity here is crucial and plays the same role as Smith's "attention and approbation." It builds on the social nature of our existence and on our individual validation in and through the eyes of others. The public arena of exchange and interaction—the realm of civil society—is not simply a "neutral" space of market exchange where already-fully-constituted individuals meet to exchange property and develop commerce, manufacturing, or the arts. It is itself an ethical arena in which the individual is constituted in his individuality through the very act of exchange with others. Vanity is that which links us to the social whole as we become who we are through the other's perception of us (a sort of Median social self *avant la lattre*).

Following the tradition of such thinkers as the Third Earl of Shaftesbury, who posited "a thousand other springs" to the governance of the world than mere self-interest, Ferguson stresses:

> What comes from a fellow-creature is received with peculiar emotion; and every language abounds with terms that express somewhat in the transactions of men, different from success and disappointment. The bosom kindles in company, while the point of interest in view has nothing to inflame; and a matter frivolous in itself, becomes important, when it serves to bring to light the intentions and character of men. . . . The value of a favor is not measured when sentiments of kindness are perceived; and the term misfortune has but a feeble meaning, when compared to that of insult and wrong.[43]

Insult and Wrong. Like vanity, these two sentiments are beyond the province of meager interest and achieve their full meaning only in the web of human interaction.

What is novel in the thought of the Scottish Enlightenment is of course not the mere positing of shared social space as an ethical arena. This had always existed within the political and philosophical traditions of Western civilization. The polis of classical antiquity was one such model. It was, after all, only in the polis that real human existence was deemed to reside. The great hierarchic edifice of Thomas Aquinas, where human means served godly ends, was another. Calvin's Geneva and the "community of saints" founded on the shores of the New World were yet a third variant of this ethically articulated vision of the social world. Common to all schemes was an articulation of social existence in terms of some vision of ultimate good. In its Christian variants this good was posed in terms of Divine purpose (albeit interpreted differently in terms of the diverse soteriologies of medieval Christendom and Reformation religion). Common to all visions is of course a transcendental if not transcendent source of moral action as the bases of social existence. In Christianity, this rooting of the shared and ethically constituted social arena in an otherworldly realm continued, as we have seen, into the seventeenth century and the thought of John Locke. The use of Reason in human affairs brought us—with Locke—to a true understanding of the "revelatory" dimension of our shared world. It did not, alone, serve to constitute that world.

As we have intimated, this transcendent grounding of the social order was no longer sufficient in an intellectual climate defined by Deism and the concomitant distancing of God from human affairs. Consequently, what was new in the eighteenth century was the very terms in which that ethically validated and validating social space could be conceived. Not yet totally casting off its moorings in a Godly benevolence, it nevertheless came to be characterized by increasing inner-worldliness, that is to say, by human attributes which themselves had to support a vision of the social good.

And here, of course, we are back to what Durkheim, some 150 years later, termed the "duality of human existence," that is, the existence of both interest-motivated action and altruistic-idealistic sources for social action. Both innate to human existence, these two sources of human motivation both defined the problem of social existence and, for the thinkers of the Scottish Enlightenment, pointed the way to its solution.[44] If the Deism of the eighteenth century no longer accepted a model of human, this-worldly activity framed in theological terms, it had no recourse but to posit in its stead a new philosophical anthropology. In fact, this move or turn inward to a natural, in-worldly, and ultimately humerman source of social order can be seen by a brief comparison of the opening chapters of Locke's *Second Treatise* and of Adam Ferguson's *An Essay on the History of Civil Society*. Both begin with the "State of Nature." But whereas for Locke this state of nature is, following Hooker, based on the common subordination of humans to God, for Ferguson it is nothing more than a short course in natural history with no reference, or indeed need of reference, to a divine being. Ontology has, as it were, been replaced with epistemology.

The Deistic model of the sources of civil society, of course, must not be confused with later, atheistic thought. The world was still understood in terms of a providential order ruled over by a Godly benevolence. Indeed, Alasdair MacIntyre has made a convincing case for just how important a continuing theological perspective was in the thought of a Scottish moralist like Francis Hutcheson.[45] Yet, what nevertheless distinguishes this period—of the classic image of civil society—was the disengagement of the moral sense from a direct theological linkage. And it was, as we have seen, precisely this moral sense (as an almost protopsychological datum) which stood at the core of the image of civil society. Its sources are a natural benevolence that we must recover from within.

Of course, by positing the sources of natural benevolence within the human world, the distinction between public and private lives attained a saliency, indeed a recognition, it had never had before. When the sources of morality and of constitutive good lay beyond the human world, the distinction between both realms was irrelevant for the conduct of the good life. The field of morality—precisely because it was defined in transcendent terms—embraced both spheres equally and in fact obviated any distinction between them. When, however, the field is inherently human, that distinction within the human world, between the individual and the social, the private and the public, takes on a new resonance and must be addressed in terms of the moral basis of the social order. (Needless to say, this "idealist" reading of the relationship between ideas and structure can be reversed with no detriment to the argument. Feudal society, with no distinction

30

between public and private, has need of an all-embracing moral code. The emergence of capitalist market relations, with its incipient distinction between public and private, posed a new set of problems for the conception of the social order. In either reading, what emerges is the need to articulate a new ethical vision). In many ways the idea of civil society can be seen as an attempt to overcome this problem, if sometimes by fiat more than anything else.

To be sure, we are in fact dealing with two sets of problems that cannot be conflated. The set of oppositions contained in the individual/social is not exactly the same as that contained in the public/private. The idea of civil society as a model for social order set out, however, to overcome both sets of oppositions. The distinction between the individual and the social is, in the classic civil society tradition, easily reconciled, as mentioned above, by anthropological fiat. Thus for Ferguson "man is by nature, the member of a community; and when considered in this capacity the individual appears to be no longer made for himself. He must forego his happiness and his freedom, where these interfere with the good of society. . . . He is only part of a whole . . . and if the public good be the principle object with individuals, it is likewise true, that the happiness of individuals is the great end of civil society."[46]

The public/private divide is a more serious problem, which brings us to the heart of the image of civil society as a moral vision. What I wish to argue is that what made the classic vision of civil society unique was its positing of the social space of human interaction as a moral sphere—that is, not simply as a neutral arena of exchange—where moral attributes were derived from the nature of man himself. What was unique was precisely the coupling of a vision of society with that moral field implied by the term "civil society" while, at the same time, rooting this field in an inner-worldly logic and not in a transcendent reality. This, as history has shown, was a fragile synthesis that could not support either the expansion of capitalism or the growth of rationality. It rested on a particular view of the relations between men's passions and their interests and of the crucible of civil space where a synthesis between them could be achieved.

There are, in that tradition of political economy which we as-

31

sociate with the idea of civil society, two readings of this relation, which contain very different resonances. One is to be found in Mandeville's *Fable of the Bees* and the in the Smithian notion of the Invisible Hand. The former, a rather well-known model, has it that through the evolution of appropriate institutional frameworks and under the direction of sagacious statesmen "private vices" would be transformed into "public benefits."[47] While Adam Smith did not exactly follow the moralism of Mandeville, it was precisely through reliance on the Invisible Hand that he took his position against State regulation of the grain trade, even in periods of extreme duress. Setting himself up against the natural law tradition, which legitimized the "policing" of grain in terms of God's dominion and the (natural) "right to sustenance" that the poor enjoyed, Smith articulated an idea of reasoned self-interest that would provide for the proper distribution of grain with no recourse to a moral economy of human benevolence, but with recourse solely to the Invisible Hand of market relations.

At first sight the Smithian account would seem to relegate to the shared space of civil society no normative or representative dimension. It is but the arena where the Invisible Hand works its alchemy, turning the dross of rational self-interest into the gold of the public good. This is, however, a one-sided reading that ignores certain salient aspects of Smith's moral vision, aspects that he shared with the other moral philosophers of the eighteenth century—which constitute the second "reading" of men's passions and interests noted above. What it ignores is precisely that aspect of the moral sentiment which for Smith (as for Ferguson and others) severely attenuated any attempt to imagine rational self-interest in terms of either disengaged reason (i.e., reason or interests freed from the "passions") or of the self, freed from the eye of the other. We have seen above how, for Smith himself, the very focus and motivating force of economic activity, of the hustle and bustle of worldly affairs, was the search for recognition from others. The need for respect and approval, man's very *amour de soi*, rested on the praise of others. Therefore, the individual self could never, in this reading, be totally disengaged from society, nor could reasoned self-interest be abstracted from those passions which, through the moral sentiment, rooted man in society. If, in

32

his discussion of the grain trade, Smith sought to base the proper workings of the social order on the rational pursuit of profit and the juridical notion of "perfect rights" (such as property), in his *Theory of Moral Sentiments* he nevertheless remained within the tradition of the Scottish moralists, which framed the social order in terms of men's mutual recognition in the realm of civil society. Indeed. as A. O. Hirschman has claimed, the first position was ultimately dependent on the second.

We have perhaps, with Smith, run a bit ahead of our story, for the distinction between law and virtue, between juridical rights governing the public sphere and a more private or individual sphere of virtue and morality, already prefigures the writing of Immanuel Kant. Smith, writing in the last third of the eighteenth century, shares the idea of civil society as an ethical entity and has also pushed it somehow beyond these limits. If benevolence was no longer seen as a prerequisite for the workings of the social order, as it was in Hutcheson, the critical idea of an interdependence between men that went beyond interest-motivated action remained. This interdependence and mutual validation of selves through the very workings of the market invested the public arena of civil society with a critical representative dimension, as an ethical locus where private interests and passions were not only realized but were themselves constituted through mutual recognition. Here the public/private distinction has been recognized and met through a conception of privateness whose very sources are deeply rooted in a public recognition. This is the very core of the eighteenth-century idea of the individual and a point well worth stressing. Though not "organic" in the late-nineteenth-century romantic sense of the term, the whole tradition of eighteenth-century ethical speculation or moral philosophy rested on cognizance of the social embedding of individual existence and the manner of strengthening those social bonds through which both the individual and society were constituted.[48]

What the idea of civil society meant to the thinkers of the Scottish Enlightenment was thus primarily a realm of solidarity held together by the force of moral sentiments and natural affections. It was these that set men over the animals and the basic life of

33

material substance and which "reserved for man to consult, to persuade, to oppose, to kindle in the society of his fellow-creatures, and to lose the sense of his personal interest or safety, in the ardor of his friendships and his oppositions."[49] The natural law tradition played a significant role in the taking of these intellectual positions, as did the Deistic image of a benevolent Creator whose "natural benevolence" was the source of our own. Significantly, however, these two intellectual traditions were transformed, as it was in the workings of society itself (and not in a transcendent entity) that these sources could be found.

The crux of this transformation lay in the idea of reason or, perhaps more properly, Reason, which, while embracing the concept of interest, went far beyond any utilitarianism. Indeed, the idea was not of reason governing the passions so much as, with Shaftesbury for example, Reason which was itself an element of the natural affections. Reason and rationality in such thinkers as the Third Earl of Shaftesbury simply brought us, through our innate benevolence, to an understanding and hence a love of the whole—of the universal.[50] Natural affections, which bound societies together (that solidarity we spoke of earlier), emerged from a happy confluence of Reason and benevolence, which allowed us to put the good of the whole above the good of the parts and so the public or social good above our individual interests. The whole force of the civil society tradition is in fact aimed against any restriction of reason to what we would now call, following Max Weber, instrumental rationality. Ferguson makes this more than clear when he reminds us:

> Mankind, we are told, are devoted to interest; and this, in all commercial nations, is undoubtedly true: But it does not follow, that they are, by their natural dispositions, averse to society and mutual affections.[51]

Rather, it is a "benevolent heart" joined with "courage, freedom, and resolute choice of conduct," and not "fortune or interest" (indeed a "contempt" for the latter), that encourages us to actions directed to the good of mankind and so to the good of a particular society. Reason, in its universal sense, takes us beyond particular

34

interests to affirm the universal good (which, we must continually remember, is also constitutive of the very individual actor in his existence within civil society—recall the above-quoted passages from Adam Ferguson and Adam Smith).

This idea of a unitary framework of both Reason and the passions (of moral sentiments and natural affections) is, as we can see, quite beyond the Lockean vision, which was still rooted in (albeit rationalized) theology. Natural law, for Locke, was still rooted in Divine Revelation, and human agents were still Godly subjects. These principles were, for Locke, at the sources of his understanding of the rights and contracts, privileges and liberties of civil society. In the Scottish Enlightenment, civil society was loosened, if not yet totally freed, from its transcendent anchor, and that universal (basis for the good) which for Locke was to be found only in God was, by the eighteenth century, displaced. The universal was no longer beyond the world, but within it. It was, further, in society as in philosophy, not to be sought through the proliferation of general theories and abstract speculations, through "the parade of words and general reasoning which sometimes carry an appearance of so much learning and knowledge."[52] Rather, the knowledge of the universal was to be attained through a collection of particulars under general headings.[53] And it was, within the thought of the Scottish Enlightenment, precisely through the study of particular human agents acting in society that the universal attributes of the moral sentiments and natural affections could be ascertained.

In more abstract terms, the universal could be found within the particular, the social in the individual, and the public (good) within the private (realm of interests—in its nonutilitarian sense). It was, finally, in such a way that the thinkers of the Scottish Enlightenment managed to articulate a representative vision of civil society where the particular and the universal, the private and the public, were indeed united within one field of meanings. The public good was represented in terms of the workings of reason as the reality of individual existence was itself secured in the public realm. Central to this idea (of civil society and the public arena as the validating realm of individual existence) was the unity of Reason and moral sentiment, which, as we have

35

hinted at above, was not to stand the test of time and had in fact begun to unravel in the thought of David Hume.

IV

Hume, it would do well to recall, aimed his criticism at precisely that natural law tradition that was so central to the moralists of the Scottish Enlightenment. Writing before Ferguson, but in pointed opposition to the moral philosophy of Shaftesbury and Hutcheson, he subjected both the "naturalist" assumptions of the latter on human benevolence and their ultimate grounding of morality in a transcendent (i.e., Godly) providence to scathing attack. Hume died the same year that Smith's *Wealth of Nations* was published—the same year as the American Revolution—and this symbolism should not pass unnoticed. It was as a follower of Hume that Smith, in his concern with justice rather than morality, abjured the principles of benevolence in his analysis of the grain trade, and it was very much on Humean—rather than solely Lockean—principles that the liberal individualism of the United States of America was to be based.

Indeed, it may seem strange on first sight to include Hume in a discussion of the civil society tradition, as he is generally not understood in this context, nor is he seen as the father of nineteenth-century liberalism (especially when the latter is seen to emerge from the former strain of thought). I would like to submit that it is precisely in his rejection of the fundamental premises of the civil society tradition that Hume is to be understood as the precursor of later liberal thought. The point is that it is only in the devolution or disintegration of the civil society tradition that we can understand the growth of liberalism or, rather, liberal-individualism, with all its attendant problems in the "representation of society." These problems of the fundamental difficulty, if not impossibility, of a society founded on the principles of liberal-individualism or the contractarian tradition in articulating a representative vision of the whole rests on its Humean heritage and the challenge of Hume's thought (that same challenge which awoke Immanuel Kant from his many years of slumber).

The challenge posited by Hume was disarmingly simple. He

simply tore asunder the unity of Reason and moral sentiment upon which the whole tradition of civil society had been based. Hume's distinction between "is" and "ought," upon which was based what Alasdair MacIntyre has appropriately termed his "subversion from within" of the Scottish Enlightenment, was, as well, an outright attack on the tradition of moral sentiment and universal benevolence upon which the idea of civil society rested.[54] In terms most germane to our own problematic, of the moral basis of the social order, the most succinct formula, taken from *A Treatise of Human Nature*, (subtitled, *Being an Attempt to introduce the experimental method of reasoning into moral subjects*) proposes:

> Since morals, therefore, have an influence on the actions and affections, it follows, that they cannot be deriv'd from reason; and that because reason alone, as we have already prov'd, can never have any such influence. Morals excite passions, and produce or prevent actions. Reason of itself is utterly impotent in this particular. The rules of morality, therefore, are not conclusions of our Reason.[55]

Thus, for Hume, "the ultimate ends of human action can never . . . be accounted for by reason, but recommend themselves entirely to the sentiment and affections of mankind."[56] A strict "boundary" in Hume's phrase, is posited between what is *ascertained* by reason and the *motives* for human action, which can be understood only in terms of sentiment. The fragile concomitance of both, upon which the unity of the individual and society, private and public had been seen to rest, no longer holds. Reason has no place in a psychology of human motivation—which is relegated solely to the passions, which in turn have no privileged knowledge, indeed none at all, of universal truths.

The philosophical implications of this distinction are, however of less interest to us than its sociological derivatives. For if the working of Reason can only bring us to universal truths that are beyond the field of morality or virtue, how can a representative vision of the social good be posited? How, in this reading, can society be conceived as a normative order? It was Hume's answer to these questions which had such a strong impact on later liberal theory. For, in fact, Hume abstained from positing the social order in terms of any morally substantive good. The universal good was nothing beyond the calculus of individual or particular goods, and the public good was supported solely by the workings of private interests.

The role of Reason in the Humean idea of society was fixed within this calculus—allowing the individual to ascertain his own benefit as deriving from following certain universally applicable rules of conduct. In itself, Reason has no other role and certainly no autonomous moral validity. Of these rules, the three fundamental ones for the workings of society are the stability of possessions, their transfer by consent, and the performance of promises.[57] These, Hume emphasizes, are "artifices" of society—necessary for its workings—but not rooted in any historical, mythical, logical, or transcendental status. ("In the state of nature, or that imaginary state, which preceded society, there be neither justice nor injustice").[58] Foreshadowing Hegel, Hume well realized that "justice" as well as the rules governing the exchange of property and indeed the whole edifice of civil society (of which the obligations to fulfill promises and thus secure a realm of continued human interaction was central) "takes its rise from human conventions."[59] They are decidedly not to be found in any set of natural principles—cosmic, transcendental, or otherwise ("those impressions, which give rise to this sense of justice, are not natural to the mind of man, but arise from artifice and human conventions").[60] Moreover, and crucially in terms of the impending deathknell of the Scottish Enlightenment, men, in the Humean reading, would follow the rules of justice not because they represented some universal, constitutive good, but simply to maximize their self-interest. In the social reality as Hume conceived it, characterized by people's "selfishness and limited generosity" joined with the scarcity of goods "in comparison with the wants and desires of men," men's only recourse, to realize their *own* interests, was to follow universally validated rules of justice.[61]

It is this proposition, Hume asserts, and not a "regard of public interest or a strong extensive benevolence," which leads us to follow the rules of justice.[62] Not only is moral sentiment here distinguished from the *rules* of justice, but the *sense* of justice, which is historically contingent and takes different forms in different societies, is divorced from Reason. It is founded, Hume argues, not on any set of "eternal, immutable, and universally obligatory relations between ideas" but solely on our "impressions."[63] In this reading what is *deemed* moral has no foundation in Reason, as the latter is indeed uncoupled from any moral sentiment. And while it is reasoned self-interest that leads us to follow the rules of justice, justice itself has no more than an instrumental value and no autonomous standing beyond those particular interests which are served by following its dictates (those three rules quoted above).

To get a sense of just how far we have traveled from the tradition of moral sentiment and natural sympathy that characterized the civil society tradition, it may be instructive to compare Ferguson with Hume. I have chosen a representative passage from Ferguson bearing on the threat to civil society and one by Hume dealing with the ties of common society. Ferguson:

> But apart from these considerations, the separation of professions, while it seems to promise improvement of skill, and is actually the cause why the productions of every art become more perfect as commerce advances; yet, in its termination and ultimate effects, serves, in some measure, to break the bands of society, to substitute mere forms and rules of art in place of ingenuity, and to withdraw individuals from the common scene of occupation, on which the sentiments of the heart and the mind, are most happily employed. . . . if nations pursue the plan of enlargement and pacification, till their members can no longer apprehend the common ties of society, nor be engaged by affection in the cause of their country, they must err on the opposite side, and by leaving too little to agitate the spirits of men, bring on ages of languor, if not of decay. The members of a community may, in this manner . . . lose the sense of every connection, but that of kindred or neighborhood, and have no common affairs to transact, but those of trade: Connection, indeed, or transactions, in which probity and friendship may still take place; but in which the national spirit . . . cannot be exerted.[64]

And Hume:

> 'Tis certain, that no affection of the human mind has both a sufficient force, and a proper direction to counter-balance, the love of gain and render men fit members of society, by making them ab-

stain from the possessions of others. Benevolence to strangers is too weak for this purpose; and as to the other passions, they rather inflame this avidity, when we observe, that the larger our possessions are, the more ability we have of gratifying our appetites. There is no passion, therefore, capable of controlling the interested affection, but the very affection itself, by an alteration of its direction. Now this alteration must necessarily take place upon the least reflection; since 'tis evident, that the passion is much better satisfy'd by its restraint, than by its liberty, and that in preserving society, we make much greater advances in the acquiring possessions, than in the solitary and forlorn condition, which must follow upon violence and universal license. The question, therefore, concerning the wickedness or goodness of human nature, enters not in the least into the other question concerning the origin of society; nor is there any thing to be consider'd but the degrees of men's sagacity or folly. For whether the passion of self-interest be esteemed vicious or virtuous, 'tis all a case; since itself alone restrains it: So that if it be virtuous, men become social by their virtue, if vicious, their vice has the same effect.[65]

While Ferguson is afraid that mere commerce and interest-motivated action will destroy the common ground of civil society and the sentiments upon which this ground rests, Hume blithely refers his readers to (reasoned) self-interest as the sole guarantee of the social order. We are here far from the world of universal benevolence and natural sympathy and are treading the ground of Adam Smith's Invisible Hand.

I would like to close this discussion of Hume with yet another extensive quote from Hume on the mutual interest and advantage to be gained from the exchange of services. (Hume is so succinct and straightforward that one cannot resist the temptation to quote him at length). Hume sets out the following moral tale on those aspects of social life which, I believe, more than anything else will convince of his role in articulating those values of liberal individualism which we have come to see as our own:

> Your corn is ripe today; mine will be so to-morrow. 'Tis profitable for us both, that I shou'd labour with you today, and that you shou'd aid me to-morrow. I have no kindness for you, and know you have as little for me. . . . Hence I learn to do a service to another, without bearing him any real kindness; because I foresee,

40

that he will return my service, in expectation of another of the same kind, and in order to maintain the same correspondence of good offices with me or with others.[66]

Here we indeed seem to have traversed the distance of two hundred years as Hume resonates with the sentiments of the Fortune 500 or *Forbes* magazine. In a later chapter we shall analyze this affinity between Humean principles and the modern or perhaps postmodern condition and its concurrent problems of articulating a representative and normative vision of the social order that, I would claim, he did so much to articulate.

With Hume (and after him Smith) the distinction between justice and virtue, between a public sphere based on the workings of self-interest (in conformity to law) and a strictly private sphere of morality, is presented in its starkest form. It was this distinction and its attendant dilemmas that the Scottish Enlightenment and the whole civil society tradition had attempted to avoid. The ensuring dilemma, of how to posit a prescriptive and not just descriptive model of the social order, given this distinction between abstract and general rules of justice on the one hand and the particular desiderata of rational self-interest on the other, has defined the modern period from Hume onward. Its theoretical challenge was first addressed by Kant, who, as we shall see, seemed, despite his theoretical innovations, to remain very much within a Humean problematic.

With Kant a number of themes that had been central—if still somewhat latent—in the thought of the Scottish moralists achieve a new recognition. The problem of the relation between the particular/individual and the universal/social, and with it the problem of the proper mode of representing social life, which were inherent in the civil society tradition, take on a new rigor. It was, in fact, only in the writings of Immanuel Kant that the above-noted problems, of properly representing the public and private spheres (as well as the relation between this and the idea of Reason) was first fully articulated.[67]

In terms of our previous inquiry into the civil society tradition, Kant can be understood as fighting an almost rear-guard action to salvage that connection between the workings of Reason and the moral sphere that scientific thought (and the writings of Hume) were increasingly questioning. Our interest in Kant, however, lies less in an appreciation of the relative success or failure of this philosophical project than in its implications for the idea of civil society as a representative and ethical vision of the social order.

In certain respects Kant continued (and of course substantially deepened) the thought of the Scottish philosophers, making the themes of freedom and equality central edifices of his philosophical anthropology. Similarly, and of equal if not greater importance, he united these ideas with the progressive workings of a universal (or more properly transcendental) Reason through which individual rights (to civic freedom and political equality) were articulated. Reason supplied that ideal (or model, *Urbild*) through which our judgment is guided by the moral law.[68] Right (*Recht*, embracing both personal "rights" and the very notion of justice) is ensured through the autonomous and agentic individual subject following the dictates of a Reason that, in its very universality, bridges the distinction between private and public, individual and social. As mankind comes into its own, the autonomy, freedom, and equality of each individual (which must be assured in the juridical community of citizens) themselves engender—though a universal reason—the workings of the moral law. In Kant's words, from *The Critique of Practical Reason*:

> He is the subject of the moral law which is holy because of the autonomy of his freedom. Because of the latter, every will, even the private will of each person directed to himself, is restricted to the condition of agreement with the autonomy of the rational being, namely, that it be subjected to no purpose which is not possible by a law which could arise from the will of the passive subject itself. This condition thus requires that the person never be used as a means except when it is at the same time an end.[69]

Kant's famous strictures on never using any individual as only a means cut to the heart of the civil society debate. They provide a new, more analytic formulation of the realm of moral sentiment and natural sympathy upon which the Scottish philosophers constructed their idea of civil society. In Kant however, this injunction is not founded on any "natural" endowment but—and this is precisely its critical importance—on following the strictures or formal conditions of reason itself. For Kant reason, more concretely practical reason, was realized in the juridical community of citizens and as such represented the crowning achievement of human freedom in the modern world.[70] Reason and equality were thus firmly united in the representative vision posited by Kant of the social or political order.[71]

Moreover, and central to the whole Kantian conception of practical reason, was the existence of a shared public arena where the workings of reason were substantiated.[72] As Hannah Arendt has made clear, the category of the "public" was central for the Kantian synthesis of reason, equality, and freedom.[73] It was, for Kant, within the public arena of critical discourse that reason and equality, and with them the preconditions for the "kingdom of ends," were validated.[74]

The notion of publicness has been central in the renewed debates over civil society and the public sphere initiated in recent years (and partially influenced by the belated English translation of Habermas's *Structural Transformation of the Public Sphere* and a reexamination of the writings of Hannah Arendt.) It was, of course, in the Kantian reading only through participation in the civil structures of political activity that man's autonomy, and with it that of reason, were guaranteed.

On one level, Kant's notion of publicness would appear as a more fully developed and more highly theorized concept than that mutuality inherent in the Scottish Enlightenment idea of natural sympathy. With Kant, a labile and subjective idea takes on a rigor and objective form in and through its unity with Reason. Similarly, with Kant, a new, more rigorous vision of social differentiation began to develop. The State, as the embodiment of political society, is no longer viewed as coterminous with civil society, as the publicness of rational debate and critique is seen (and indeed emphasized) as the province of civil society in its distinction from the State.

In Kant's objections to the absolutist state, this role of a critical citizenry freed from civil constraint is salient. The very legitimation of constitutional rule rests on the idea that its laws would be such that had all the (rational) citizenry debated them, they would have arrived at the same.[75] Kant thus would appear to overcome (through his very synthesis of Reason with the public realm) that distinction between individual (interests) and social (good) with which the moralists of the Scottish Enlightenment wrestled.

This synthesis, however, contained the critical <u>distinction between the juridical and the ethical,</u> which was to prove so important for further theoretical attempts to articulate an ethical vision of societal representation.[76] The public arena was for Kant the sphere of right (*Recht*), of mutual and rational consent to the individual and collective will (*Willkür*) of others.[77] It was not however the realm of the ethical, which was reserved for the private workings of inner life. As Susan Meld Shell explains:

> The juridical community is not a "kingdom of ends." It does not assume coincidence of motives nor does it abolish internal conflicts over ends. No person has any rightful concern with the inner motives of his fellows. The laws of rights require only that every action (whatever its moral incentive) which outwardly affects others gain their rational consent.[78]

In Kant's writings the (private) sphere of morality and ethics is thus divorced from the representative vision of society as juridical community.[79] The public arena as the realm validating the juridical equality of citizens is thus invested with value, while concomitantly remaining removed from the realm of the ethical. Kant then, more than anything else, absolutized that distinction noted by Hume, rather than overcame it. This solution (and distinction) to the dilemma of how to represent the public good, still critical in the discourse of liberal political theory, perpetrated rather than resolved the tension between public and private realms. By distinguishing right or duty from ethics and reserving the latter for the private realm, Kantian theory left unresolved the critical issue of ethical representation—of the status of the public sphere.

V

It was in fact this separation of the juridical from the ethical that gave rise to the Hegelian critique of Kant. Hegel's criticism and development of Kant's philosophy turned precisely on this point—the divorce of public right from private morality

44

and so the mediated and incomplete realization of reason this entailed.[80] Leaving morality as a "regulative principle" only, and not fully integrated into the domain of Right, meant, in Hegel's reading of Kant, the abdication of the former from its proper place in the ethical representation of society. Marx, as is well known, followed in Hegel's footsteps in attempting to unite the private realm (of individual interests residing in civil society) with the public realm (of political concerns). As opposed to Hegel, he posited this unity as prescriptive for future development and not as embodied in the actually existent state. What unites both thinkers, however, is a concern with the proper integration of (private) morality or ethics within the public arena.

Given the importance of the current debate between Habermas and his critics over his attempt to renew an Enlightenment project of reason—as well as the whole, contemporary debate over civil society—the thought of Hegel would seem especially pertinent to our theme. Our own interest, however, lies less in an analysis or comparison of the Kantian, Hegelian, and Marxist systems than in understanding how the thought of these philosophers influenced the very idea of the civil society as ethical ideal and its attendant problems of representing social life.

With Hegel and Marx we come in fact to the end of the civil society tradition proper. Both, in different ways, seek to overcome that distinction between legality and morality, between juridical community and ethical life that was first posited by David Hume in opposition to the thought of the Scottish Enlightenment and "absolutized" by Immanuel Kant. For both Hegel and Marx this distinction was a fatal flaw in the idea of civil society and both sought to provide the theoretical means for a reconstruction of civil society as idea and praxis. In their different reconstructions, however, the very distinction of the idea of civil society as it had been articulated in the eighteenth century was overcome and transformed. However great the difference between Hegelian and Marxist models of civil society, they can only (both) be understood in terms of an attempt to reintegrate the two realms of legality and morality, which stood at the core of the original idea of civil society. In so doing both sought, in different ways, to realize that model of civil society for which the ideas of moral affections and natural sympathy were no longer sufficient.

45

Thus for example it is important to note that Hegel's notions of ethical solidarity based on the unity of public right with private ethics find a strong resonance in the earlier tradition of the Scottish Enlightenment (of "natural sympathy" and "sociability"), as well—it might be added—as in the thought of such disparate thinkers as Burke and Rousseau.[81] In a similar vein, Marx's (ethical) condemnation of the workings of market relations in civil society, where men treat one another as means and are denigrated to such in turn, are precisely an attack on the Kantian distinction of legality and morality discussed above.

In the most general of terms, and striking from today's perspective, is in fact the shared components of the classic–modern synthesis starting from Adam Ferguson and running through G. W. F. Hegel, which recognized society (conceived of as a civil society, including what Habermas has termed the public sphere) as invested with value. Thus, and to take only one, albeit centrally important, example: the phenomenon of property exchange that takes place in the market is, for Hegel, itself imbued with a value that subsequent Marxist and utilitarian theories have, in different ways, occluded.

In Hegel's writings it becomes clear that the individual need for recognition (and hence existence) is attained through the recognition of property.[82] Indeed, for Hegel property—in the realm of civil society—takes the place of love—in the realm of the family.[83] Through both (as different moments in the actualization of the spirit) a universal will is constructed through recognition, and as Hegel observed at the end of Part I of the Jena lectures, "The will of the individual is the universal will—and the universal will is the individual. It is the totality of ethical life [Sittlichkeit] in general, immediate, yet [as] Right."[84] It is thus, according to Hegel, precisely through the mutual recognition involved in property exchange that the individual as self-consciousness (für sich) is constructed, which is the closest we can come to an ethical realm in a world defined by the mutual exchange between different entities (as opposed to the ideal self of the Greek polis, undifferentiated from community).[85] In this latter-day world, the realm of ethics is constructed in and only in the mutual recognition that defined civil society.

The point here is that for Hegel, as well as for the thinkers of the Scottish Enlightenment, the realm of civil society is one of mutuality and reciprocal recognition. This "core" of civil society was what gave it normative status in all the thinkers of the civil society tradition.

With Hegel, this model of mutual reciprocity is of course posited in terms quite beyond those of moral sentiments or natural affections. Rather, the basis of community—through mutual recognition—is the universal (Idea of Freedom) working through the particular (livelihood, happiness, and legal status) of each concrete individual. What Hegel attempts in the *Philosophy of Right* is, however, not simply to go beyond the natural law doctrines of the Scottish Enlightenment, but to overcome the Kantian antinomies and with them the distinction between public Right and private morals upon which the Kantian system was based. This he attempted through the positing of a theoretical framework which, while recognizing the differences between particular and universal interests, nevertheless united them in a system of right which is "the realm of freedom made actual."[86]

This "actualization of freedom," and so of ethical life in the concrete workings of the world, is the beginnings of his critique of the Kantian relegation of morality to the private sphere as merely an "ought to be," and without "execution."[87] The foundation of this critique is Hegel's notion of the will, which is seen as the unity of the particular and the individual. "It is particularity reflected into itself and so brought back to universality i.e. it is individuality."[88] And it is precisely this individuality as the expression of the particular (individual) will within the universal (social) framework that serves as the foundation of Hegel's idea of civil society. This latter is one "moment" in the progressive realization of ethical life, achieved through the mutual recognition, which, as pointed out earlier, the exchange of property implied. Civil society represents—in its developmental logic—both elements, particular and universal, through whose ultimate unity Hegel hoped to overcome the Kantian distinction of public Right and private morality. In Hegel's terms:

> The concrete person who is himself the object of his particular aims, is, as a totality of wants and a mixture of caprice and physical necessity, one principle of civil society. But the particular person is

47

essentially so related to other particular persons that each establishes himself and finds satisfaction by means of the others, and at the same time purely and simply by means of the form of universality, the second principle here.[89]

There is one crucial caveat in this Hegelian reading of civil society, which in itself forms the basis of the Marxist critique of Hegel. This is in the very arena where the universal interest, or the Idea of Freedom, is realized. For though Hegel clearly distinguishes civil society from the State and provides an acute analysis of the workings of particular interests within civil society, civil society is not, in itself, that realm of ethical realization. As he makes clear, civil society as such is the realm where the Idea of Freedom is present only in its "abstract moment," as an "inner necessity."[90] "It is the system of the ethical order, split into is extremes and lost."[91] The heterogeneity of interests and classes that make up civil society are, in Hegel's thought, ultimately self-defeating—so long as they remain within *that* "moment" where universality is not concretely (but only abstractly) realized.

> Particularly by itself, given free rein in every direction to satisfy its needs, accidental caprices and subjective desires, destroys itself and its substantive concept in this process of gratification. . . . In these contrasts and their complexity, civil society affords a spectacle of extravagance and want as well as of the physical and ethical degeneration common to them both.[92]

Hegel's whole analysis of civil society turns in fact on the overcoming of these contradictory desiderata of particular interests and so the realization of ethical life through its embodiment in a universal framework, which begins *but* does not end with the sphere of civil society.

For Hegel, civil society and its attendant mass of conflicting individual and group interests embody on the one hand the principle of particularity and on the other the principle of universality, which, however, exists only *in status nascendi*. Civil society contains, at its two poles, both the origins of true particularity and individual identity as it "tears the individual from his family ties, estranges the members of the family from one another and recognizes them as self-subsistent persons" and intimations of the universal, through the Corporation, which organizes particular interests, needs, and satisfactions as universal, abstract rights.[93] Corporations unite the particular interests within universal social frameworks and are thus the "second ethical root of the State, the one planted in civil society" (the first is in the family).[94] Through corporations the individual participates in communal life, and through such participation his individual and particular wants and needs are mediated by a recognition of the communal (and incipient universal) framework. The corporation acts both to achieve security and other benefits for its members through the promotion of group interests and to inculcate in its members a sense of belonging and membership in a body, a group beyond each particular individual. In this way particularity, in Hegel's terms, is returned to itself through participation in the universal.

The Corporation, however, is limited and restricted to diverse groups within civil society (and in fact cannot encompass either the casual day laborer or the poor, those not organized into "Estates" and so not yet part of the whole). As a representative of these interests it does not yet encompass the whole of society. This is the province of the State proper, within which, and only within which, the Idea of Freedom and so of ethical life is fully realized. "Particular interests which are common to everyone fall within civil society and lie outside the absolutely universal interest of the state proper. The administration of these is in the hands of Corporations. . . . however these circles of particular interests must be subordinated to the higher interests of the state."[95] The move from civil authority (police) and corporations that serve individual or groups interests to public (or political) authority that serves the people as a whole is the move from the ultimately centrifugal force of particular wills in civil society to the centripedal force of the State, where the true unity of particular and universal is achieved. Here we see, in starkest contrast to Kant, the attempt to unite particular and universal injunctions—not, however, in a realm of private morality, but in a public space which is ethical life—or concrete freedom. This unity of wills has taken us beyond the particular interests of burghers, corporations, or Estates, which constitute civil society, and into the realm of the State proper (and more concretely the universal interests represented by the class of civil servants), which is the sole representative of the universal idea.[96]

One way of reading Hegel is to see in his writing an attempt to maintain the reciprocity and mutuality of the classic civil society tradition while placing it on a firmer foundation than that of innate and natural sentiments. Indeed, he artfully shows how civil society is itself the object of historical development and not a predetermined natural state. Moreover, his new synthesis seeks to sidestep the critical Kantian (and Humean) distinction between legality and morality, which left the latter beyond the realm of concrete ethical action in the world. In squaring this circle and overcoming the dichotomies of both the Scottish Enlightenment and Kantian theory, Hegel also "overcame" the very autonomy of the concept of civil society, positing its full realization in the State.

With Hegel the very concept of civil society thus achieves a transformation on a number of different levels. First, its existence is posited historically—itself an object of historical development and not a natural or metahistorical reality in which one can seek a normative order beyond the exigencies of history. Second, it is conceived as an arena of mutually conflicting particular interests, which in themselves cannot overcome their particularity to attain the universal (value or the Idea of Freedom). Conflict, which is endemic to civil society, is ultimately destructive of the very ties of civil society, whose only partial existence (in the Corporation) is not yet a sufficient guarantee of social order and stability. Third, civil society as an ethical or normative order is, finally, "realized" only through its transformation, or rather sublation (*aufhebung*) in the State, which is the realm of the truly ethical made concrete. The proper synthesis between the particular and the universal— what for the thinkers of the Scottish Enlightenment was the problem of the private and public, individual and society—is thus attained not in the realm of their conflict (civil society) but beyond it, in the State. The ethical ideal that previous thinkers had sought to root in society itself—an attempt which, following the thought of Hume and Kant, proved impossible—is here transformed from society to the State. Here, the very attempt to maintain a concrete ethical representation of society ends up positing such representation beyond society and in the workings of Reason as embodied in the State. In Hegel's attempt to save civil society as an ethical

50

entity, civil society, at least as it was classically conceived, disappears.

And however strange this Hegelian logic may seem, we must recall that at least one of its sources (and we are not, as mentioned, interested here in explaining the Hegelian system *tout court*) was the perduring challenge posited to the civil society tradition by the thought of Hume and Kant. With the distinction between legality and morality, between right and virtue, the eighteenth-century edifice of civil society, built on the idea of natural sympathy—i.e., on the innate workings of virtue *in the public realm*—came tumbling down. For if one could no longer posit a public virtue or morality (and by the late eighteenth century this could no longer be rooted in a transcendent reality as it was in the natural law tradition), those ideational conditions upon which the whole concept of civil society rested were no longer valid. Hume, Smith, and Kant (and the whole liberal-individualist tradition that developed from their thought) accepted this distinction, within which "value" was relegated to the private sphere and rested essentially within the individual conscience. Within this tradition, civil society as an ethical space has no intrinsic meaning, and its regulative and attendant values are there for the protection and preservation of individual liberties. Here ethical value is the province of the particular individual and not of society as such.

Hegel and, following him, Marx sought a different way out of the impasse posed by Hume and Kant: that is, they sought to preserve the public space as an ethical entity—albeit in very different ways. For Hegel, as we have seen, this was achieved only in the sublation of civil society into the State; for Marx, as is well known, it was in the very eradication of the distinction between them—posed, in contradistinction to Hegel, not as an existing historical reality but as a future desideratum, to be achieved after the Revolution, when true human history would begin. Both, however, in their different solutions to the Kantian antinomy, mark the end of any idea of civil society as it was classically conceived.

If Hegel "resolves" civil society into the existent and ethical (universal) entity of the State, Marx, it can be said, resolves it into itself. That resolution, however, will be achieved only in the fu-

51

ture negation of the existent distinction between civil society and the State and a future unity of human existence within which true freedom will be achieved. Following Hegel, Marx rejected all "myths and fantasies" of the eighteenth century regarding the natural origin of civil society.[97] He was aware of the abiding contradiction of modern existence between the philosophically posited autonomous and isolated individual and his (and with Marx and Engels we begin to have her) social existence. For Marx, the eighteenth century, that epoch of civil society, produced both the isolated individual and the most highly developed forms of social relations. This dichotomous reality stands in contrast to that view of a "society of free competition" where "the individual *seems* detached from the nature ties." Marx's castigation of the eighteenth-century philosophy of the Scottish Enlightenment stems from its penchant to resolve both aspects of modern existence into a mythical and abstracted reading of human nature.

> The prophets of the eighteenth century, on whose shoulders Smith and Ricardo were still standing with their whole weight, envisaged this eighteenth-century individual—the product of the dissolution of feudal society on the one hand and of the new productive forces evolved since the sixteenth century on the other—as an ideal whose existence belonged to the past. *Not as a historical result, but as history's point of departure. Not as arising historically but as posited by nature,* because this individual was in conformity with nature, in keeping with their idea of human nature.[98]

Thus he follows Hegel in his historical account of the emergence of civil society and his rejection of the philosophical and anthropological fictions of the eighteenth century.

However, as Marx himself asserted, he did turn Hegel on his head, reversing the "abstract and idealist" form of Hegel's thought, which made of the development of world history "only the test" of the idea."[99] Nowhere is this more evident than in Marx's systematic analysis and critique of the Hegel's *Rechtphilosophie,* published as the "Contribution to the Critique of Hegel's Philosophy of Law." In this early work, Marx sets out (what would fashionably be today termed) to "deconstruct" the Hegelian edifice—practically verse by verse—to show how Hegel reversed the relations between the proper subjects and predicates of world history, making the Idea (*Begriff*, of Freedom) the subject and the real, concrete historically determined individuals, in their interrelations, conflicts, and different modes of existence, merely predicates of the Idea. In one of the famous passages from this work, Marx asserts:

> The idea is made the subject and the actual relation of family and civil society is conceived as its internal imaginary activity. Family and civil society are the premises of the state; they are the genuinely active elements, but in speculative philosophy things are inverted. When the idea is made the subject, however, the real subjects, namely, civil society, family, "circumstances, caprice, etc.," become unreal objective elements of the idea with a changed significance.[100]

This, which Jean Cohen has called the "immanent critique" of Hegel, is well known and centers, in the main, on showing the absurdity of Hegel's belief in the universal interests of the State (and of the bureaucratic class of civil servants) and in the embodiment of freedom in such organized (and for Marx class), corporate bodies as Estates.[101]

If for Marx the conflicts of particular wills that constitute civil society cannot be resolved into the universal ethical entity of the State, they are not, for all that, any less existent. In his "On the Jewish Question," Marx devotes long passages to an analysis of the particular and separate interests (based in the main on ownership of property—not yet of the means of production) that define life in civil society. Those conflicting interests were, for Marx, neither overcome nor resolved in the State. Rather, the modern state (of which the Declaration of the Rights of Man of 1793 was paradigmatic) legitimized them through the sanctity of property and its relations. In Marx's terms the very abolition of "birth, social rank, education, and occupation" as political distinctions "presupposes" their continual existence in society. The political state as universal entity exists only "in opposition to these elements of their being."[102] Instead of overcoming them, the State, as we shall see, is, at least partially, subservient to them.

The State, and with it the political realm of citizenship and participation, is not, in Marx's early work, reduced solely to an epiphenomenon of the productive forces of society. And it is in

these early writings—especially in "On the Jewish Question"—
that we can find Marx's most telling critique of civil society in its
distinction from the State. For here, the political realm, in its
abstraction from civil society, is still posited as a realm of freedom, in contrast to the life of civil society. What gives it this
character is precisely the *communal* nature of political life and
citizenship. Membership in the political community imbues the
individual with a *public* character, which is not so distant a cousin
from the reciprocity and recognition between social actors that we
found in the thought of the Scottish moralists.

The crucial difference, of course, is that here, with Marx, this
communal and public character is to be found *only* in the political
sphere of citizenship and *not* in civil society, where the individual
exists as an egoistic and isolated actor pursuing his interests in
opposition to those of other actors. In the words of an oft quoted
passage from "On the Jewish Question":

> Where the political state has attained its true development, man—
> not only in thought, in consciousness, but in reality, in life—leads
> a twofold life, a heavenly and an earthly life: life in the *political
> community*, in which he considers himself a *communal being*, and life
> in *civil society*, in which he acts as a *private individual*, regards other
> men as a means, degrades himself into a means and becomes a
> plaything of alien powers.[103]

Here, of course, we see Marx not only turning Hegel on his head
but adding a historical specificity to the Kantian injunction, thus
illuminating the incomplete nature of Kantian ethics, which leaves
morality (treating individuals only as ends never as means) beyond the pale of the public sphere.

For Marx, modern society is defined by this abiding contradiction between the abstract citizen (a communal being, participating in public life through citizenship) and man as a concrete
individual, a member of civil society, i.e., the egoistic individual
existing as Bürger, in opposition to the juridical existence of the
citizen. However, as noted above, the public realm exists not only
in abstraction and in opposition to civil society but, for Marx, in
subservience to it. In his analysis of the French Convention of
1793, Marx never tires of pointing out how "the so-called rights of
man, the droits de l'homme as distinct from the droits du citoyen,

are nothing but rights of a member of civil society, i.e., the rights of egoistic man, man separated from other men and from the community."[104] Consequently, "the citoyen is declared to be a servant of egoistic homme, . . . the sphere in which man acts as a communal being is degraded to a level below the sphere in which he acts as a particular being, and that, finally, it is not man as citoyen, but man as bourgeois who is considered the essential and true man."[105]

This division of human existence into disparate realms of civil society and political life was, for Marx, the defining characteristic of modernity as a civilization and belied any attempt to posit the autonomous, individual pole of this dichotomy in terms of true human nature. Marx thus rejected both the anthropological naïveté of the eighteenth century and the abstract idealism of Hegelian thought. He saw the very emergence of civil society as identical with the political emancipation of the eighteenth century and not as in any way preceding it (ontologically or historically). The emergence as well as differentiation of both resulted ulti- mately from the overthrow of the unified feudal order, where "the vital functions and conditions of life of civil society remained . . . political."[106] In feudalism the components of civil society were not individuals as such but estates, corporations, guilds, and privileged groups. These were the participatory actors in a public sphere. The destruction of feudalism "abolished the polit- ical character of civil society" and at the same time broke up civil society into its individual components—setting up, on the other side, the realm of political community as "the *general* concern of the nation, ideally independent of those *particular* elements of civil life."[107] Consequently "a person's distinct activity and dis- tinct situation in life were reduced to a merely individual signifi- cance. They no longer constituted the general relation of the individual to the state as a whole."[108] Existence in civil society thus became a matter of conflicting individual interests devoid of that communal mutuality which was relegated to the political province proper, as "Public affairs . . . became the general affair of each individual, and the political function became the individ- ual's general function."[109] This atomization of society—conceived of as "the emancipation of civil society from politics"—is at the same time a removal of those "bonds which restrained the egoistic spirit of civil society," i.e., the mutual responsibility that was part and parcel of feudal ties and obligations and was based on the relative "holistic" model of the social order represented by feudalism.[110]

Marx, as we can see here, is fundamentally concerned with the same set of problems that led his philosophical forerunners, one hundred years earlier, to their own idea of civil society. With them however, the very idea of civil society was a solution to the problem of how to posit a social whole beyond the particular interests that define individual existence. With Marx (here following Hegel), civil society it itself that realm of conflict between particular interests that must be somehow overcome in another (ethical) unity. And while we have been so conditioned by the divisions of twentieth-century academic disciplines, as well, I should add, as by the manifestly revolutionary character of Marx's writings, to view the Scottish moralists and Marx with quite different spectacles, to pigeonhole them in different analytic loci— the defining *problematique* of their writings was the same. From the eighteenth century through the nineteenth, of major concern to all social philosophers was the possibility (that is to say, the normative possibility) of positing a unified (or universal) vision of the social order that, at the same time, recognized the legal, moral, and economic autonomy of its component parts. The idea of civil society emerged at the beginning of this period as just such a solution. Its fundamental premises, rooted in a theological anthropology and combined with a naïve belief in the congruence of reason and sentiment, were critically undone within a short sixty years, as the writings of Hume and Kant testify. The problem first addressed by Hutcheson, Shaftesbury, and Ferguson, that of the proper relations between the individual and society, between the public and private realms, remained as the defining problem of social thought (and in fact continues to pursue anthropologists, sociologists, and philosophers into the last decade of the twentieth century).

The writings of Hegel and Marx, however, attest to the continuation (of sorts) of the civil society paradigm into the nineteenth century. In their own work, its viability as a concept and model of social representation disappears. In Hegel it disappears into the universal state, in Marx into the future reunification of civil and

political society. "Only," Marx asserts at the end of "On the Jewish Question,"

> when the real, individual man re-absorbs in himself the abstract
> citizen, and as an individual human being has become a species-
> being in his everyday life, in his particular work, and in his par-
> ticular situation, only when man has recognized and organized his
> "forces propres" as social forces, and consequently no longer sep-
> arates social power from himself in the shape of political power,
> only then will human emancipation have been accomplished.[111]

With this, the classic idea of civil society comes to an end. Its
shadow, however, continually remained in the background of
both liberal and socialist theory and politics into the twentieth
century. In liberalism, the idea of the morally (and economically)
autonomous individual, which served as the basis of the idea of
civil society, remained as the fundamental premise of political
life. However, as we shall see in coming chapters, the loss of the
early, eighteenth-century notion of natural sympathy and moral
sentiments made it increasingly difficult to root this individual in
a community and so to present a coherent vision of society beyond its individual members. This difficulty of representing society as such has plagued liberal theory down to this day. Marxist
and socialist thought in general remained within the original
Marxist formula of overcoming the contradictions of civil society
in a new unity of social and political life. Developments in Eastern
Europe have proved this unity to be not only morally untenable
but, more recently, unworkable as well. The unity has proved, in
Lesek Kolakowski words, a "soteriological myth" with terrible
consequences.[112]

This modern condition, characterized in both its liberal and its
socialist variants by a fundamental crises of representing society,
has led contemporary social theorists to return to the original
Scottish Enlightenment idea of civil society as a possible resolution of contemporary impasses (of both socialist and liberal
thought). Posited as a panacea, the idea of civil society has reap-
peared among writers across the political spectrum and in many
different countries, and the works of the Scottish moralists are
being reissued in paperback editions, even retranslated into the
languages of East-Central Europe. (The first edition [1767] of Fer-

guson's *A History of Civil Society* recently sold for the record price of £1,870.)[113] Having reviewed here the main arguments upon which the idea of civil society was based, we shall turn to a more analytic consideration of the historical conditions of its emergence and of the ideas or world-images that accompanied its emergence. Such an exercise will, I believe, aid us in assessing the possible continuing validity of the idea of civil society both as a normative ideal and, more concretely, as a set of institutional practices defining social relations in the contemporary world.

CHAPTER 2

The Sources of Civil Society

Reason and the Individual

I

In the previous chapter we traced the course of the idea of civil society from its early modern origins in the thought of John Locke to its theoretical dissolution in the late eighteenth and nineteenth centuries. This devolution took the form of a three-pronged attack, each prong building on the previous one, though analytically distinct from it. Here we may think of the names of Hume, Hegel, and Marx as signposts on the way toward the increasing loss of coherence in the civil society idea. Hume, we recall, distinguished between the "is" and the "ought" and in so doing broke with the naïve anthropology of moral sentiments and natural sympathy upon which the idea of civil society rested. Hegel, aware of the contradictions within civil society (the true essence of the "is"), sought to overcome it in the ethical entity of the State. Marx, as is well known, followed the Hegelian critique

59

of civil society, positing its "sublation" not in the existing political State of the nineteenth century but in a future metahistorical entity where the "true" essence of man would unfold.

In our analysis of the civil society tradition a number of themes have emerged as central concerns to those writers who joined the debate over civil society. One of those themes was the perduring need to articulate some vision of the individual that would both uphold his (and ever so much later, her) autonomy and agentic nature and at the same time present a vision of a "public" —that is, a group of individuals sharing core ideas, ideals, and values. An important point, one that must be kept in mind, is that the ties binding this public, uniting these autonomous individuals, were not conceived as solely instrumental ties of market relations and commercial exchange. Rather, as we have seen again and again, it was a common set of moral sources, of sentiments and sympathy, that the eighteenth century writers invoked to express this mutuality.

Yet another of these themes, connected to the above, was the concern with rooting social order in a representative vision of Reason that was prescriptive of social norms and values of mutuality. Through this vision of shared Reason the individual as well as the public aspects of social existence were maintained— especially in the thought of Immanuel Kant (with the caveat that morality proper was relegated to the private sphere, and the public arena lost its ethical character). Finally, there was the progressive articulation of Reason as embodying universal principles valid for all people at all times. (This development was concomitant with the growth of scientific thought and the application of rational principles to the problems of the natural world.)

Already with the writings of David Hume an irreconcilable contradiction was perceived to exist between the last two of these ideas. The very universalism of Reason precluded its normative elements. (We recall again the Kantian solution to this problem and its derivatives in terms of the idea of society as an ethical entity). In many ways the later-nineteenth- and twentieth-century trajectory of the idea of civil society rested on attempts either to live with this contradiction (in the liberal-individualist tradition) or to overcome it (in the socialist one). Each tradition can record its successes and failures. However, before we turn to latter-day expressions of the idea of civil society within these traditions and to their social embodiments, we must first explore in greater depth the historical and analytic foundations of the original idea of civil society. More concretely, we must return to those ideas of the individual and Reason as embodying universal principles of justice and morality and analyze both their historical development and their place in the idea of civil society.

How, we must ask, did these ideas come, in the eighteenth century to provide the foundation for that representative vision of society which we identify with the idea of civil society? Civil society, as a model for the social order, rested on these ideas, which were invested with a transcendental (and earlier transcendent) dimension, and that is precisely what provided them with their unifying force and (in more social-scientific terms) civil society with its legitimacy. How then did the ideas of universal Reason and the individual come to be invested with this transcendent dimension? How did they come to be seen as truths beyond history, space, and time?

This chapter is devoted to providing some tentative answers to these questions through an analysis of Christian, more especially ascetic-Protestant, ideas of the individual and the manner in which they informed the natural law speculation of the early modern period. The synthesis of Protestant individualism and natural law doctrines as providing the basis for the idea of civil society will be studied in the context of eighteenth-century America, where, many argue, the idea of civil society was most fully embodied.

The United States would in fact seem a perfect case for exploring both the sources of the idea of civil society and its current problems. In our analysis of the sources of the idea of civil society we shall thus pay special attention to developments in seventeenth- and eighteenth-century America. For if the "theory" of civil society received its fullest articulation in the Scottish Enlightenment, the historical model of this theory was seen to reside across the Atlantic. There, more than anywhere else, the new idea of the individual invested with transcendental qualities emerged as the basis of the social order. Moreover, in eighteenth-century America the relations between these individuals were seen to rest upon the foundation of a shared appeal to the laws of reason as exemplified by those natural law doctrines that, as we have seen, played so salient a role in the Scottish Enlightenment idea of civil society.

It was for this very reason that the United States provided for the philosophers of the eighteenth and nineteenth centuries (and for many thereafter) the model of civil society, with its voluntary associations, separation of Church and State, federalist (as opposed to Statist) concepts, and protection of individual liberties. More significantly, the singular lack of a salient socialist movement there in the nineteenth and twentieth centuries would seem to point to the very "success" or achieved synthesis of civil society there. The socialist movement emerged in nineteenth-century Europe from precisely the failure of the idea of civil society—as a protest against its inherently (class) particularism and positing in its stead a new (supposedly) universalism (of the working class). The absence of such a movement in the United States would seem to attest to the achievement of the classical idea of civil society there.

In America, then, a synthesis of reason and revelation informed the basis of civil society in a manner that was both salient and unique. To appreciate more fully the sources of the idea of civil society, it is thus best to contextualize them within that social formation that has been, for so many, the model and paradigm of modernity as a civilization.

In the final section of this chapter we shall explore the more analytic or theoretical implications of this synthesis as well as the problems adhering to it in more contemporary attempts to re-present society in these terms.

II

In the broadest of terms what the modern ideas of Reason (and of the individual) implied was the relocation of the perceived source of the moral order, seen from the late seventeenth and eighteenth centuries as resting within society and not in a transcendent, ~~other~~ otherworldly realm. Indeed, when we consider the importance of the contract tradition of government so central to the liberal-individualist tradition, we realize just how

62

important this newly articulated idea of the moral order has been to the political traditions of the past two hundred years.

These assumptions about the source of moral action are in fact linked to some of the major modern intellectual traditions to emerge from Western Christian civilization. We may think, for example, of Vico's immanent historicist conceptions of natural equity and universal jurisprudence or of the republican tradition of civic humanism, as among its intellectual cousins.[1] These examples notwithstanding, the notion of the moral order as rooted in a society of individuals, as a strain of political thought in the Western tradition, calls for some inquiry, for a number of reasons. First, this tradition continues to be but one of a number of political traditions that defined the locus of moral authority in very different spheres. In this context Burke's traditionalism, Hegel's World Spirit, and the Marxian dialectic of history exemplify alternative notions of the sources of moral action[2] (all, we might add, emerging from the problems and contradictions inherent to the civil society tradition, studied above). Second, the conception of the moral order as resting in the community must be differentiated from the contract-tradition *per se*. That is, the very positing of society in ethical terms contains a moral dimension that was not found in the idea of the contract as developed by the Utilitarian followers of David Hume. (Again, we recall the problems that inhered to the idea of civil society following the Humean critique.) Finally, this notion goes well beyond the concepts of natural law, which—in their various forms—characterized Western political thought for close to two millennia. Natural Law, upon which moral action had been based, was, until the empiricism of Hume, rooted in a transcendent order.[3] As Otto Gierke pointed out, *Lex Naturalis*, which "radiated from a principle transcending earthly power," stood above all notions of popular sovereignty and of representation (the exercise of the power entrusted to the Community of the Faithful by a General Council).[4] While its rationalization in the late eighteenth and the nineteenth centuries divested it of all "transcendental dignity," in the Christian era it had been rooted in the concepts of *lex aeterna* and *lex divina*, and among the Stoics, in the world-immanence of the Logos.[5]

Thus we see that from a historical perspective, the "deification" of society, and of the agentic and autonomous individual on which it stood, as the ultimate matrix and source of the moral good in Western civilization is not unproblematic. It is precisely this problem—of the "transcendent" aura invested in society as a source of morality, ethics, and the normative vision of the social order—that we shall deal with in the following. To do so, however, we must elaborate somewhat on the contradiction inherent in the positing of society as the locus of a transcendent morality.

It is best to begin by exploring what we mean by the very idea of a transcendent morality. The Christian tradition, within which the idea of civil society developed, was one of the great religious civilizations or world-historical religions. By civilizational or world-historical religion, we are referring to one of those civilizations in which there emerged and became constitutionalized in the period between 500 B.C.E. and A.D. 600,

> . . . a conception of a basic tension between the transcendental and the mundane orders, a conception which differed greatly from that of a close parallelism between these two orders or their mutual embedment which was prevalent in so-called pagan religions, in those very societies from which these post-Axial Age civilizations emerged.[6]

The emergence of these Axial civilizations followed a period of institutional breakdown characterized by a similar breakdown of cosmological symbolism. This period, in Eric Voeglin's terms, of "cosmological disintegration" during different "times of troubles" resulted in a new appreciation of the relations between the individual and society and the cosmic order.[7] The change was accomplished through the fundamental restructuring of the terms of relations between mundane and transcendent orders.[8] As has been noted by S. N. Eisenstadt and others, the emergence of this conception in the civilizations of Ancient Israel, Christianity, Ancient Greece, China, Hinduism, Buddhism, and Islam constituted a major force in the restructuring of the terms of collective life and of the principles of political legitimation.[9]

In the context of the present study, the emergence of Christianity as an Axial civilization is of utmost importance. For the Axial break (and the emergence of what in other contexts has been termed the Great Civilizations or Historical Religions) presumed a fundamental reordering of the nature of relations between society and the powers governing the cosmos.[10] Breaking down their mutual interpenetration, the Axial age posited a new conception of the social order, autonomous from, but in tension with, the cosmic (henceforth conceived as transcendent) sphere. The institutionalization of this conception of a chasm between mundane and transcendent orders (between society and the cosmos) and, more importantly, the search to overcome this chasm—in Weberian terms, to attain "salvation"—became in Axial civilizations in general and in Christianity in particular the matrix of those social visions within which social and political activity was conceived.[11]

In most general terms, once society was oriented to a transcendent vision, and once monistic world views gave way to a "rational metaphysic and religious ethic," the sources of the moral order became intimately linked with that vision.[12] When the undifferentiated "magic garden" of the world was supplanted by the conception of a chasm between transcendent and mundane spheres, ethics, morality, and hence also the ideal image of society were thenceforth linked to the particular type of religious vision that ordered the relations between the two spheres.[13]

Within those world-historical religions in which the transcendent sphere was posited in terms of a personal-creator God, the source of moral authority was conceived as rooted in the transcendent sphere.[14] While the moral injunctions of more immanent world-historical religions, such as Confucianism, saw morality as rooted in an achieved harmony with the mundane spheres of existence, the more otherworldly and transcendent Judeo-Christian tradition rooted its moral imperatives in the Logos of a creator God.[15]

Within these civilizations a dichotomy was thus posited between the exigent and mutable world of man and a transcendent order. The ultimate sources of both morality and social authority were thenceforth conceived as rooted in this transcendent order. Given the existence of this conception, in one form or another, for more than 1,500 years of West European history, how, we must ask, was the locus of moral imperatives redirected in the eighteenth century to the more mundane sphere of society? How was the mundane sphere of society, and more especially of civil society, invested with that moral suasion which previously had been the province of the transcendent? What, moreover, were the historical dynamics that informed this fundamental restructuring of moral action in the Christian West in the seventeenth and eighteenth centuries? To answer these queries and so gain an understanding of both the moral sources of the idea of civil society and the problems currently attendant upon these sources, we must follow the path opened up by Max Weber and Ernst Troeltsch into the analysis of Christian civilization as providing those "world-images" which stand as the source of our own.

We have seen that the sources of moral authority as resting in a society of autonomous individuals sharing the vision of a universal reason was central to the idea of civil society as it developed in the modern era from John Locke to Immanuel Kant. Broadly stated, these ideas were rooted in a particularly Christian, indeed, even more a Calvinist, vision of man and society and cannot be understood apart from this referent and the unique way this vision was instituted in certain West European societies and most especially in the United States, where the roots of the civil society idea in Christian revelation are easiest to assess. There, however, as elsewhere, the sources of civil society are to be found in a set of ideas that predate not only the emergence of the *Novus Ordo Seclorum*—but even of the migration to the American Strand in the 1620s.

One of these sources, as noted above, was the unique view of the individual as an autonomous entity secure in his or her individuality beyond communal ties and referents. This idea of the individual, which stands at the core of civil society, was preeminently a Christian idea.[16] We have in fact seen these Christian sources in the thought of John Locke as well as in the development of the natural law tradition in European political thought. The idea of the individual as value originated in the Christian vision of what Ernst Troeltsch has termed the "individual-in-relation-to-God" and in the soteriological (salvational) drama which defined this existence. What this meant is that the individual was in Louis Dumont's terms an "outworldly-individual," that is to say, individual value was achieved through *imitatio Deo* and the concomitant rejection of this-worldly concerns and pursuits.[17] That value attached to the individual was here attendant on his or her relation with the transcendental otherworldly realm

66

and not through existence in the world. In more schematic, and perforce simplistic, terms, Grace, which was the source of value, was otherworldly and was attained through otherworldly pursuits. Thus from the writings of Saint Augustine the schema of salvation was defined by a growing separation of Nature and Grace (this-worldly and otherworldly realms) and of the World and the Church, a separation that formed the ideational basis of the individual's life activities.[18]

The separation of this-worldly and otherworldly salvational activities reached its apogee in the thirteenth century with the crystallization of an embracing sacramental theology. This doctrine, which rooted the definition of both collective and individual identities in the religio-moral community of the Eucharist, effectively divorced the scheme of salvation from all this-worldly and mundane referents.[19] Grace, posited beyond time and history, continued to define the locus of individual existence in the *corpus mysticum* of the Church.

This doctrine would undergo radical changes during the Protestant Reformation. Indeed, what I wish to suggest is that our notion of the ethically autonomous individual—upon which the idea of civil society rested—is predicated on the introjection within the individual of a particular dimension of grace which had previously been defined in otherworldly terms. More specifically, the emergence of the concept of the individual as, *pace* Durkheim, "a touchstone" of morality "partaking in a transcendental majesty" was the outcome of a redefinition of grace from an out-worldly attribute to a function of life within the world.

This transformation of the terms of grace and with them of individual identity was, within certain Protestant communities of the seventeenth society, rooted in the primacy of the "Word" and a renewed emphasis on the indwelling of grace as the basis for individual and social existence. Negating the efficacy of externally applied grace, Calvinism did away as well with the mediating function of priestly authority. In terms of sacramental theology, this was expressed in the "de-sacralization" of the Eucharist and its annulment as a means of grace.[20] Doing away similarly with the soteriological efficacy of externally enforced norms, Calvinism posited voluntary obedience to God's law as the only true basis of Christian life.[21] This doctrine served as the basis of a new conception of cosmic order with significant implications for the redefinition of individual identity and with it the basis of moral authority.

The basis of the new ideal social and moral order, the new *ecumene*, was thenceforth to be the "Holy Community" of "saints," voluntarily participating in Christ.[22] This new definition of community was to form the basis of a new, ideal model of Christian society. Subsequently, the boundaries of Christian community were not those of common participation in the sacrament of the Eucharist, but common, voluntary subjugation of each individual will to the Will of God. By willful participation in the Body of Christ, a new community was defined, which, like that of the early Church, existed in the body of the old, but was distinct from it. In Calvin's words: "It is the godly man's duty to abstain from all familiarity with the wicked, and not to enmesh himself with them in any voluntary relationship."[23] Such a code of conduct led to the effective separation within each parish between two bodies of communicants: "On one side there were the true, genuine, faithful and active Christians, and on the other those who were merely nominal and worldly." There thus was effective, in Troeltsch's words, "the separation of the pure body of communicants from the impure."[24]

For our concern with the development of new models of the moral order based on the autonomous and agentic individual, the changes in the fundamental terms of Christian society engendered by Calvinism are of utmost significance. On one level, Calvinist thought prepared the way for a breakdown of the existing solidarities of Christian society and posited a new set of ties between people—in Donald Kelly's telling phrase, "a kind of sublimation of blood into belief."[25] Implied in this dictum is precisely that "freeing" of the individual from traditional, primordial and particular solidarities based on kinship and territorial identities that we identify with the forms of modern society. Within the Calvinist communities of the sixteenth and seventeenth centuries a new locus of social solidarity, trust, and mutuality was posited—one based on sharing ideological commitments to the work of Reformation as exemplified most saliently in the covenants contracted between English and, later, North American Puritans in the late sixteenth and early seventeenth centuries. These

68

covenants, which, in the words of the Puritan divine Richard Rogers, . . . "did knit them in that love, the bond whereof could not be broken either on their part which now sleepe in the Lord, whiles they heere lived, nor in them which yet remaine, by any adversarie power onto this day"[26] provided a new "metaphysical universe" where individual identities were conceived in terms of a community of saints—each standing in unmediated relation to the source of transcendent power and authority.

What was transformed, however, was not only the "status" of the individual—imbued with a new autonomy and agency—but the nature of the ties between these individuals, that is, the nature of society itself. For these ties were defined no longer by a tradition of primordial "givennes" (membership in a territorial or kinship collective) but by what may be termed ideological ties of, as Kelly noted, a shared set of beliefs. These beliefs were still, in the sixteenth and seventeenth centuries, defined by their transcendent referents (i.e., by the salvational doctrines of ascetic-Puritanism), but, already, we can glimpse the emergence of that model of individual identity and shared (moral) commitments with which we have been familiar in the thought of the Scottish Enlightenment and whose sources was to be found in the Protestant Reformation of the sixteenth century and its redefinition of the nature of both social and individual identity and meaning.

As part of this dynamic, and with great significance for the future, it should be noted that the Reformation also articulated a new notion of the relationships of authority within society. For, while accepting in practice the need for positive law and structures of domination (until the establishment of the Kingdom of God), it negated their locus in any ultimate principles of order (as articulated in Thomist philosophy).[27] Instead, it posited in the sphere of Church polity a conception of the ministry based on consent, collective agreement, and the fundamental equality of believers and ministers before God.

These new terms of social existence were moreover defined by the profoundly this-worldly thrust of Protestant soteriology. In medieval Catholic Europe, the only "life-calling" legitimized in sacred or otherworldly terms was that of the monastic orders. However, as noted by Weber and others, the importance of the Reformation lay precisely in its "endowment of secular life with a new order of religious life as a sphere of "Christian opportunity.' "[28] It was thus only with the Reformation that secular callings were given religious legitimation and perceived as possible paths to salvation.

The orientation toward a greater this-worldliness, toward the "justification" of the whole person and his everyday life in terms of salvation, was, of course, at the center of Weber's famous Protestant Ethic thesis.[29] Its implications, however, are broader (as Weber himself realized) than the mere rationalization of economic activity. For, with the "demise of the older images of 'Religion' and World, Law and Grace" and with mundane life imbued with soteriological efficacy, the way was open for rebuilding secular society in the same image of perfection that had characterized monastic life.[30] As Benjamin Nelson pointed out,

> . . . a fundamental reorientation of the social and cultural patterns of the Western world could not occur until the medieval administration of self and spiritual direction fell before the onslaughts of Luther, Calvin and their followers. So long as a distinction was made between the special calling of monks who lived "outside the world," systematically observing a rule in their pursuit of the status of perfection and everyone else in the world, who lived irregularly, without benefit of a rule, in the midst of continued temptation; so long was there a brake on the incentive of ordinary men and women to forge integrated characters with a full sense of responsibility.[31]

This new sense of moral authority and with it of individual responsibility was expressed in pursuit of a state of perfection within the orders and institutions of the world. The basis of this pursuit was, as Benjamin Nelson has indicated, the specifically Protestant form of illuminism, rooted in the immediacy of grace.[32] No longer mediated by the sacraments (and thus no longer contained within the institutions of the Church), grace became present in the immediate, this-worldly historical present. Consequently, as noted by Nelson, there

> . . . developed a new integration of life, both personal and political through the rearrangement of existing boundaries . . . older maps were redrawn, fixing new co-ordinates for all focal points of exis-

tence and faith: religion-world, sacred-profane, civil-ecclesiastical, liberty-law, public-private. [In this rearrangement] New scope and authority were given to the Inner Light, sparked by the Holy Spirit. This was the Holy Spirit within each individual and within groups. This inspiration came to serve as the basis for vastly expanded involvement of new participants in a variety of different relations of self and world: charismatic activism, quietistic mysticism, covenanted corporate consensualism, natural rights individualism, a religion of Pure Reason.[33]

The strong impetus toward social and institutional restructuring that characterized ascetic or sectarian Protestantism and resulted in a new vision of the individual as a moral and autonomous agent was linked to this introjection of grace within the orders of the world. As various studies of English Puritanism clearly indicate, the activities of the community of the elect set them apart from and, ultimately, in conflict with previously existing definitions of communal solidarity and terms of membership.[34] For it was not solely in the separation of the community of the elect from the "imperfect world"—i.e., from existing communal loci—that the "Holy Commonwealth" could be realized. Rather, only by imbuing the world beyond this community with a similar attitude of "election" or "inner grace" could mundane activity be rendered soteriologically efficacious.[35] This implied, in more analytic terms, that the particular ascetic-Protestant conception of grace and illuminism had to be instituted beyond the boundaries of the community of the religiously elect and within the social world at large.

III

The only society where these principles were, at least partially, institutionalized was in the Puritan communities of North America. It was only there, on the shores of the New World, that the religious and social principles of ascetic-Protestantism became a viable and salient component of a new political tradition, one which, not surprisingly, we identify with the idea of civil society. The communities of "visible saints" founded in the New World in pursuit of the Holy Commonwealth

71

were structured around the kind of religious orientation Troeltsch termed the particularism of grace and Dumont characterized as ascetic-inworldliness.[36] That is to say they were conceived as communities founded on the principles of grace and oriented to the construction of a "Holy Commonwealth" of covenanted saints. The foundations of this community were, as John Winthrop preached aboard the *Arabella,* a"double lawe, . . . the lawe of nature and the lawe of grace, or the moralle lawe and the lawe of the gospell."[37] The "Cittie upon the Hill" founded on the American Strand was thus an attempt to realize grace within mundane, historical, and worldly actions and institutions (and not in otherworldly or sacramental rituals). As explained by John Winthrop in 1637: "Whereas the way of God hath always been to gather his churches out of the world: now the world, or civil state, must be raised out of the churches."[38]

As opposed to other "communities of saints" (such as the Anabaptists in Munster, for example), one of the unique features of New England's "errand into the wilderness" was that though New England Congregational Puritanism attempted to remake the world in the image of grace, it nevertheless maintained the autonomy of law (and so also of representative institutions) within the political and social structures established in the New World. In their search to establish not only the "true Church" but also a Christian or Godly Commonwealth, New England Puritans established a political order based on a particular cooperation of civil and ecclesiastical institutions, existing "in co-ordinate state, in the same place reaching forth mutually to help each to other for the welfare of both according to God." Implying neither the unification nor the opposition of civil and ecclesiastical spheres, the Puritans maintained that "God's institutions (such as the Government of Church and of Commonwealth) may be close and compact, and co-ordinate one to another and yet not confounded."[39] The bases of this coordination were the covenants drawn up in the civil and social realms "to profess and practice one truth according to that most perfect rule, the foundation whereof is everlasting love."[40]

The Puritans founded their social venture on two distinct forms of the covenant. One was the Church covenant, governing the ordering of the religious realm, while the other was the social or

72

federal covenant, drawn up before the foundation of town or Church and intended as the basis for the civil polity. The coordination between the two covenants and their respective realms provided the basis for the Puritan notion of theocracy, that

> . . . Form of Government where 1. the people that have the power of chusing their Governours are in Covenant with God: 2. Wherein the men chosed by them are godly men, and fitted with a spirit of government: 3. In which the Laws, they rule by are the Laws of God: 4. Wherein Laws are executed, Inheritances alloted, and civil differences are composed, according to God's appointment: 5. In which men of God are consulted with in all hard cases, and in matters of Religion. . . . The form which was received and established among the people of Israel whil'st the Lord God was their Governour . . . and is the same that we plead for.[41]

This form of government, which kept the ungodly from participation in the political realm and limited both election to office and the right to "choose among themselves magistrates and officers" to the company of saints, was a theocracy only in a very special sense of the term. For rather than the establishment of a sacerdotal order under the rule of ministers, it was an attempt to constitute a pure social order, untainted by the corruption of history. It was indeed this very desire which drove them to the New World, for as Edward Johnson declared, "We chose not the place for the Land, that our Lord Christ may raigne over us, both in Church and Commonwealth."[42]

And it was this vision that informed the unique political and legal structure legitimizing, in terms of biblical precedent, the judicial basis of life in the Massachusetts colony. With it, the colonists tempered the principles of fundamental law that they brought with them from England.[43] As stated clearly in the open sentences of the 1648 *Book of General Lawes and Liberties:*

> So soon as God had set up Political Government among his people Israel he gave them a body of Lawes for judgement both in civil and criminal cases. These were brief and fundamental principles.[44]

Fundamental laws were here rooted in Godly commandments, and human laws were rooted in the Laws of God, for

> . . . God was said to be amongst them or neer to them because of his Ordinances established by himselfe and their Lawes righteous because himselfe was their Lawgiver.[45]

Going one step further and modeling their commonwealth on the "Judicial laws of Moses," the leaders of the Massachusetts colony combined the notion of fundamental law, existing beyond any specific institution and common to all nations, with the covenant of grace (and so with their own models of Church organization) that they may "injoyne the special presence of God in the puritie and native simplicity of all his ordinances by which he is so near to his own people."[46] Basing their own ordinances on the "Lawes of God," they thus conceived of Church and Civil States as

> . . . planted and growne up (like two twinnes) together like that of Israel in the wilderness by which we were put in minde (and had opportunitie put into our hands) not only to gather our Churches, and set up the Ordinances of Christ Jesus in them according to the Apostolick patterne by such light as the Lord graciously afforded us: but also withall to frame our civil Politie, and Lawes according to the rules of his most holy word whereby each do help and strengthen other (the Churches the civil Authoritie, and the civil Authoritie the Churches) and so both prosper the better without such aemulation and contention for priviledges or priority as have proved the misery (if not ruine) of both in so many other places.[47]

Authority in the World (in the form of the civil magistrate), no less than in the Church (in the form of ministers, elders, and deacons) was therefore rooted in a particular model of communal identity based on the covenanted church of visible saints. Submission to this authority was based on acceptance not only of the moral law of God (or the law of nature, common to all humanity), but of that positive law of God revealed first in the Mosaic injunctions of the Old Testament and later transformed by the covenant of grace at the time of Christ.[48] The organization of social life according to the later emanations of God's positive law were seen to define the peculiarities of the New England Way, with its unique calling of covenanted Churches and definitions of the nature of the relations between the Church and the World. This is amply attested to in Sheppard and Allin's defense of Congregational policy in 1648, where they declare that

> . . . civil societies and governments thereof is herein left to rules of human prudence by the Lord and Government of the Whole World; and therefore may admit various forms of Government, various Laws and Constitutions, . . . but here in the Kingdom of Christ we must attend to what kind of Churches he hath instituted, so we must cleave to such rules, priviledges and forms of government and administrations he hath ordained.[49]

As can be seen, a distinction is posited here between two laws—the law of nature, common to all societies, and the law of grace, the distinct province of New England. The fulfillment of the latter in addition to the former is, indeed, presented as the imperative of New England's divine mission, of realizing therein the Kingdom of Christ.

Characteristic of New England (in both Church and Commonwealth) was thus a particular interweaving of natural law doctrine with the covenant of grace—imbuing the former with soteriological efficacy while rooting the latter in the structures and orders of the world. Existing as neither an ordered hierarchy (as in the Thomistic system) nor in opposition (as in other communities of saints), this very interweaving of natural law and Godly ordinances served two purposes. It drew political authority and institutions into the salvational drama of new England's mission but, at the same time, maintained the autonomy of those institutions (and the law upon which they were based) from sacerdotal interference. The implications of this unique synthesis on the future role of natural law doctrines in the eighteenth century was, as we shall see, significant. No less important for both this development and the idea of civil society was the particular manner in which the original Puritan conception of grace—upon which the Puritans' social and political order was founded—as transformed over the course of the seventeenth society.

For as in other sectarian Protestant communities, one of the fundamental problems faced by New England Puritans lay in ordering the concrete relations between the Church and the World—that is, between the Church of the elect and the unregenerate members of the community. Once the initial expectations that all members of the community would join the Church of covenanted saints was disappointed, this problem took on an urgency that was to continue throughout the seventeenth century.

The urgency can be understood only if we take into consideration the importance of the notion of a community sharing in the experience of grace in the structuring of the social order in seventeenth-century Massachusetts. For the very basis of the Puritan "errand into the wilderness" was, as we have seen, to constitute a commonwealth based on grace.[50] Membership in the political community was predicated on the experience of regeneration and infusion of grace. The covenant of sainted individuals who could give evidence of this experience represented the ideal model of collective identity as well as the outer boundaries of membership therein.

The problem of constructing a social order based on the "particularism of grace" became apparent, however, in the first years of settlement and persisted throughout the century. For, as John Bossy once remarked, the spirit "bloweth where it listeth" and, following a mass of conversions to the Church (of regenerate saints) in 1633, there was a drop in conversionary experience.[51] Moreover, the second generation, which came of age in the 1650s, did not provide the same evidence of saving grace as its fathers. The economic growth of midcentury, which brought demographic change and structural diversification, also contributed to the breakdown of communal norms and solidarities.[52]

With the fragmentation of communal life following the early decades of settlement, adherence to the original values declined. The realization by midcentury that the second generation could not provide the same testimony of grace as its fathers, engendered a major crisis in mid-seventeenth-century Puritanism. This problem of maintaining an ideal model of the social order was ultimately met by a radical redefinition of the normative order (of the ideal *ecumene*), which had originally been identified with the Church of regenerate saints. By the end of the century this normative order was seen to reside within each individual soul and not within the community of the elect. This development was a complicated process that evolved over the course of the seventeenth century and involved the transformation of many of the fundamental religious precepts and practices of early seventeenth-century New England Puritanism.[53]

It involved in fact a transformation of the Congregational

Churches themselves. While the Congregational Churches themselves became more sacerdotal and sacramental with such developments as the Half Way Covenant and Stoddardism (and thus
lost their "sect" character), the locus of the community of saints
representing the particularism of grace moved from membership
in the Church to membership in the community.[54] Progressing
through such developments as the covenant ownings of the 1670s
and later through the various "little Awakenings" (1733–35) leading up to the Great Awakening itself, a new sense of national
identity developed, uniting all members in a communal identity
of both religious and civic dimensions.[55] The Puritan sect as an
instance of the "particularism of grace," defining membership in
the "Holy Commonwealth," gave way to a secularized form of
civic virtue embracing the whole of the collective.[56]

The crux of these changes, out of which a new collective identity emerged, was in the way in which, over the course of the
century, grace, no longer defined in otherworldly terms but as an
attribute of the very this-worldly attempt to construct the Holy
Commonwealth and originally seen to reside in the community of
regenerate saints, was interiorized into individual conscience.

By this I mean a growing sense of the privatization of grace
beyond the boundaries of the community of saints. By the end of
the seventeenth century, in New England (which provides after
all the only attempt to institute the Congregational Puritan vision
of the polity based on grace) the earlier distinction between Nature and Grace and the World and the Church, which had divided
society in two, distinguishing, that is, between regenerate saints
and the unregenerate members of the community, had become
transformed. Instead, the "boundaries" of the normative moral
order (based on grace) were "displaced" from within the community to within each individual. As the Congregational
Churches lost their sect character and as grace was transformed
into conscience, so too the earlier distinction between regenerate
and unregenerate members of the community became a distinction with each individual. This process resulted in a new concept
of the moral order as resting, ultimately, not on grace but on the
moral behavior of each and every individual, who carried within
the possible sources of salvation as well as damnation. Signifi-

77

cantly, by the end of the seventeenth and in the early years of the eighteenth century, the criteria for membership in the Churches of New England came to rest less and less on the attestation of saving grace and more on the (public or civic) moral rectitude of the individual communicant.[57] Personal morality rather than collective grace had become the defining term of the normative order and of participation therein.

If we recall here our earlier analysis of the idea of civil society and of the need to reconcile interest and value, egoism and altruism, private and public, individual and social existence, we can appreciate just how important the Reformation tradition was, in both setting out the problem and pointing the way to its solution. If the rise of private interests was a feature of the growing market economy of the late seventeenth and eighteenth centuries, the terms of the potential conflict between individual and social interests were posited in ethical terms taken from religious sources.

IV

The unified (what Louis Dumont would call "holistic") society of traditional norms, values, and commitments had broken down into one of individuals freed both from the organic/particular and primordial identities of kith, kin, and territory and from their identity in the universal Catholic Church. The modern individual who emerged in the eighteenth century continued, however, to embody that transcendental status of an individual-in-relation-to-God. What had changed and changed drastically was the arena of this relation. No longer defined in an other-worldly *ecumene*, the individual was henceforth of the world as well as in it. On the one hand the individual social actor carried within that universal value which had previously been the province of the whole (Christian society and later, with the Reformation, the "Holy Commonwealth" of visible saints). This (universal) value, still in the seventeenth century articulated in terms of grace and the privatization or internalization of grace within the communicant, was, by the eighteenth century, already joined with a more secular morality and pre-Christian ideas of natural law (as for instance in John Wise's 1717 *Vindication of the*

78

Government of New England Churches). On the other hand, the individual in this period also emerged as a bearer of private interests and goals, which were perceived as standing in potential conflict with those universal values (whose definition was slowly changing from a religious to a secular idiom, i.e., from grace to morality).

What is nevertheless critical for the idea of civil society is the continuity, into the eighteenth century, of both the transcendental status of the individual (and of a society of said individuals) and the division of individual identity into universal/moral and private/egoistic components. Rooted in the particular manner through which ascetic-Protestantism was institutionalized—in less sociological jargon, in the way it became part of our tradition, one of our moral sources—this division within the individual was, as we have seen earlier, one of the foundations of the idea of civil society—of its problems and well as of their solution. For if the source of moral action rested within the individual conscience, its realization pointed back to the community of saints and to a this-worldly realm nevertheless defined by grace. If, as anthropology replaced theology in the eighteenth century, this community was no longer defined in terms of grace but in terms of moral sentiments, it was nevertheless posited in those universal terms stemming from the Christian tradition.

Not surprisingly this confluence of traditions—Christian grace and secular morality—as the basis for the polity found unique and exemplary expression in the integration of natural law philosophy with the now secularized visions of the Holy Commonwealth in eighteenth-century New England. Thus, for example, John Wise's 1717 *Vindication of the Government of New England Churches*, mentioned above, provides the first example of the use of Lockean arguments drawn from natural law philosophy (with its strong orientation to Reason as the sole arbitrator of the "good") in eighteenth-century New England. Intervening in the debate over Church policy, Wise nevertheless draws the bulk of his argument from natural law theory. Referring not only to Puffendorf, but to Plato and Aristotle as well, Wise develops the ideas of Grotius on the confluence of the Laws of Nature and Natural Reason.[58] For Wise man's "Original Liberty [is] Instampt upon his Rational Nature. He that intrudes upon this Liberty, Violates the Law of

79

Nature." Quoting Plutarch to the effect that "Those persons only who live in Obedience to Reason, are worthy to be accounted free," Wise posits Reason and the Law of Nature as the sources and goals of human endeavor. Drawing on diverse sources, from Puffendorf to Ulpian (whom Wise quotes on man's natural right to be free), Wise was instrumental in redefining the sources of the moral order in early-eighteenth-century New England to include not only the Christian idea of grace but the principles of reason based on natural law.

Of course, Wise was not alone, and as the eighteenth century progressed more and more political arguments in the colonies were drawn from the classical and early modern corpus of natural law theory. By the 1750s and 1760s such preachers as Jonathan Mayhew, Daniel Shute, Jason Haven, and Samuel Cooke were referring to a new "trinity" of God, Nature, and Reason as the foundations of politics and government.[59] In 1775 John Adams, in "Novanglus: or, A History of the Dispute with America, from Its Origin, in 1754, to the Present Time," refers to Grotius, Puffendorf, Barbeyrac, Locke, Sidney, and LeClerk on natural law and the duty to resist tyranny.[60] Arguing the natural equality of man and the delegation of ministerial authority by the people, John Adams weaves together in such statements as the following the English tradition of civic virtue with the classical natural law tradition based on reason and nature:

> These are what are called revolutionary principles. They are the principles of Aristotle, Plato, Livy and Cicero, of Sydney, Harrington and Locke. The principles of nature and eternal reason.[61]

It was precisely these principles that the colonists invoked in their arguments for political independence. In the words of James Wilson, in his 1774 *Consideration on the Nature and Extent of Legislative Authority of the British Parliament*:

> All men are, by nature, equal and free: no one has a right to any authority over another without his consent: all lawful government is founded on the consent of those who are subject to it. . . . This rule is founded on the law of nature: it must control every political maxim: it must regulate the legislature itself.[62]

80

Here the law of nature, posited as superior in obligation to any other, is woven into the fundamental terms of the civic polity—a theme to which we shall return in our discussion of the arguments over independence. For Wilson as for other judges and lawyers of the last decades of the eighteenth century, the law of nature was "immutable, not by the effect of arbitrary disposition but because it has its foundation in the natural constitution and mutual relations of men and things."[63] Thus, the "supremacy of Divine Natural law" provided for the revolutionary pamphleteers of the 1760s and 1770s the same type of argument for equality and freedom in the sphere of political society as it had for John Wise fifty years earlier in the sphere of Church policy.

However, central to the later development of America as a model of civil society was the manner in which a religious idiom maintained its presence, entering in and in a sense molding the emergent secular political discourse of the eighteenth century based on rationalized natural law principles. This idiom with its particular interweaving of religious and secular definitions of the polity found expression in a new, more secular vision of the "Holy Commonwealth" built on grace. The continuing importance of this particular vision of the polity was felt in the developing rhetoric of civil (or, in E. L. Tuveson's term, "Whig") millennialism during the Seven Years War (in the 1750s) and later during the Revolutionary period.[64] Those millennial expectations articulated by Jonathan Edwards during the Great Awakening (1740s), and published posthumously as the *History of the Work of Redemption* as well as in his *A Dissertation Concerning the End for Which God Created the World* (1746) and *An Humble Attempt to Promote Explicit Agreement and Visible Union of God's People* (1747), have been presented as crucial in the modeling of later millennial visions, such as those of Joseph Bellamy, Jonathan Edwards, Jr., Timothy Dwight, and Samuel Hopkins.[65]

Significantly, the Great Awakening of the 1740s, which envisioned the whole community as impregnated with redeeming grace, giving rise to "a new state of affairs, one in which justice, charity and truth are the common motives for conduct," was a period that also fused together secular notions of collective and individual identities with religious intimations of divine grace.[66]

81

Such historians as Alan Heimart, Nathan O. Hatch, and Ruth Bloch have noted the strong interpenetration of religious-millennial themes (rooted in seventeenth-century Puritanism) with civic-republican ones in the decades from the 1740s to the Revolution.[67]

While the precise nature of the relation between the millennialism of the Awakening and later forms of civil millennialism remains a subject of historical debate and controversy, the very construction of a tradition of civil millennialism would seem to support our idea of the continued influence of Puritan religious orientations on the political doctrines of the eighteenth century. The move from Church to community, to national polity, as the model of the social order was expressed over the eighteenth century in the developing forms of a civil millennial tradition, which defined the "Children of Israel" in terms not of covenanted members of a Church but of civil membership in the nation. All of these contributed to millennial orientations becoming, in J. G. A. Pocock's phrase, "a mode of civil consciousness."[68] It was, I maintain, this new form of civic consciousness that contributed to the unique manner in which natural law, the idea of reason, and the religious heritage of asectic-Puritianism were all integrated into the American political ideology of the eighteenth century.

Thus we can find in the same work by John Adams (*A Dissertation on the Cannon and Feudal Law*, 1765) both a clarion call to the study of natural law and that "enthusiasm" (associated earlier with the millennialism of the Awakening preachers) transferred from the religious to the civil realm, and from a term of abuse to a source of (national) pride.[69] This, what David Lovejoy has termed "enthusiasm of liberty," that "noble infirmity" which suffused the discourse of civic virtue, tied the natural law tradition of the civic-humanists to the more indigenous Puritan traditions of the seventeenth century.[70] It finds expression in such works as John Adams's "Novanglus," where we can find an example of that uniquely American ideology to which E. L. Tuveson has given the name "apocalyptic Whiggism."[71] By this he means a whiggish political discourse of natural rights and liberties and fear of corrupting influences interwoven with the notion of America's apocalyptic role in maintaining religious liberties—in Pocock's terms, "Whiggish tolerance merging into the holy common-wealth."[72] Thus, John Adams asserts:

> I have always considered the settlement of America with reverence and wonder, as the opening of a grand scene and design in Providence for the illumination of the ignorant and the emancipation of the slavish part of mankind all over the earth.[73]

We can find here the latterday secular and civic manifestation of those religious visions which have been traced (notably by Pocock and Tuveson) to the concept of visible saints, the Puritan commonwealth and the workings of the Great Awakening. Significantly, however, we find these in a text replete with references to the natural law tradition and to the writings of Aristotle and Plato, Grotius and Puffendorf, Locke, Harrington, and Sydney.[74] It is this unique interweaving of religious and civil traditions that characterized the civil society tradition in the United States, setting it off from those of other nation-states and giving to the unity of natural law doctrines and religious themes their particular saliency in eighteenth-century America.

What characterized the ideological developments traced above was indeed nothing less than a unique merging of Christian ideas of grace with the civil polity on the one hand and, on the other, the later-eighteenth-century infusion of these ideas with a belief in Progress, natural law, and individual virtue. This symbolic vision became central to post-eighteenth-century American national character, informing and structuring the unique components of what Robert Bellah has termed the American civil religion.[75]

In Bellah's reading, the American civil religion comprised a collection of beliefs, symbols, and rituals with respect to sacred things, "a genuine apprehension of universal and transcendental religious reality as seen in or revealed through the experience of the American people." These beliefs and rituals marked the parameters of the American value system founded on a unity of natural law principles (based on reason) with those of a "higher law" drawn from Biblical religion (or revelation). In the words of James Wilson, "The law of nature and the law of revelation are both divine, they flow, though in different channels from the same adorable sources."[76] Both sources formed the basis of legitimacy upon which the civil republic rested and by which national identity was defined.

Lending these ideas their particular force was their integral connection the broader fabric of what Bellah defined as the American "Myth," through which historical experience was interpreted in light of transcendent reality.[77] Of major importance to this myth was the notion of the origins of the American nation. The very "newness" of America and its concomitant associations of pristine purity were woven together with a vision of man and nature that drew on Biblical images and symbols. The American wilderness was viewed in terms of the "promised land," of "the New Canaan" and of "paradise." This image of the land was moreover tied to a new, paradigmatic image of man "emancipated from history" and imbued, like Adam *revividus*, with a sacred *telos*.[78]

Together, these visions tended to imbue the founding political doctrines of American society with a certain "sacredness." They also affected the American conception of history and the place of America and Americans therein, especially vis-à-vis Europe, which symbolized a "corrupt" past. It was ultimately upon this reading of history that Americans appealed to natural law doctrine in dissolving their contracts with the English crown.[79]

The debates over independence were carried out largely in terms of natural law theory and an appeal to Reason against the corruption of history. As Bernard Bailyn has noted, "in pamphlet after pamphlet, the American writers cited Locke on natural rights . . . Grotius, Puffendorf, Burlmarque and Vattel on the laws of nature and of nations."[80] Thus, for example, James Otis in his *A Vindication of the British Colonies* (Boston, 1765) argued for the supremacy of natural law over the colonist's charter with the English Crown: "Life, liberty and property are by the law of Nature as well as by the common law secured to the happy inhabitants of South Britain and constitute their primary civil or political rights."[81] A year earlier, in *The Rights of the British Colonies Asserted and Proved* (Boston, 1764), he had stressed the universal, fundamental, and transcendent character of the Law of Nature:

There can be no prescription old enough to supersede the law of nature and the grant of God Almighty, who has given to all men a natural right to be free and they have it ordinarily in their power to make themselves so if they please. . . . The Law of Nature was not of man's making nor is it in his power to mend it or alter its course. He can only perform and keep or disobey and break it. The last is never done with impunity.[82]

In these writings as in others of the pre-Revolutionary decades, civic virtue was tied to natural law, as Plutarch and Cicero, Puffendorf and Grotius, Locke and Vattel were all invoked by such writers as Stephen Hopkins (*The Rights of the Colonists Examined*), Samuel Adams (*Natural Rights of the Colonies*, 1772), Richard Bland (*Inquiries into the Rights of the British Colonies*, 1766), John Adams, and others. Among all these writers natural law principles were used to analyze and argue the rights of the colonies toward the mother country. John Adams declared in 1774: "Great Britain by his despotic Edicts has forced us to the Alternative of either becoming Slaves or recurring to the Principles of Nature for Protection."[83] It was precisely in the return to these principles that the law of nature was invoked by such men as John Adams and Richard Bland to justify a new social compact of the new political society in the colonies. Appeals by John Adams (in his debates with Governor Hutchinson), to Vattel and the Law of Nature, to Hooker and Locke on the fundamentals of law and tyranny, and to Puffendorf and Grotius on the rights of colonies as regulated by the Law of Nature—all formed the ideological basis of the new order in the new world.[84]

The argument for colonial rights against the English crown was based, as we can see, on arguments drawn on natural right theory (together with the British constitution and "usage"). It was also drawn from Scripture and the firm belief that the American settlers were a chosen people. We have seen the roots of this tradition in the seventeenth-century belief in the "Holy Commonwealth." By the end of the eighteenth century, the very destiny of the American republic was itself firmly identified with the course of redemptive history. America had become both the locus and the instrument of the great consummation. The equation of the Kingdom of God with the American nation, which was inherent to this belief, substituted the nation for the Church, which, as we have seen, played a similar role a century earlier.[85] In this sense the nation emerged as the primary agent of God's meaningful activity in history—contributing a central tenet to the "religion of the republic."

The more concrete implications of these beliefs were to be found in the uniquely American ideal of civil society and the manner in which European social and political ideas were transformed as they merged with the developing political ideology of the American republic. Thus, for example, in terms of natural law doctrines (and so the role of Reason as the arbitrator of the social good), one can contrast its difference in Europe as well as between North and South America. The importance of natural law doctrines in the thought of the Enlightenment have of course become a historical axiom. Yet, as is pointed out by Yehoshua Arieli, in Europe "the theory was accepted as interpretation, justification—or even criteria and guide—for existing institutions and political actions."[86] In Latin America, the use of natural law theory to legitimize existing political arrangements was even more salient. In North America, however, natural law doctrines "dissolved existing loyalties and traditions and atomized society in order to build it anew on the most generalized, abstract and universal principles of the Enlightenment."[87] This very dissolution of existing loyalties and traditions was itself, however, an outcome of the prior restructuring of identities and commitments engendered by the Reformation. The formation of new communities of "visible saints," studied above, who broke with the existing patterns of social and religious structuration, was thus essential in the radical rearticulation of natural law doctrines in North America, especially in respect to the new notion of the individual—what in essence may be termed the transcendental individual—as constitutive of the political community.

This fact was both noted and analyzed by Georg Jellinek, whose work served as an inspiration for Weber's own. Already in 1895, Jellinek compared the American Bill(s) of Rights (from different states); the French *Decleration des Droits de L'Homme et du Citoyen*; and, more significantly, the English Bill of Rights of 1689, Habeus Corpus Act of 1679, and 1628 Petition of Right. His conclusions are worth quoting:

86

> The American bills of rights do not attempt merely to set forth certain principles for the state's organization, but they seek above all to draw the boundary line between state and individual. According to them the individual is not the possessor of rights through the state, but by his own nature he has inalienated and indefeasible rights. The English laws know nothing of this. They do not wish to recognize an eternal, natural right, but one inherited from their fathers, "the old, undoubted rights of the English people."[88]

In English law there is, for Jellenik, no autonomous grounding of individual rights in a set of natural principles but solely in tradition, "the laws and statutes of this realm."[89]

In attempting to explain how the "inherited rights and liberties, as well as the privileges of organization, which had been granted the colonists by the English kings," became transformed into "rights which spring not from man but from God and nature," Jellenik had recourse to the defining traits of Congregational Puritanism that we examined above.[90] While, Jellinek, in analyzing the origins of natural right in New England in terms of religious doctrine, emphasized freedom of conscience, we have here stressed the interweaving of natural law doctrine with the idea of the community of saints (that is, a polity built on grace) as the essential background to this aspect of American rights.

Moreover, as Jellenik has emphasized, it was in the original compacts, more properly covenants, contracted by the Puritan saints for the furthering of the vision of the Holy Commonwealth that—for the first time in history—compacts as the source of states "were not merely demanded by actually concluded."[91] It was these which bound everyone to "respect the self-created authority and the self-created law."[92] Here then we see how the early-seventeenth-century structures of political authority and of law lent natural law doctrine in the colonies its particular saliency and meaning. We see also how the heritage of Puritan individualism transformed the very idea of the compact as the source of society.

For as opposed to Europe, where the compacts formed between independent and rational agents tended to take precedence over the contracting parties, in America the individual in his autonomous state as moral agent remained the fundamental component of the political order. Rather than the collectivity, State, or organic community, it was the individual himself who served as the fundamental unit in American interpretations of natural law doctrines. The protection and sanction of the individual—rather than of the community (or State)—because the guiding force in the North American synthesis of natural law with the religious tradition noted above.

Here, then, it is not only the different meanings of compacts (or contracts) that distinguish the United States from European societies, but, of no less importance, the different meanings of the individuals forming those compacts. In the United States, the individual—and indeed individualism—was invested with an intense moral dimension that was lacking in Europe. There the continuity of traditional communities (as well as legal powers) mediated the autonomous moral dimension invested in the individual across the Atlantic. This was the underlying dimension of Jellenek's analysis of British and American concepts of rights, where, as we have seen, "ancient rights and liberties," the laws and statutes of the realm, are what defined individual right and not the autonomous right of man as a natural, moral agent.

In other European countries different traditions militated against the moral dimension of individualism that characterized America. In the German tradition, for example, it was the circumscription of the individual by the family or clan.[93] (Here we should also recall that Rousseau's *Contrat Social* does not recognize individual rights apart from the *volonte generale*, which implies the "complete transfer to the community of all the individual rights.")[94]

If in Europe individual rights were seen to stem from the State as concessions or special permissions, or at best to be the province of that measure of liberty granted the individual when it does not conflict with the common good (and so the province of the State), in the United States rights were rooted in the moral attributes of individual conscience, the result of the particular manner in which grace was internalized into conscience at the same time that the boundaries of the Holy Community expanded beyond the regenerate saints to include all members of the community.

This new moral dimension not only defined the uniqueness of the individual in eighteenth-century America, as opposed to the

88

traditional and more *Statlich* Continental thought, but also permitted a unique interpretation of the concepts of liberty and equality, which in Europe were seen as antithetical, but in America were integrated in a novel structure to become one of the defining characteristics of civil society in America. Rooted in pre-Revolutionary traditions of English radicalism, common law, natural rights, and the Puritan values of the "equality of believers," the value of equality was central to the very conception and legitimation of the early Republic. A similar interweaving of secular and religious themes was to be found in the emerging eighteenth-century discourse on liberty—which, as we have seen, combined the religious "enthusiasm" of the Great Awakening with English Whig tradition based on concepts drawn from natural law theory. In the debates over English infringement of colonial rights, this interweaving continued as religious themes joined with the "conspiracy theories" of the English radical tradition. By the revolutionary decades, the preservation of natural liberties became, as noted above, both the justification for the Revolution and an example of that "republican virtue" preserved only in the New World. By the end of the century the sovereignty of the individual conscience, united with notions of political liberty and equality, all rooted in the natural law tradition and imbued with religious sanctions, became a potent ideology of American national consciousness.

The crystallization of the American civil polity witnessed, in effect, the transformation of the European concept of individualism as its original negative associations were metamorphosed into political virtues. Indeed, it was through the unique American articulation of the doctrine of individualism that the "European" contradiction between liberty and equality was resolved. That individualism which Tocqueville viewed negatively as the expression of an atomized society was rearticulated in America along different lines, drawing on those indigenous traditions of the moral individual outlined above.

For from the early decades of the eighteenth century, republican liberties had been viewed as correlates of the Puritan tradition, based on the individual and the freedom of conscience. To this, the early-nineteenth-century Transcendentalists and Unitarians added their own vision of the perfectibility of man, based on the growth of Enlightenment and education. To quote Arieli again, "individualism, liberty and self-government were the main vehicles in the progress towards perfection."[95] A new concept of the individual and of individualism was thus expressed in the writings of Channing, Garrison, Thoreau, and Emerson. In this conception "the rights of man and democracy were the political expression of religious and philosophical truth . . . aimed at the vindication of the greatness of man in each individual." Here too we see a latter-day manifestation of that particular conception of the moral individual imbued with sanctity at the basis of the civil polity in North American political thought. Underlying this unique American conception of the individual was the synthesis of eighteenth-century Enlightenment ideas of contract, natural rights, and liberties; the limited role of government; the dependence of government on society; and of course equality, with the religious heritage of the "Holy Commonwealth" and the transcendental individual who stood at its center.

It was, as is well known, to this newly articulated notion of the individual that many scholars have turned, following the work of Max Weber, for an understanding of the new civilization of modernity that emerged from the European background, based ideologically and politically on the assumption of equality and of growing participation of the citizens in the social and political center of society. This was most clearly manifest in the tendency to establish universal citizenship and suffrage, and some semblance of a participant political or social order based on the premise of mass participation in the decision-making process. It is moreover precisely this ideological premise of universal equality that contributed so much of the idea of America as a paradigm of civil society. We must remember, however, that the natural law doctrines upon which this equality of individuals was based were interpreted and integrated into social and political thought in a very specific manner. The very stress on the "metaphysical equality" of citizens, on representative government and individual rights, resulted from a merger of natural law philosophy with a very different, religious, tradition, and together they formed a unique synthesis.

Our analysis of the sources of civil society—or at least of its preconditions (in the idea of the individual and Reason as a new expression of universal injunctions to the good)—has concentrated, perhaps unduly, on seventeenth- and eighteenth-century America. The historical development there was, however, paradigmatic of a broader and more general change in sensibility, values, and world views, the outcome of which we explored in our discussion of the Scottish Enlightenment and the idea of civil society in eighteenth- and nineteenth-century political philosophy. It remains for us here to return to the more analytic components of the developments studied above in the North American context and to outline their relevance for the civil society tradition. We must therefore return to the idea of the individual and of Reason as constitutive, in the eighteenth and nineteenth centuries, of a new definition of universal value upon which a representative vision of society could be based.

V

The idea of the individual that emerged in the eighteenth century was, as we have seen, one of a moral individual whose very autonomy rested on following the dictates of a Reason that was both transcendental and constitutive of individual existence. What emerged, most especially in the thought of Immanuel Kant, was the notion of moral personhood—the moral aspect of which was precisely what allowed the existence of that publicness to be found in civil society.[96] In his *Introduction to the Metaphysics of Morals*, Kant sketched out the attributes of this personhood, which drew heavily on the tradition of ascetic-Protestantism:

> Moral person-hood is then nothing other than the freedom of a rational being under moral laws (psychological person-hood is by contrast merely the capability to become conscious of one's own identity in various states of existence). The consequence is that a person is subject to no laws other than those which he gives himself (either alone or at least jointly with others).

Here we see, in more analytic terms, that secular version of the autonomous individual conscience following the dictates of an "inner light" and no longer bound by the sacramental doctrines of the Church. Here too we see the emergence of precisely those new terms of universalism that characterized the thought of the eighteenth and nineteenth centuries, especially in the United States; and were based on the transcendental qualities of a universal Reason and no longer on those of a universal Church. It is to this transformation of the defining terms of universal values (and truths, we might add) that we must refer to appreciate both the emergent concept of civil society and its ultimate failure to present a viable model for the social order. Both developments are in essence part of the long-term implications of the Reformation of the sixteenth and seventeenth centuries in which the very constitutive terms of individual existence in society were cast in a new mold beyond the existing definitions of Christian universalism.

The Catholic Church as *Universitas Fidelium* was through its sacramental doctrine a potentially universal and inclusive framework (as illustrated by the first millennium and a half of Christianity). Protestant sects, the source of our modern notions of both individualism and rationality, were, on the other hand, rooted in exclusivity and particularism. One was not born into a sect, but had to undergo an internal transformation—the experience of grace—to attain membership. The universality it espoused was one of particular subjects, each rooted in the experience of grace.

Ultimately, however, the institutionalization of Protestantism and hence its universalization resulted in the loss of its transcendental referent. This process, essentially of secularization, was inherent to the logic of Protestantism, if the community of saints was to expand beyond the narrow boundaries of those defined by the experience of grace. In this universalization or institutionalization (which we generally refer to under the broad category of secularization), the terms of the universal and the particular were transformed as Reason replaced the Deity as locus of universalist values and injunctions in both the ethical and the social (interpersonal) sphere. Less perhaps the this-worldliness of Protestant soteriology and more its individual emphasis thus stands at the core of its secularization. For the need to posit new universal terms of association between transcendentally constituted subjects could be met only by a universal Reason, which could replace the transcendent (Deity, recall the individual-to-relation-to-God) and so constitute individuality—but at the same time unite these individuals into a type of (universal) community once represented by the Christian *ecumene* and now precluded by the very particularism of grace in Protestantism. What emerged in the later sphere of community was the idea of the individual whose only transcendence is that of a morality "immanent in [but] transcending" the individual self.[97] Morality here is founded on the very dialectic of Reason, itself inherent to but transcending individual conscience. The governing notion of sociability here thus becomes that of the moral subject constituted by transcendental Reason.

The development we have traced is thus one where the essence of individualism was seen to be in the transcendent subject or, framed more theologically, in the direct relation of the individual to God. Men and women were, in this reading, constituted by their individual relation to the transcendent source of meaning and order. This idea, inherent to early Christianity, developed through the soteriological doctrines of ascetic-Protestantism. It continued in the devotional movements of the late seventeenth century and in the privatization of grace beyond the boundaries of a community of saints. Indeed, a similar movement to that noted above in the North American context can be found in the "ethical inwardness" of the Cambridge Platonists. Their stress on moral activity as partaking of a "Universal Righteousness" and on the bifurcation of individual identity by a Reasoned virtue (which is "natural") and the vice of excessive appetites marks a similar move toward the interiorization of Puritan beliefs, this time in English Protestantism of the Restoration period. Benjamin Whichcote's dicta that "Hell arises out of a Man's self: And Hell's Fewel is the Guilt of a Man's Conscience" and that Heaven "lies in a refin'd Temper, in an internal reconciliation to the Nature of God, and to the Rule of Righteousness. So that both Hell and Heaven have their foundation within Men" was a fundamental tenet among all the Cambridge Platonists.[98] It resonates with the selfsame interiorization of grace as conscience that we studied above in late-seventeenth-century New England and points forward to the ideas of Shaftesbury (who in fact published Whichcote's sermons) and the moral basis of the civil society idea in the Scottish Enlightenment. Ultimately these ideas, which stressed the appre-

93

hension of God (as the source of our natural goodness) through reason, led in the late eighteenth and nineteenth centuries to our more contemporary ideas of the individual as possessing metaphysical and moral value founded on the premise of universal Reason.[99]

What emerged together with this modern idea of the individual was, however, a new idea of the universal no longer rooted in a transcendent and otherworldly sphere but in the immanent this-worldly workings of Reason. And with this individual-as-constructed-by-Reason emerged or rather, reemerged, the problem of society, of how to represent the ties and relations between morally autonomous and agentic individuals.

This problem, which Otto Gierke analyzed in terms of the development of modern natural law theory, was rooted in the change wrought by Protestantism in the defining terms of Christian universalism.[100] The effect of the Protestant Reformation was to replace what Gierke termed the *universitas* (or corporate unity) of the Catholic *ecumene* with a *societas* (or partnership, association) of distinct individuals defined by their particular relationship to the sources of grace and otherworldly transcendence. The hierarchic edifice of the Christian Commonwealth had become atomized into one of individual "saints," each containing within his or her own conscience the terms of Christian universalism.

To better appreciate the problems this entailed in terms of positing a model of social life, we would do well to recall that in premodern Christian civilization the universal was conceived of transcendentally. That is to say, it was radically separated from humanity by the "Axial" or "transcendental chasm." The particular took the form of the individual believer bound to society through sacramental communion, which represented the universal terms of social inclusion based on the mystery of the Corpus Christi. In the words of Corinthians, "For as the body is one, and hath many members, and all the members of that one body, being many, are one body, so also is Christ. For by one Spirit are we all baptized into one body, whether we be Jews or Gentiles, whether we be bond or free; and have been all made to drink into one Spirit."[101] Through participation in the Eucharist "each individual formed a part of the community of true communicants, sharing together the promise of eternal life."[102] Through the Eucharist each individual joined with others in a representation of that universal Christian *ecumene*.

In more social and political terms this was expressed as the Principle of Unity (*principium unitatis*) and so of the primacy of the whole over its parts. To quote Gierke:

> In the Universal Whole, Mankind is one Partial Whole with a final cause of its own, which is distinct from the final causes of Individuals and from those of other Communities. . . . Christendom is set before us as a single, universal Community, founded and governed by God Himself. Mankind is one "mystical body"; it is one single and internally connected "people" or "folk"; it is an all embracing corporation which constitutes that Universal realm, spiritual and temporal, which may be called the Universal Church or, with equal propriety, the Commonwealth of the Human Race.[103]

(Needless to add, this doctrine was mediated by the corresponding one of the two swords, referring to the spiritual and temporal orders—the *Sacerdotium* and *Imperium* respectively. Though this latter doctrine served as one important source of Western political pluralism—in the continuing struggles to define the nature of the relations between both orders, institutions, and principles of legitimacy—their ultimate reconciliation as an aspect of Christian universalism was a fundamental tenet of medieval political belief and so of central importance to understanding the defining character of modernity as well.)

For in modern, post-Reformation societies the representation of the universal was radically transformed. Here the particular is no longer constituted as the individual. Rather, what becomes a universal in the individualist ethic of modern societies is the individual him/herself. Society itself is no longer a universal but exists only as a derivative of the individual, that is, of the growing recognition of the individual as subject and society as the amalgamation of these "universally" constituted subjects. That the particular becomes the universal is the reigning ethic of individualistic societies, hence the emergence of the problem of representing the social sphere—that is, of representing a *societas* of individuals rather than a *universitas* of constitutive parts (of a whole).

95

The issue of societal representation is first and foremost one of the symbolization of society. And the problems that emerged in the centuries following the Reformation turned precisely on how to represent as a unity or *universitas* a society constructed of individuals. For, as noted, with the Reformation the representation of the universal became increasingly problematic as each and every individual came, in a sense, to represent the universal, as each conscience internalized that *ecumene* which had been the sacramental community.[104] This can be better understood if we recall Max Weber's famous characterization of the unique religious features of ascetic-Protestantism:

> It demands of the believer not celibacy, as in the case of the monk, but the elimination of all erotic pleasure or desire; not poverty, but the elimination of all idle enjoyment of unearned wealth and income, and the avoidance of all feudalistic, life-loving ostentation of wealth; not the ascetic death-in-life of the cloister, but an alert, rationally controlled conduct of life and the avoidance of all surrender to the beauty of the world, to art, or to one's own moods and emotions. The clear and uniform goal of this asceticism was the disciplining and methodical organization of conduct. Its typical representative was the "man of vocation" or "professional" and its specific result was the rational, functional organization of social relations.[105]

We see here perhaps the prototypical example of that universalized particularity noted above. The "universal" values of celibacy, poverty, and a devotional life, in essence of *imitatio Deo,* are incorporated into the particular, becoming constitutive of each believer̦s *Lebenswelt.* The universal is here collapsed into the particular. In this collapse it becomes increasingly difficult to articulate a model of the social whole, as the relations between individuals become those of autonomous, distinct, and particular entities each carrying within him/herself the universal values (first of grace, then of Reason). This is precisely that move "from Tribal Brotherhood to Universal Otherhood" charted by Benjamin Nelson.[106] At a different level it is reminiscent of Hegel's insights into the loss of the "absolute morality of the Greek polis" as it was transformed into the "formal legal relations of the Roman universal monarchy."[107] With this move, "this spirit of substantial universality, which has died and split up into the atoms of many absolute isolated individuals, has decayed to become the formalism of law."[108] Whatever the truth of Hegel's understanding of antiquity, two millennia later, a similar set of problems, of legal formalism, procedural rationality, and the disengagement of purposefully rational action from its matrix in an ultimate set of shared meanings, is still with us—indeed forming the background of the current wish to return to civil society, to reassert a social solidarity that would affirm community no less than individuality.

The sources of these problems and current concerns cannot be ignored or brushed aside. They lie in that identity of universal and particular (characteristic of late-eighteenth-century thought and indeed a modernity as a civilization) which is far different from the universal's *representation* in the particular, which had characterized medieval Christendom. The result has been an isolation if not exclusion of (as well as between) particular individuals based on their *identity* (as embodying universal values), as opposed to a (hierarchic) inclusion (of/between particular individuals or estates/*Stände*) based on their *representation* of the universal Christian *ecumene*.

Here it is perhaps appropriate to recall our discussion of natural law theory in eighteenth-century America. There, natural law ideas of individual equality and the compacts formed between individuals provided the basis for the civil polity. There, the challenge of modern natural law theory, of providing a representative vision of the social whole (*universitas*) from the idea of the individual taken as an autonomous being (whose existence was "logically prior" to the State or society) was most successful. The nascent American republic represented, more than any other society, those premises of modern civilization within which the

> . . . State was no longer derived from the divinely ordained harmony of the universal whole; it was no longer explained as a partial whole which was derived from, and preserved by, the existence of a greater: it was simply explained by itself. The starting-point of speculation ceased to be general humanity; it became the individual and self-sufficing sovereign State; *and this individual State was regarded as based on a union of individuals, in obedience to the dictates of Natural Law, to form a society armed with supreme power.*[109]

97

Indeed, in this quote from Gierke we see the ideas of Adams, Otis, and Jefferson given more analytic form.

In its very construction of the political community on the ideas of natural law and the moral individual, the United States can in fact be seen as giving concrete form to Hegel's understanding of individual "right" (and in fact social existence) in civil society. For Hegel notes, "A man is counted as a man in virtue of his manhood alone, not because he is a Jew, Catholic, Protestant, German, Italian etc."[110] As Albrecht Wellemer has pointed out, nowhere has this idea as a principle of citizenship rights been true to a greater extent than in the United States.[111] And the fact that Hegel's quote resonates with the verse from Corinthians quoted above should not surprise us, for this is precisely the new universalism of the individual as moral entity which replaced the earlier Christian idea.

However, and this is a crucial caveat, the very success of the natural law doctrine—based on self-sufficient individuals endowed with Reason—as the foundation of the American political community rested on the synthesis of these ideas with the tradition of the Holy Commonwealth of visible saints, that is, of the transcendent subject of Protestant belief. Not only (transcendental) Reason, but (transcendent) grace (that illuminism of sectarian Protestantism noted by Nelson) now redefined in this-worldly terms of individual conscience, continued throughout the eighteenth century to define the terms of individual and social existence in the civil polity. It was, I would maintain, the very continuity of this particular religious heritage that made the posting of a *universitas* of isolated individuals—united by compacts— possible in eighteenth-century America. This, in essence, was Jellinek's conclusion as well when he stated:

> In the closest connection with the great religious political movement out of which the American democracy was born, there arose the conviction that there exists a right not conferred upon the citizen but inherent in man, that acts of conscience and expressions of religious conviction stand inviolable over against the state as the exercise of a higher right. This right so long suppressed is not "inheritance," is nothing handed down from their fathers, as the rights and liberties of Magna Charta and of the other English enactments—not the State but the Gospel proclaimed it.[112]

It is the continuity of this tradition that has led some to see America as the expression par excellence of civil society.

Yet the problem of civil society (whether in the eighteenth century or today) remains that of positing a model of the social whole that would overcome (while not negating) the inherent universal/particularity of its members. The problem of civil society is thus, in its essence, the problem of modern natural law—of constituting a *universitas* that would include (or rather, represent the ties binding) a *societas* of individuals whose very compacts or contracts tend to highlight the autonomy and independence of each rather than their fundamental communality. We have seen that as long as this attempt was carried out in transcendent terms, either with John Locke or in the natural law philosophy of eighteenth-century America (which, and again I stress this point, was uniquely tied to a secularized virtue and the traditions of ascetic-Protestantism), such a synthesis was possible. With the loss of the transcendent dimension and its replacement solely by Reason (and thus, in the civil sphere the ties of market exchange and strategic or instrumental action), the moorings of a unified social vision broke lose. The naïve anthropology of the Scottish Enlightenment was insufficient ground upon which to construct new and universal terms of solidarity and mutuality. The search for such unity as both philosophical principle and social desideratum continued within and beyond the civil society tradition throughout the nineteenth century. To both aspects of this search and their attendant problems we must now turn.

CHAPTER 3

Civil Society, Citizenship, and the Representation of Society

I

The problem of uniting individual and social wills—of articulating a model of society that would at the same time represent the autonomy of its individual members—that is, the essence of the problem of civil society, continued into the nineteenth century. In the second half of that century, following the critique of Marx, the growing capitalist economy of West European societies, and the rise of socialist movements there, the terms of these problems changed, even if the problems themselves remained the same. Thus, in the second half of the nineteenth century there is less concern with civil society and more with the idea of citizenship. In that period the definitions and meanings of citizenship replace the problem of civil society as the locus of social conflict and concern in all industrial countries. Citizenship, and with it the values of membership and participation in collective life, become, in this period, the new model for representing the values of

101

both autonomy and mutuality within the boundaries of the nation-state. The great struggles of the nineteenth century over the definition of citizenship were thus, in fact, over participation in civil society. In these struggles the challenge posed by the socialist movement to the civil society tradition was of utmost importance and thus a proper place to begin our analysis.

In this chapter we shall in fact use the case of socialism, or rather a highly abbreviated analysis of the socialist movement in Europe and the United States, to view the defining terms of citizenship in these countries. The very failure of socialism in the United States provides—as we shall see—an important illustration of the unique existence of a civil society there. In contrast, the impingement of the socialist movement in nineteenth-century European societies will be explained as an attempt more fully to institutionalize the idea of civil society in the polity—through opening up and expanding the reigning definitions of citizenship.

To appreciate the very emergence of the socialist movement and its attempt to broaden the terms of civil society and make them more inclusive of all members of the national polity, we shall concentrate on some of the contradictions that defined the terms of citizenship in nineteenth-century political thought. The contradiction between liberty and equality, between the autonomous individual and the mutuality existing between individuals, in essence between the terms of justice and those of social solidarity, will form the substantive locus of the remaining sections of this chapter and the next. We shall approach these from different sides and different perspectives (historical, sociological, and philosophical) in order to appreciate their role in problematizing any contemporary principled "resurrection" of the idea of civil society. It was, we argue, these contradictions that stood at the core of the civil society idea once its supporting struts in reason and revelation were removed. Not surprisingly, it was these conflicts that formed the substance of the nineteenth- and early-twentieth-century debates on political and social theory.

In this chapter we shall approach this set of contradictions in two of their rather well-known sociological guises, which cut to the heart of the conflicting demands of citizenship and of civil society. We shall review some aspects of the thought of Emile Durkheim as providing not only the founding moment of the sociological discourse but, more importantly, as returning to a set of ideas similar to those of the Scottish moralists in an attempt to square the existence of the autonomous individual with some embracing conception of solidarity and mutuality between individuals. In the final section we shall see how a similar set of problems was perceived and analyzed in the thought of Max Weber, who, however, remained much less sanguine than Durkheim on their ultimate reconciliation. Weber's analysis of the "iron cage" of rationality brings us in fact to a new appreciation of the contradictory terms of citizenship, equality, and solidarity in contemporary life. The implications of this for the idea of civil society are explored through the changing definitions of the public and private realms in the United States. In Chapter 4 we shall return to these problems again, stressing their different articulation in different societies as well as a more highly theoretical attempt at their reconciliation among certain contemporary thinkers.

II

We have already noted, somewhat in passing, the connection between the lack of an organizationally strong, ideologically coherent, and politically autonomous socialist movement in the United States and the paradigmatic role that the United States played as a model of civil society. Those two themes bear more than a coincidental relation to each other. For the socialist movement as it grew and developed in different European societies in the nineteenth and early twentieth centuries represented, more than anything else, an attempt to broaden the basis of membership and participation in society—and, in a sense, through such broadening, to extend the "civil" component of civil society beyond a circumscribed meaning of polished manners or caste-conscious civility.

The rights of unionization; the freedoms of speech, of the press, of assembly; the freedom of movement (within the confines of the nation-state), of association (or combination); and, most importantly, the right to organize political parties and the right of the franchise—all of which had been denied to members of the working class in West European societies (to different extents and in different forms) throughout the nineteenth century—represented in a concrete and meaningful way the venues of individual participation in collective life. The right of individual workers to organize collectively as an interest group within society was one of the fundamental demands of the socialist movement and indeed of any concrete "realization" of civil society within society. It was in fact these demands, rather than a coherent policy of implementing collectivization, that characterized socialist policies up until World War I. As Adam Przeworski has noted, this period was characterized, on the whole, by socialist efforts to win the suffrage and to organize workers as a class.[1] Indeed, many of the great general strikes of the turn of the century, in Austria in 1896 and 1905, in Finland in 1905, Belgium 1902 and 1913, and Sweden in 1902, were called to force changes in the electoral laws.[2] Bearing in mind the generally ecstatic response to the first free elections in East-Central Europe in 1989, we should recall that the principles of universal citizenship that we in the West take for granted are not of all that long a standing and were not won without a struggle. To take the case of England as an example, suffrage was extremely limited and was broadened only gradually throughout the nineteenth century. The first Reform Bill of 1832 left five out of six adult males disfranchised, and the Reforms of 1867–68 increased male suffrage only to about 30 percent of the population. The further reforms of 1884–85 left a population of 31.5 million with an electorate of still only 5 million males, that is to say, it left about one-half of the male urban working class beyond the pale of citizenship.[3] The principle of universal political citizenship was not recognized even in England until 1918.[4]

It is against this background of the exclusion of a significant part of society from the very "rights of reason" formulated in the eighteenth century that we must view the expansion of socialism in nineteenth-century Europe. It is against this same background, or rather its absence, that we must compare it with the case of American exceptionalism. This exceptionalism began, however, not with the lack of socialism, but with the absence of feudalism.[5] In Walter Dean Burnham's famous phrase, "no feudalism, no socialism." As study after study has shown, it was the persistence into the industrial era of a "feudal baggage," most especially of strong status lines and barriers, of a politics of *Stände*, that en-

104

couraged the growth and crystallization of a strong socialist movement in European countries. Not economic inequality *per se* but the continual traditions of exclusion from political, civil, and social membership in the community is what stood at the root of the development of nineteenth-century socialist movements. It was, as Seymour Martin Lipset has convincingly argued, the absence of a feudal tradition in the United States, Canada, Australia, and New Zealand that "sharply differentiated the working class movements of these countries from those on the European continent."[6]

In terms of our own concern with civil society, what had persisted into the nineteenth century was a severely restricted definition of citizenship, and with it of those legal and social (not necessarily solely economic) badges of individual equality which constituted membership in society and so made of it a truly civil society. These distinctions ran, in Selig Perlman's telling phrase "like a red thread between the laboring class and the other classes in society."[7] They were exemplified in such practices as the carrying of the "livret" (a form of internal passport) by members of the French working class, whose freedom of movement was restricted (by, among other factors, their employers' permission). Their source was in the very continuity of feudal status hierarchies defined by particular codes of honor, life-style, family ties, and privilege, which, as Arnold Meyer has pointed out, continued, in some cases, into the middle of the present century.[8] The great theoretical edifice of civil society—of legal rationality and formal equality—was, as socialists had been arguing for decades, severely mediated by the continuity of cultural values as well as political practices rooted in the feudal past.

In fact, Lipset has argued that the very concomitance of these cultural codes and political practices on the part of European ruling elites led to the radicalness of socialist party politics in countries where those codes and practices were most salient. He notes: "Where the working class was denied full political and economic citizenship strong revolutionary movements developed. Conversely, the more readily working-class organizations were accepted into the economic and political order, the less radical their initial and subsequent ideologies."[9] Significantly, Lipset goes on to show how, even where *de jure* recognition of working class political rights was achieved (as in France, Italy, and Spain), the

105

absence of any *de facto* recognition of working class organizational structures, such as trade unions as economic bargaining partners, led to radical, syndicalist, and revolutionary actions on the part of working class movements.

These findings bear contemplation in terms of our own concern with the idea of civil society as it was classically conceived. For revolutionary ideology and syndicalist activity represent a total rejection of existing society, of its institutional as well as its symbolic and cultural orders. This rejection and total condemnation of the existing social order is of course very different from the type of social democratic and reformist policies that characterized British (and even to an extent early German) working class parties at the end of the nineteenth century. It is of course in direct opposition to the logic of collective bargaining in the United States, where, as Paul Jacobs has shown, mutual acceptance of negotiated contracts on the part of labor and management implied, for the former, a recognition of its responsibilities to the social order and a rejection of radical tactics.[10] Where civil society and citizenship existed and the working class was therefore integrated into the body politic, there was little need to advocate (or attempt to implement) the overthrowing of existing society. Where the working class was excluded from membership in the national community and hence from civil society—either formally, through legal means, or informally, through various social and political practices—revolutionary ideology and activity were strong. Citizenship, legal and (increasingly at the beginning of the twentieth century) economic membership in the community, provided the most concrete indexes of civil society—whether in Western Europe in the nineteenth century or Eastern Europe at the end of the twentieth. The major struggles of the socialist movement, as well as its successes in nineteenth-century Europe, were around these issues of citizenship and inclusion (or membership) in civil society.

The socialist movement in Western Europe thus arose and developed in the nineteenth century in response to the continued exclusion of the working class from full membership in the nation—one might almost say in response to the failure to universalize and to institutionalize (in concrete social practices) those sources of moral sentiment and natural affections which, for Ferguson and the Scottish thinkers, stood at the core of civil society.

The gradual extension of civil freedoms to all membership of society, over the course of the nineteenth century, marked, as Reinhard Bendix has noted, "the transformation from the estate societies of the 18th to the welfare state of the 20th centuries."[11] This transformation was characterized by a struggle, often against "feudal remnants," for the full implementation of citizenship, that is, of participation in the national community. The continuity of a feudal heritage based on the representation of estates (from which the fourth estate was excluded) was, as we have seen, a salient factor in the vehemence and violence of these struggles over the extension of civil status to all members of society. The corporate, group-based terms of feudal political culture (that very basis of the medieval *universitas* studied above) precluded the full institutionalization of a civil society of autonomous, moral, and economic individual agents—or rather subjected it to constant struggle. Even in those cases where formal, legal guarantees of individual rights were recognized, the basic right "to join with other individuals in pursuit of legitimate private ends," that is, the right of association, continued to be denied to workers in such countries as France, England, Belgium, and the Netherlands. Recognition of individual autonomy and so of the very principles of Reason as the *summum Bonum* of collective life was thus of a restricted nature throughout the nineteenth century and into the twentieth. In this respect we can not point to the full institutionalization of those analytic aspects of civil society based on civic freedom, economic autonomy, and moral agency discussed in the previous chapter as having been completed until after World War I. In the struggle over their realization, civil society was viewed alternatively as an illusionary entity, hiding the continual exclusion of one class of citizens from participation in national life—as in the socialist tradition—or, conversely, as an acceptable model of social life whose full implementation was perhaps not yet realized but certainly on the way to fulfillment.

This latter vision of the inherent perfectibility of existing society, indeed of mankind *tout court*, was most salient in the United States, where—not coincidentally—socialist ideology never really took hold and the restrictions on membership in civil society were markedly less than in West European countries. Indeed, in some

107

sense the very future-orientated and messianic components of the socialist vision were already present in the "Religion of the Republic" studied previously. However, and beyond these ideological similarities, which led Leo Sampson to term the ideology of Americanism as a "surrogate socialism," the failure of socialism in the United States is a strong indication of the very existence of civil society there—at least as this idea was classically conceived.[12]

Many factors have been adduced to explain the failure of socialism in the United States, ranging from the ideological heterogeneity of the movement, its organizational diversity, and its social base (that is, the absence of members of the working class among its adherents) to the American political system (its pluralism, mobility, and flexibility in dealing with protest), the American economy, and the nature of social classes.[13] These, together with additional, structural factors, such as social mobility, the open frontier, the status-striving of immigrants, and the nature of the two-party system, have all been used to explain the failure of American socialism.

However, if we take a comparative perspective we shall immediately see that the uniqueness and exceptionalism of the American experience lies neither in the major characteristics of the Socialist Party there nor in any set of structural factors alone. Socialist parties and movements throughout the world have always suffered splits and divergent ideological positions. The movement as a whole emerged from nineteenth-century Utopian thought, and even a perfunctory glance at French, Spanish, or Russian socialism, for example, immediately reveals the wide divergence in sociopolitical orientations and organizational frameworks. The point, then, is not that such ideological or organizational heterogeneity existed in the United States, but that crystallization or coalescence of ideological positions and organizational frameworks did not occur.

Similarly, a comparison with other societies lacking "feudal baggage," such as Australia and Canada, where socialist parties with some political strength and saliency did develop, emphasizes that it is not simply the lack of a feudal heritage that played a role in the failure of American socialism—but the very terms of civil identity which developed in its absence. (In Canada, as in the United States, manhood suffrage existed prior to the emergence

108

of a mass working class movement, yet since the 1920s a viable socialist movement with influence in parliamentary politics has existed.) A comparison of America with New Zealand, Australia, or even Brazil also reveals the need to reassess the importance of the "open frontier" in influencing the development of socialism, as those societies, which developed around and in tension with a frontier, also experienced radical and socialist politics.[14]

Furthermore, studies focusing on the importance of upward social mobility and the "embourgeoisment" of the American working class as a factor in limiting the development of socialism have increasingly stressed that the awareness or perception of mobility is *as important* as mobility itself in structuring social and political attitudes. Stephan Thernstrom has stated that "mobility data are meaningless except within a context of well-defined attitudes and expectations about the class system."[15] Here too we see the importance of that "metaphysical equality" among citizens which was central in constructing the terms of civil society in America.

Finally, as various scholars have noted, one cannot fully understand how certain features of the American political system structure social development without relating them to the broader realm of American values and beliefs. The American Constitution is a case in point. Although the United States is certainly not the only modern nation state with a constitution, its uniqueness, in that for more than two hundred years it has continued to be the central tenet of American values and institutions, distinguishes it from other constitutions, which have been changed and adapted by various political regimes. This, together with the "sacredness" with which the American Constitution is imbued, has accounted for its unique role in American life.

From a comparative perspective it thus becomes clear that a full understanding of the failure of socialism in the United States is to be found not in any set of structural factors or political constraints *per se*, but in the overriding terms of American ideology, with its inclusive definitions of citizenship and its integration of the working class as members of the national collective. More than anything else it was the very ideology of Americanism, its civil religion, in Bellah's terms, that precluded the development of a socialist movement there. The uniqueness of this civil religion as

109

a form of national identity, which in its very essence precludes a socialist ideology, was expressed by Leo Sampson as follows:

> When we examine the meaning of Americanism we discover that Americanism is to the American not a tradition, or a territory, not what France is to a Frenchman or England to an Englishman, but a doctrine—what socialism is to a socialist . . . a highly attenuated, conceptualized, platonic impersonal attraction to a handful of final notions—democracy, liberty, opportunity, to all of which the American adheres rationalistically, much like a socialist adheres to his socialism.[16]

The set of beliefs that made the American ideology so different from that of other nation-states was a crucial factor in the integration of the working class as citizens in the civil polity. These beliefs centered upon a number of core ideological components, which can be traced to the ascetic or sectarian Protestant background of the United States. These include:

1. The ideological terms of membership in society, i.e., acceptance of the principles of American values and beliefs and not the existence of primordial or ascriptive criteria of individual inclusion in the polity (those criteria rooted in the feudal Ständestaadt)
2. The stress on individual autonomy and agency as the core principles of social solidarity
3. The high degree of commitment and participation of these individuals to society and to its social and political orders— that is, in essence, the right of all members of the national community to participate in public life (Here too we see the absence of the feudal heritage, where the traditions of territorial and not individual representation which while overthrown in the French Revolution [law of August 11, 1792], continued in different types of restrictions based on status groupings [land value or capital], household restriction, restrictions based on literacy, formal education or public office, residency, and so on.)[17]

It was primarily these ideological factors that informed, structured, and gave unique saliency to those structural factors which,

110

by themselves, existed in other societies but did not prevent the growth of socialist movements.

In the eighteenth and nineteenth centuries civil society came to imply a form of universal citizenship within the nation-state, based on the one hand on the principles of individualism and on the other on the participation of these individuals in public life, a participation that was in turn based on the mutuality of citizens in the form of compacts, contracts, and the moral, economic, social, and political ties binding these individuals. In these terms, the United States would indeed seem to be the society where these principles were most fully realized. The failure of the socialist movement to take root in America presents perhaps the most striking illustration of this phenomenon. Moreover, and of equal if not greater significance, here we see the continuing importance of those two sources of civil society, Reason (as the equality of citizens) and the individual—as well as the locus of these ideas in the traditions of ascetic-Protestantism—as enduring components of the idea and practice of civil society. Here more than anywhere else the unique terms of Protestant universalism based on the individual (and not on a collective or organic entity of the people), that universal/particularism noted above, became the basis of the religion of the republic and so of the civic polity. In this religion of the republic the terms of universal citizenship were based on the existence of individuals freed from any corporate identity and defined by their autonomous status vis-à-vis society as a whole.

An interesting corollary to this aspect of American political culture, which will serve to illustrate its concrete implications in terms of social action is that, as Lipset has argued, social movements and not political parties have been the chief form of articulating and furthering demands for social change in the United States—the uniquely American response to social crises.[18] This phenomenon, which Lipset presents as part of an explanation for the failure of socialism in the United States, has deep implications for the understanding of civil society there as elsewhere. For the contemporary concern with politics on a manageable scale, with loosely organized and semiformal venues of political organization, with new forms of protest movements, independent of existing political and institutional structures—all, knowingly or not, hark back to this very American model of protest and participation in the political process.

The current East European "nostalgia" for a civil society beyond the pettiness and politicking of party politics (that is, the form of protest and political action that existed, by necessity, before the revolutions of 1989) is in fact a wish to duplicate this American form of political action, which is presented as a model for civil society everywhere. Often the particularly American aspects of this model of citizenship are ignored, however. That is a mistake. For the tendency to articulate participation in terms of social movements and not political parties is deeply rooted in precisely that historical development which sets America off from other nation-states of both Western and Eastern Europe. Here, as in other realms, the traditions of Protestant individualism, the stress on individual autonomy and on the "metaphysical equality" existing between individuals, and the lack of a hierarchic, feudal tradition of the politics of estates all contributed to the defining terms of the political culture. Similarly, the stress on the moral nature of this individual identity and by implication the deep moral hue attributed to the political realm (not necessarily, or not at all, to political parties), those "creedal moments" of political and moral intervention in civil life studied by Samuel Huntington are all rooted in the traditions of the community of saints and the Puritan vision of a reformed social order.[19]

In fact, we can find deep resonances of the Scottish Enlightenment model of civil society as embodying an ethical representation of society, of the moral affections binding autonomous individuals, in the very moral tenor of American politics—or perhaps more correctly of those social movements American politics has spawned, from Garrison's burning of the Constitution through the civil rights and anti–Vietnam War movements of this century and down to the current popular movements to ban smoking in public places, to punish drunk drivers (MADD), or the "war" against drugs. In all cases (and the abiding differences between the first and second set of cases will be discussed shortly), a high moral tone is invoked, and that is precisely what so many identify with the meaning and workings of civil society. Thus, the very fact that America is taken as a model for civil society (and the example of political movements is but a concrete

112

illustration of this) attests, as does the failure of socialism there, to the particular definitions of citizenship and participation in public life that existed in the United States. These were, as we have seen, ideological in their essence. They rested on adherence to a set of principles and beliefs, to an ideological *ecumene* (and not to a set of primordial or ascriptively defined set of criteria), and so admitted the possibility of a universalization of citizenship to a degree unknown in other modern nation-states.

Thus far we have been viewing the idea of citizenship, *qua* membership in the national community, as coterminous or at the very least as the *sine qua non* of civil society. The extension or universalization of citizenship and the institutional spheres of its realization (in the legal rights of individuals and later of social groups) has been analyzed as the concrete and practical forms that the idea of civil society has taken in the nineteenth century. The question of American exceptionalism to the socialist movement and ideology has been presented as a theoretical foil against which the complementarity of citizenship and civil society could be best understood.

In the preceding analysis we have taken the attributes of citizenship and of participation as relatively unproblematic and have viewed the existence of civil society in terms of their realization in concrete social practices (individual legal rights, extension of the franchise, etc.). This simplistic account occludes the different analytic dimensions of citizenship of their implementation and universalization, which nonetheless must be considered, especially in light of contemporary concerns with civil society in both Eastern and Western Europe as well as in the North Atlantic communities. What I have in mind is precisely that distinction made by T. H. Marshall more than forty years ago between the political, civil, and social aspects of citizenship, which he defined as follows: "The civil element is composed of the rights necessary for individual freedom—liberty of person, freedom of speech, thought and faith, the right to own property and to conclude valid contracts, and the right to justice [that is] the right to defend and assert all one's rights on terms of equality with others and by due process of law." The political element comprises "the right to participate in the exercise of political power as a member of the body invested with political authority or as an elector of the members of such a body." And the social element includes "the right to a modicum of economic welfare and security [and the] right to share to the full in the social heritage and to live the life of a civilized being according to the standards prevailing in society."[20] The benchmarks used by Marshall to identity the founding moments of the first and second aspects of citizenship in England were the Reform Act of 1832 and the Electoral Act of 1918. The social aspects of citizenship were still, in the middle of the twentieth century, being fought over. (Here too the expansion of social rights was, in England, gradual, from the Workmen's Compensation Act of 1906 to the Old Age Pension Act of 1908, the National Insurance Act of 1911, and the Unemployment Insurance Act of 1920. It is perhaps only in the National Health Service Act of 1946, whose implementation began in 1948, that we can speak of a full recognition of the principles of social citizenship, of sharing that common material culture which, for Marshall, was the hallmark of social citizenship.)[21]

If we follow Marshall's scheme, the universalization of citizenship thus involves the progressive extension not simply of civil and political rights but of certain social desiderata as well. And if we view the contemporary scene in both the East and the West, we see that the meaning of civil society—as normative concept—in both places reflects these different meanings of citizenship. Denied both civic and political rights during forty years of state socialism, civil society is, for many in contemporary Eastern and East-Central Europe, simply a model of civil and political citizenship that never existed. The demand for a return to civil society is—where it is not nostalgia for the high modernism of early-twentieth-century bourgeois culture (complete with its strong feudal element and working class exclusion) or for the solidarity of the samizdat—in a sense not for a "return" at all but for the full realization of the universal principles of political and civil citizenship that developed in Western Europe and earlier in the United States but never really existed east of the Elbe. In all of those countries, with the only partial exception of Czechoslovakia, the liberal-individualist tradition based on the principles of universal citizenship was extremely weak and never fully instituted.

In Western Europe and the United States the demand for civil

114

society is rooted in a very different set of circumstances and problems. There, the principles of political and civil citizenship have
been, since the early decades of this century, taken for granted.
The nuts and bolts of social citizenship and participation are,
however, the sources of the contemporary demand for a "truly"
civil society—a demand examplified most vividly in the contemporary concern for entitlements.[22] Here the case of public health
services provides a good illustration of these deep-seated differences in the meaning of civil society in the East and the West. In
the United States, as in Britain, the provisions of the public health
care system remain the focus of ideological debate and controversy on all sides of the political spectrum. In the United States,
where over 30 million people are without any form of health
coverage, the debate over individual entitlements to health care
facilities goes to the heart of liberal-individualist values and the
role of the State as in essence a guarantor of crucial aspects of
individual existence in society. In England, the debate over privatization—private beds and private hospitals—reflects similar, albeit more English, concerns with the emblems of status and
privilege.[23] (More recent conflicts over the extension of market
principles to the organization of the NHS has brought this debate
to a much more principled level involving the very fundamental
definitions of individual and social responsibility—of the very
terms and definitions of civil society). However, when we come
to contemporary Eastern and East-Central Europe, the situation is
very different. There medical care, though free to all the citizenship, is also depressingly lacking, suffering from acute shortages
of drugs and of the most elementary forms of equipment. Moreover, in the turn to economic privatization there is no appreciation of its implications for the health care system. In the
"discourse" of civil society the problem of social entitlements
finds little space, and the problem of health care (to take but one
example) is divorced from the principled, ideological concerns of
civil society, of its reconstitution or indeed its establishment.[24]

The contemporary differences in the meaning of civil society in
Eastern and Western contexts are rooted in the abiding differences that characterized the liberal-individualist and socialist traditions in their respective relationship to the conflicting demands
of modern society—that is, of the private and public aspects of

115

social existence. Those tensions between private and public, individual and social demands and desiderata, were perceived throughout the nineteenth century and into the twentieth as the ideological tension between liberty and equality. Full implementation of the principles of individual liberty (as for example in a totally laissez-faire market economy) would, given the different social position, capabilities, resources, etc., of individuals, preclude the achievement of social equality. On the other hand, any guarantee of social equality would, by necessity, involve the imposition (by the State) of myriad constraints on the (market) activities of individuals to ensure a totally equitable distribution of social wealth and resources.

Of course, within the liberal-individualist tradition, equality was perceived as equality of opportunity and not equality of condition and was guaranteed by the formal mechanisms of equality before the law, precisely those civil and political rights which formed two components of Marshall's definition of citizenship. The nineteenth century was in fact characterized by what may be called a "strong" reading of this definition of political and formal, legal equality, which excluded what we would now call social entitlements. Thus, for example, in England the Poor Law of 1834 offered a minimum of social relief and security only to those who had, in effect, renounced the rights of citizenship. This was in marked contrast to the so-called 1795 Speenhamland System of poor relief, which sought to maintain the integrity of family, village, and parish as centers of solidarity and the mutality of relief and welfare.[25] The Poor Law of 1834, by contrast, dissolved the bonds of mutuality by treating the poor as individuals who had lost or rather forfeited their communal ties. Marshall states:

> The Poor Law treated the claims of the poor, not as an integral part of the rights fo the citizen, but as an alternative to them—as claims which could be met only if the claimants ceased to be citizens in any true sense of the word. For paupers forfeited in practice the civil right of personal liberty, by internment in the workhouse, and they forfeited by law any political rights they might possess.[26]

Note too the date. Two years after the Reform Bill extending (albeit minimally) the franchise. Here we see how the demands of political citizenship, based on political and legal equality, were

116

perceived to exist only in opposition to the social aspects of mutuality (and sympathy) and a less formal, generalized, and abstract concept of social solidarity.

In a similar way the early Factory Acts were designed to protect the social condition of women and children—again, those members of the community who were not enfranchised and were denied the rights of citizenship. Here too social entitlements were seen to stand in contradiction to the autonomy of the individual citizen and to his (very much "his" throughout the century) right to conclude contracts with other legally defined citizens on the market. So, too, the restrictions on workers' organizations in England and in France (Loi le Chappelier) were justified and legitimized in terms of the principle of individual autonomy.

It was thus only very gradually that principles of citizenship were extended—within the liberal-individualist tradition—to include a modicum of, it not equality, then at least some form of social entitlement that came to be seen as part and parcel of citizenship and not an alternative to it. Many, though by no means at all, of the struggles in contemporary Western societies over health-care, better public education, and racial and gender inequalities are centered on different forms of social entitlements. The often polemical positing of these demands for greater social equality in the above-mentioned realms, in terms of a return to civil society, reflects the desire by some part of the populace to include ever broader areas of social entitlement within the defining terms of citizenship in the late twentieth century.

Once posited in these terms, the different positions of conservatives and liberals in contemporary America over such issues as affirmative action, public health policy, or federal spending on poverty programs can be seen to reflect deep-seated (if often unarticulated) philosophical differences on the meanings of citizenship and the proper mean to be found between the conflicting demands of liberty and equality. In passing we may note that what is unique in the American experience is that these differences have been and continue to be presented as differences on the level of concrete social programs and not of different "metaphysical universes." Consequently, the struggle over these various issues is carried out on the whole within the institutional and legal venues of political parties, representative government, and

117

of course the court system. In European countries, including those of Western Europe, these differences were, especially in the nineteenth century, perceived as embodying different and contrasting ultimate goods, hence different visions of the very constitutive core of society. As such, they were subject to conflict whose violence and vehemence broke through the existing and established channels of participatory action (in the form of general strikes and syndicalist or revolutionary practices, for example). However, in one form or another and in different ways in different societies (often, in Germany, Austria, and Sweden, for example, in the wake of World War I), the principles of social citizenship—today's entitlements—have become accepted aspects of our understanding of citizenship. This broader understanding of what it means to be a citizen in today's nation-state adds a new dimension to the very idea of universal citizenship based on civil or formal legal-rational equality that in itself warrants further analysis.

III

With this broader understanding of citizenship, which included an element of shared solidarity and not simply of individual rights, the problems that concerned the Scottish moralists of the eighteenth century reemerged within political and social thought. What reemerged was the classical problem of squaring the demands of the abstract right of the individual with the desiderata of social entitlements and mutual welfare. In many ways this problem has been at the center of social and political thought from the late nineteenth century until today—defining and molding contemporary debates over civil society. For, as should be clear by now, the idea of civil society stands or falls with their reconciliation, or even the theoretical possibility of such a reconciliation, given the reigning definitions of individual and social existence in the modern world.

We have seen in the previous chapter how the legacy of the Protestant Reformation fundamentally transformed the definitions of universalism and particularism within the cultural orientations of Western Christendom. Instead of the particular

118

individual (or corporate body) representing the universal values of the Christian *ecumene*, the individual in a sense incorporated within him/herself (through the interiorization first of grace and then of moral precepts) the ethical value of the universal whole. In a sense, each individual came to be seen in and of him/herself as a universal and thus endowed with a sanctity and value that are at the core of the liberal tradition (recall here our earlier discussion of seventeenth- and eighteenth-century America).

This understanding of the individual involved, however, the bifurcation of individual identity that was noted above in the writings of Shaftesbury and Ferguson. That is to say, the perceived divide within the individual of interest-motivated and altruistic sources of action (the latter emerging from that aspect of universal morality internalized into conscience). The distinction within the individual of particular-private and what was invariably seen as interest-motivated sources of action and universal, social, and by implication altruistic sources of action has become seminal to modern consciousness. Its expression has taken many different forms among different writers and thinkers; we may think, for example, of Freud's division of the personality into superego, ego, and id as one important variant on this theme.

Closer to our own concern with the attempt to revitalize the idea of civil society we should recall Emile Durkheim's writings on *Homo Duplex* and the different meanings of individualism. For Durkheim, as is well known, there exists within the individual consciousness a divide and conflict between the utilitarian demands of self and the sacred or moral dictates of society. The dualism that characterizes human existence is, for Durkheim, an internalized duality rooted in the conflicting demands of self and society on the individual. These "two classes or states of consciousness," the one "purely individual" and the other "nothing but an extension of society," are the source of constant tension in individual life.[27] Recalling the thinkers of the Scottish Enlightenment, for Durkheim individualism was not to be defined by the "utilitarian egoism" of Spencer and the economists or of that ultilitarian individualism which apotheosized individual well-being and private interest.[28] Durkheim in fact took issue with that form of nineteenth-century individualism which, while developing out of the civil society tradition of the Scottish Enlightenment,

119

nevertheless rejected the social component of individual selfhood that was so strong a component of this tradition.[29] And, as we have seen in our analysis of citizenship, it was precisely the autonomy of the individual citizen that was stressed throughout the nineteenth century at the expense of solidarity between citizens. The attributes of citizenship were, in the mid-nineteenth century, less those of moral (i.e., universal) individual selfhood than those of abstract citizens contracting among themselves for (what was perceived to be) their mutual benefit.

Durkheim's critique of the ultilitarian tradition serves to highlight the contradiction that rested at the core of the nineteenth-century liberal tradition. For if the individual is perceived as sacrosanct and autonomous—a universal value in itself—what are the possible terms of solidarity existing between such individuals? If each is an autonomous legal, moral, and economic agent, what binds society together—beyond the calculus of mutual self-interest as presented by David Hume and Adam Smith? By the mid-nineteenth century, these concerns were not restricted to, in Durkheim's own words, "a drawing room theory or philosophical construct"; they were at the core of the whole debate over citizenship, a debate of which Durkheim, living amid the social conflicts of the Third Republic in France, was all too well aware and, in the case of the Dreyfus Affair, an active participant.[30]

Durkheim's whole theoretical endeavor (and in fact the founding of modern sociology with the idea of the precontractual basis of the social order) was an attempt to construct a theoretical edifice of mutual solidarity—of civil society—out of the idea of morally autonomous individuals. The idea of the precontractual, we recall, was the existence of rules and regulations of contract that were themselves prior to and independent of any contract. Such rules as, for example, the prohibition on selling oneself into slavery were for Durkheim socially given; they rested, ultimately, on a set of moral priorities that defined the basis of trust and mutuality in society and came to be defined in Durkheim's later thought as the *conscience collective*.[31]

The positing of a solidarity or mutual trust as existing (analytically) prior to the contract and as the basis for any contract was, in effect, Durkheim's answer to the utilitarian and contract political theory of the nineteenth century. This "precontractual" trust

120

was, for Durkheim, based on the governing terms of social solidarity, which, in modern, organic (*Gesellschaftlich*) society was based on the ethical valuation of individual personhood.[32] This "cult of the individual personality" was not, however, the individualism of Spencer and the utilitarians but a vision of the individual, which, for Durkheim, had much in common with the eighteenth-century vision of civil society, that is to say, a vision of the individual where the social is contained in the person, the universal embodied in the particular, and where the sources of moral action rest on the cognizance of the individual sanctity of each member of society.

> Since each of us incarnates something of humanity, each individual consciousness contains something divine and thus finds itself marked with a character which renders it sacred and inviolable to others. Therein lies all individualism; and that is what makes it a necessary doctrine.[33]

This quote, taken from his essay "Individualism and the Intellectuals," was in fact written in the wake of the Dreyfus Affair, in which Durkheim and his students were heavily involved. For Durkheim, public involvement in this issue was imbued with a "moral seriousness," as the affair threatened the very universalism of reason and individual rights upon which, for him, the modern terms of social solidarity were based.[34]

Via Kant, Durkheim harks back to the principles of Reason embodied in the Scottish Enlightenment account of civil society, where "the only moral ways of acting are those which can be applied to all men indiscriminately; that is, which are implied in the general notion of 'man.' "[35] In his appeal to the autonomy of Reason as regulating moral behavior (through perception of the universal moral attributes of each individual), Durkheim in fact emphasizes his debt to eighteenth-century philosophical liberalism, through which he condemns the utilitarianism of the nineteenth century.

Durkheim's formulations on the precontractual basis of the social order and on the *conscience collective* can be seen as an attempt to return, in the late nineteenth century, to the formulations of the eighteenth century on natural sympathy and moral sentiment as the core of the social order or, in the earlier formulation, civil society. Durkheim attempts to "save" that social component of individual identity which, while present in the eighteenth-century idea of civil society, was lost in nineteenth-century utilitarian theory. In this context it is not surprising to find in Durkheim's more explicitly political positions an advocacy of intermediary bodies—occupational and professional groups—standing between the individual and the State. That is precisely those type of corporate groups which the Loi le Chappelier had sought to outlaw as inimical to the principle of individual autonomy but for Durkheim were the only guarantee of social solidarity among otherwise atomized individuals.[36] It was for Durkheim only in these modern "guild" type of organizations that moral authority could exist in a society governed by the individualistic ethic. For these groups "like every group formed of individuals united by ties of interest, ideas and feelings, is capable of being a moral force over the members who comprise it."[37] Here too we find echoes of Hegel's definition of civil society as a realm existing between the family and the State—with the important difference that, as we have seen, for Hegel this entity was ethical only *in status nascendi*, while for Durkheim it was the only organizational principle through which ethical, social existence could exist.

Not that Durkheim did not share Hegel's positive evaluation of the State. For Durkheim the State was the guarantor of moral individuality. "Far from its tyrannizing over the individual, it is the State that redeems the individual from society."[38] Following Hegel, Durkheim accepts "the premise that the rights of the individual are not ipso facto his at birth; that they are not inscribed in the nature of things" and agrees that only the State can ensure, promulgate, and guarantee these rights."[39] For Durkheim, the State "must be present in all spheres of social life and make itself felt . . . It must even permeate all those secondary groups of family, trade and professional association, Church, regional arenas and so on . . . which tend . . . to absorb the personality of their members."[40] Secondary groups, the intermediary groups of civil society, are for Durkheim the venues through which the moral authority of the State, as guarantor of individual rights, enters into individual life. Without these groups the moral authority of the State was too distant from individual life to play the universalizing role (of preserving individual rights) that

122

Durkheim allocated to it. (Here we see of course the major difference between Durkheim and Hegel. Durkheim was after all concerned not with the realization of absolute spirit [in the State] but with preserving social solidarity in a society of individuals).[41]

It was, not surprisingly, this same principle that led Durkheim to advocate a particular type of socialism that stressed the universal, moral aspects of the socialist vision over and against its class, i.e., particular, aspects.[42] For Durkheim socialism, and with it the social question, "is not a question of money or force, it is a question of moral agents. What dominates it is not the state of our economy, but much more, the state of our morality."[43] And socialism and communism, both "fearing what may be called 'economic particularism,' both concerned with the dangers that private interest can present to the general interest," were for him a moral issue.[44] It was for this reason that he lent them his (albeit mediated) support. Durkheim's support for a particular brand of socialism was thus similar in nature to his advocacy of intermediary groups in society. Both were based on his belief that unbridled individualism must be mediated by an awareness of the mutuality of social life rooted in the workings of reason. Both positions stemmed from the search for those concrete mechanisms of social organization which would "subordinate the private interest to social ends."[45] Socialism was, for Durkheim, an attempt to realize this in the economic realm and in fact "to discover through science the moral restraint which can regulate economic life and by this regulation control selfishness and thus gratify needs."[46]

Durkheim and, following him, much of twentieth-century sociology thus attempted to square the circle of modern individualism (that the practice of the latter has often been unaware of the true dimensions of this problem is another matter). They attempted, that is, to posit a theoretical grounding for the solidarity and mutality of a society comprising "wholes that are self-sufficing."[47] Durkheim continually emphasized that individuals in society are not wholes, are not self-sufficing, nor are they in fact fully autonomous.[48] "The human person," for Durkheim, "forms part of the physical and social milieu; he is bound up with it and his autonomy can be only relative."[49] In emphasizing the social aspect of individual existence, Durkheim at one and the same time recalls the moral affections of the Scottish Enlighten-

123

ment and seeks to give this notion a new "scientific" form in terms of an epistemology of consciousness rooted in Kantian ideas of a universal Reason and a rational morality, where, as he stressed in his 1902 Bordeaux lectures, "the application of reason to morality is becoming the condition of virtue."[50]

In his writings Durkheim was less concerned with reason *per se* than with the social implications of the formal legal equality of citizenship. Durkheim was, after all, interested in what held modern society together. In a world of increased social division of labor, defined by an individualistic ethic, what, he queried, was the source of social solidarity? In working his way to answering this question Durkheim broke with the theoretical paradigm he had developed in the *Division of Labor* (1893) and, in *The Elementary Forms of Religious Life* (1912), posited the notion of collective representations not as a common subjectivity of ideas but as a shared normative orientation to the phenomena of social life.[51] In this move the modern discipline of sociology was founded and the nature of morality defined sociologically as the domain assumptions (fundamental premises) of modernity were integrated with those of sociology, i.e., the universality of the individual ego based on the categorical, *a priori* structure of knowledge.[52]

Our own interest in Durkheim, however, lies less in the logical consistency of his idea of *conscience collective* than in the new definition of individualism that he offered. For he presents, in the realm of theory, the counterpart to that universalization of citizenship that we noted above in our analysis of civil political and social rights. The addition of social rights to the civil and political rights of citizens manifests not only a greater extension and universalization of citizenship but also a mediation of that extreme individualism that had characterized nineteenth-century liberal-individualist political theory. It reflects an awareness or recognition of what Durkheim would call universal solidarity among citizens that underpins their very individual and particular existence.

The principle of social citizenship is thus not simply a further dimension of citizenship but a new dimension, one that recognizes the mutuality existing at the core of society. For Durkheim this mutuality was part and parcel of the very definition of individualism in the modern era, not a corrective to it. In this he was

124

not at all far from the Scottish moralists of the eighteenth century. Indeed, with Durkheim we see the continuity not only of the Scottish Enlightenment tradition but of that Puritan interiorization of grace into consciousness that we studied in the previous chapter and to which Durkheim, as his nephew Marcel Mauss noted, owed so much.

For Durkheim, as for the already Arminian-turning Puritans of the late seventeenth-century, it is within the individual consciousness that the demands of conscience (the social) and of nature (the individual) meet. The individual is for Durkheim the "touchstone of morality" and partakes in "transcendental majesty" precisely because (s)he embodies the arena of moral agency.[53] The unitary force of the ethical exists, in this tradition, within the arena of individual consciousness. Important here is not that Durkheim places the ethical within the individual, he does not— the sources of the ethical or moral are in society (as any first year sociology undergraduate knows). Rather, it is that the arena where the ethical is resolved, where its dictates struggle for primacy, contend and conflict with alternative demands and strictures, is in the individual consciousness. The individual is the center of morality because it is within the individual that the social sources of morality reside.[54] The logic of Durkheim's argument is thus of embodying the universal (public and social) within the particular (private and individual).

With Durkheim, as with the philosophers of the eighteenth century, the conflicting demands of (social) morality and (individual) interest—conceived of in terms of *Homo Duplex*—are the province of the individual conscience. In this reading, the constitutive relations and conflicts of the social order are represented in metahistorical terms, which allow for resolution only on the individual level. The representation of society (of its core values and meanings) is posited in terms of universal subjects (individuals) constituted through the workings of reason. In Durkheim's own terms, "The development of rationalism does not come about without a parallel development of individualism."[55] While moral facts and collective representations exist *sui generis*, the arena of their realization and representation is in the individual.[56] Thus, for Durkheim, while society is "the end of all moral activity," which both "transcends the individual" and is "immanent in

125

him," the field of this action, the arena of its representation, is within the individual consciousness.[57] (It is important in this context to remember that the French language contains no distinction between "conscience" and "consciousness." Thus for Durkheim the very workings of consciousness, i.e., reason, implied the realization of conscience.)

This, Durkheim's vision, has become very much part of our contemporary world, among sociologists as well as the majority of the populace in modern democratic nation-states. Its social implications were, as we have seen, expressed in the developing forms of citizenship to include a "social" component beyond the purely abstract legal equality of citizenship. Yet, for all that, we still feel the lack of solidarity, mutality, and trust in our hospitals, schools, and places of employment. The public space of citizenship—Ferguson, Kant, and Durkheim notwithstanding—still seems to be characterized by abstract legal formulae and not by moral affections. Hence the call for a return to civil society. The very continued existence of these problems points, however, to the fact that existing solutions—as well as practices—including those of Durkheim, were insufficient and we must try to assess why this has been so.

IV

Broadly stated, the continuing problem of articulating a model of citizenship that would be "civil" in the extended sense of the term, that would include the ties of solidarity existing between citizens and not just their political and legal autonomy, is to be found in the very logic of citizenship itself. The very principles of Reason upon which our idea of citizenship rests are those which, concomitantly, undermine any affective solidarity of the type envisioned by Ferguson, Kant, and Durkheim. The problem, first posed by Hume in the starkest of terms, was, as we have attempted to show, never really resolved. It would therefore be worth our while to review this ground, this time from a more sociological perspective.

As we have seen, in the modern era the concepts of reason and the legal equality of citizens have been viewed as, if not synon-

126

ymous, then at least complementary. The notion of reason as embedded in the State and expressed in the equality of citizens has been a (philosophically) given axiom since the French Revolution. It was on this basis that Immanuel Kant greeted the French Revolution and never fully removed his support for it, even during the Terror. It was the historical force of this idea that inspired the writing or conclusion of Hegel's *Phenomenology of Spirit* (1807), with the "forces of reason" knocking, as it were, on the gates of Jena. It was the desire to work through the logic of this connection beyond its abstracted ahistoricity that motivated the young Marx to undertake his work of self-clarification in *The German Ideology* (1844–45). Finally, by the end of the century it was the realization of the necessary connection between reason—as the absence of particular criteria for judgment and action—and the nature of modern life that led Max Weber to the iron cage of an *entzauberte* world. And it is perhaps in Weber that we can find the fullest understanding of the intractable contradiction that stands at the core of the modern world. Weber realized, better than most, the intimate connection among (1) the idea of citizenship as founded on the principle of Reason, (2) the social consequences of this idea in terms of any ethical representation of social life, and (3) the source of both in the religious doctrines of ascetic-Protestantism. Hence by returning to Weberian informed perspectives on the consequences of rationality we can, I believe, broaden our understanding of the contemporary forms of citizenship, civil society, and the perduring problems of integrating public and private spheres.

Weber saw in both ascetic-Protestantism and deistic reason the roots of those natural and self-evident rights upon which the modern world order is based. In his own words,

> . . . the consistent sect gives rise to an inalienable personal right of the governed as against any power, whether political, hierocratic or patriarchal. Such freedom of conscience may be the oldest Right of Man—as Jellinek has argued convincingly; at any rate, it is the most basic Right of Man because it comprises all ethically conditioned action and guarantees freedom from compulsion, especially from the power of the State. . . . All these rights find their ultimate justification in the belief of the Enlightenment in the workings of individual reason, which, if unimpeded, would result in the at

127

least relatively best of all worlds, by virtue of Divine providence
and because the individual is best qualified to know his own interest. This charismatic glorification of "Reason," which found a
characteristic expression in its apotheosis by Robespierre, is the
last form that charisma has adopted in its fateful historical course.[58]

Here, the apotheosis of Reason is rooted in the self-same form of
individual illuminism that was noted by Benjamin Nelson and, as
such, stands at the core of our modern world.

The rationalization of the world—including the social world of
citizens—to which Weber devoted so much of his writings was,
however, a Janus-faced phenomena. By bringing ever increasing
realms of life into the realm of Reason, it also denuded them of
any value (especially ethical value) beyond that instrumental calculus of means–end relationship. This famous "disenchantment
of the world," leaving us "specialists without spirit, sensualists
without heart," which is characteristic of the modern world, has
been noted by many and doesn't bear repeating here. What is less
remarked upon is the implications of this dynamic on that aspect
of universal citizenship which is so important to the idea of civil
society—if that idea is to be understood as containing an element
beyond the mere interest-motivated activities of legally free individuals. Here too, Weber can aid us in conceptualizing this problem of what may be termed the ethical status of the public sphere.
He notes:

> Precisely the ultimate and most sublime values have retreated from
> public life either into the transcendental realm of mystical life or
> into the brotherliness of direct and personal human relations. It is
> not accidental that our greatest art is intimate and not monumen-
> tal, nor is it accidental that today only within the smallest and
> intimate circles, in personal human situations, in pianissimo, that
> something is pulsating that corresponds to the prophetic pneuma,
> which in former times swept through the great communities like a
> firebrand, welding them together.[59]

Here then we see the opposite phenomenon to that characterized
above in the charisma of Reason in the eighteenth century. Somehow the universalization of value positions (embodied in the
Rights of Man) has given way to a privatization (one may almost

128

say particularization) of values. Such contemporary phenomena as the rise of consumerism, the "fall of public man," and the growth in diverse "therapies"—from orthodox Freudianism to the most current of "New Age" technologies for personal fulfillment—would all seem to indicate the basic truth of Weber's insight, at least pertaining to considerable portions of modern industrialized societies.

We may in fact note in passing that it is precisely this privatization and particularization of value positions that bears a striking resemblance to the postmodern distrust of a universal reason. Thus, for example, the recent philosophical perspectives developed by Lyotard attempt to posit normative attributes precisely to the bracketing out, indeed to the very impossibility, of constructing a universal discourse of reason. In this reading the human world is constructed of "simples" that are named (and not described). These are building blocks of what is essentially a "prelogical" universe and thus preclude any logical assertion of truth value.[60]

Drawing on the traditions of phenomenological "ontology," as well as such disciplines as ordinary language philosophy, the postmodern position challenges traditional belief in the accessibility of the "good" to the workings of reason. All stress the limits of language (reason) and its essential inability to articulate the *summum Bonum*. The "good" cannot be articulated and so cannot be subject to a discourse of reason.

The core of the postmodern position can in fact be presented in two central and related themes: (1) an attack on the existence of universals (which are either vigorously denied or, in the Wittgensteinian mode, posited beyond language and reasonable discourse) and (2) an attack on the philosophy of the subject (best illustrated by Foucault's by now famous quip that "man is an invention of recent date and one perhaps nearing its end."[61]) This position is, of course, in marked contrast to that of modernity, with its focus on the individual subject and belief in the accessibility of the "good" and the "true" (universals) to the workings of reason.

An attack on universal reason carries with it, however, with or without the acquiescence of its promulgators, an attack on the mode of representation—based on the formal equality of citizens—inherent to it. The Basic Rights of Man, including those of formal equality and economic mobility, were, as Weber showed us, the very core of the charisma of reason in its historically ascendent stage.[62] They constituted, in our terms, the ideal model of and for the representation of social life in the classic modern era. This, however, is no longer the case. The contemporary Western terms of society based on the equality of citizenship has somehow denuded citizenship of that universal solidarity of moral affections and natural sympathy which was at the core of the idea of civil society.

What I wish to claim is that this loss was inherent in the very terms of citizenship based on the principles of universal Reason. In our discussion of the Scottish Enlightenment and of the nineteenth-century institutional forms of citizenship we saw how the individual citizen was constituted in his very individuality in terms of abstract universal principles (of reason). In fact the self-same validation of the individual in and through the universal that we found (with Smith and Hegel, for example) in the realm of exchange was, according to Habermas, at the essence of the legal-normative structure as well. Thus he points out:

> The criteria of generality and abstractness that characterize legal norms had to have a peculiar obviousness for privatized individuals who, by communicating with each other in the public sphere of the world of letters, confirm each other's subjectivity as it emerges from their sphere. . . . These rules, because they are universally valid, secure a space for the individuated person; because they are objective, they secure a space for what is most subjective; because they are abstract, for what is most concrete.[63]

Here we can see that what was crucial for the whole idea of civil society and its particular way of representing the relations between public and private spheres was the development of instrumental reason. For whether in the realm of commodity exchange or of legal sanctions (or even of aesthetic standards), it is precisely the generalized, formal, and abstract nature of the rules governing intercommunicative action that afford the particular (individual) its universal (public or social) status.[64] This is, however, at the same time the paradox that stands at the core of the modern, post-eighteenth-century idea of citizenship—an "ethical" solidar-

130

ity achieved through the universalization of abstract reason. Its consequence is, as we have seen, the particular modern problem of formulating the relation of the individual to the collective in terms other than that of an instrumental reason mediating between exclusive, universalized, and particular individuals. That is, most pointedly, in terms other than those taken from the legal idiom of "rights" and no longer, we may add, of moral affections and natural sympathy.

The most telling and perhaps tragic example of this dynamic is, in America, in the realm of racial equality. It was ultimately through the court system and such Supreme Court decisions as the 1954 *Brown* v. *Board of Education* on school desegregation that black American citizens "entered" the civil polity and became recognized as legally free and equal citizens (participating in those political and civil aspects of citizenship defined by Marshall). A generation later we are witness to the fact that the extension of the formal, legal, and abstract rights of citizens to the black population of the United States has not solved the more interpersonal problem of racism and, while opening the venues of economic and social mobility for many, has left equally great numbers of the black population as a huge underclass, excluded from precisely the more informal terms of solidarity and mutuality that we have come to associate with the idea of civil society.

With this in mind we can now return to our problem of citizenship and of the representation of the bonds of social mutuality in terms of civil society—that is, in terms of a synthesis of public and private realms. This "synthesis" stood, as we have seen in previous chapters, on a unique conceptualization of the public arena. In the classical civil society tradition the arena of civil society, of law and exchange, was not viewed as simply a neutral space of interaction. It was, rather, that arena where the particular was itself constituted and so shared in the attributes of some ethical or transcendental (though no longer transcendent) validation. (This, we recall, was the very meaning of "vanity" for Adam Ferguson, of Adam Smith's "attention and approbation," of Kant's critical reason and of Hegel's characterization of property exchange.) On the other hand, the very establishment of this ethical space was based on abstract, instrumental reason (the very principles of the legal equality of citizens), oriented toward the

131

(ultimately self-referential) individual parts rather than to the whole. In fact Habermas's whole analysis of *The Structural Transformation of the Public Sphere* in the nineteenth century traces precisely this awareness (expressed albeit in class terms) of the reduction of the public sphere to an arena of private interests, incapable of representing the whole.

This development, characterized by the "collapse" of that publicness on which the idea of civil society stood, was, I maintain, inherent to the very premises of modern, liberal-individualist society. Its sources are in the contradictory terms through which individual existence in society is posited. The principled sources of modern society, founded on the realization (and increasing universalization) of Reason through the equality of citizens and the public, shared (what Habermas would term "intercommunicative") character of Reason stand in fact in contradictory and not, as so often assumed, complementary relation to each other. What I mean by this is that precisely that ethical solidarity (which the eighteenth century saw as a component of a Reason not yet divorced from the passions, and which Durkheim sought to "retrieve" from the utilitarianism and instrumentalism of the nineteenth century), realized or attained through the universalization of citizenship (i.e., through the endowment of all with universal rights), voids the area of shared public (and in the eighteenth century perforce ethical) space of any value attributes independent of the individuals inhabiting that space. This is the paradox of modern society, the sources of Weber's insights on the increased particularization of value positions as well as of the current infatuation with the "postmodern" position. This rather bold statement can be better understood through a more detailed examination of the changing relations of public and private spheres in contemporary society.

On the one hand we have seen that the principles of social citizenship—of economic inclusion in the community—have, to a certain extent, mediated the highly individualistic definitions of society that pervaded the nineteenth century. On the other, and given the protracted struggles in contemporary Western societies over social entitlements, the extent of welfare services, the nature of public health and education, and most especially the current call for a "return to civil society," the problem, in all its saliency,

132

continues to plague us. In this context—and to appreciate more fully the inability to "return" to a civil society, at least on its classical principles—it would be advisable to view how the relations between public and private spheres are currently conceived.

While this is undoubtedly only one way of approaching the problems of citizenship and civil society in contemporary societies, it is especially appropriate for our purposes. As we have been dealing throughout with the terms of the universal and the particular and the related problems of representing the ties binding society, the changing definitions of the public and private would seem the proper place to broaden somewhat our understanding of the contradictory premises that stand at the core of modern society and militate against any possibility of "reinventing" the eighteenth-century notion of civil society in today's world.

We can best approach this problem through the changing language of "rights." Of immediate if often unnoticed importance is simply that rights are no longer framed in terms of citizen or civil rights, but of human rights.[65] Moreover, a brief look at today's newspaper, a half-hour listening to the radio, or a walk around campus reveal that among these rights are "the right to wear fur," "the right to good health," "the right to bear AK-47 assault rifles," "women's reproductive rights," and of course "animal rights." Some advocates of the latter positions, as well as sections within the ecology movement, can be seen as imbuing natural phenomena, the oceans, whales, trees, etc., with "rights."[66]

Now, on first sight these latter examples would seem to be relegating to oceans, whales, trees, and kitty-cats the status of citizens. However, here I believe the articulation of rights in terms of human rights (rather than citizen rights) is central. For it is not that kitty-cats become citizens, but rather that the realm of shared public space, within which the citizen is constituted, has itself disappeared. What has taken its place is the most abstract of generalities (again instrumental or disembodied reason, what Weber refereed to as *zweckrationalität*) within which individuals exist in public only as generalized universals (humans, animals, etc.).[67] It is precisely in these terms that we are to understand the "right to wear fur" or even "women's reproductive rights." None of these are citizen rights. They are, rather, private passions and interests projected into the public arena in terms of rights.[68]

133

There is, I believe, an important lesson to be learned from this in terms of the dynamics of the public and private. For while the traditional critical reading would see the devolution of the public sphere as entailing a concomitant destructuring of the private (and this is Habermas's thesis in the work cited above), the opposite process is also at work. In lieu of the public the private is projected into the public arena, is made public, in an attempt to reconstitute itself through its representation in that sphere.

This, I would maintain, is the dynamic underlying that peculiarly American phenomenon of making private (and what in other societies would be deemed trivial) matters public concerns. In America, that paradigm of modern societies, the private is invested with a public nature in an attempt to constitute its value in the face of what is conceived to be a neutral public arena. Into this "void" the private is projected in an attempt to constitute presence. Thus, whether dealing with the drinking or fornication of a public official or the rules regulating smoking in restaurants, the private is given a public presence (and value) unique in contemporary societies. Past analyses of this characteristic feature of American life have sought to explain it by way of the "religious" or "moral" nature of the American polity. While they have not been incorrect in this, they have missed one important point. For it is precisely due to its "Protestant" nature that in America the locus of morality and ethical value is in the individual and not in the public realm. The influence of religion (or more precisely of ascetic-Protestantism) was not solely in imbuing political life with a moral tenor (though, as we have seen, this was also the case) but more in embedding an ethical character into the realm of the particular or individual subject. This was the result of that very process of the internalization of grace into conscience that we studied in the previous chapter. And, while some aspects of this process characterize modern societies as a whole (recall our discussion of the Cambridge Platonists), it was most salient in the United States, where the ethical status imbued in the individual was not in conflict and competition with prior (and more traditional) terms of solidarity and ethical action. (Here we may think yet again of the Dreyfus Affair as presenting but one example of how difficult and torturous was the institutionalization of this concept in the France of the Third Republic, other examples, of course, abound.)

134

In the United States, moreover, it is this morally validated individual subject (that modern individual) who brings into the public (social) arena those value attributes around which political life revolves. The social, or public, space as such is, there more than elsewhere, devoid of autonomous value (and I stress the element of autonomy). It is not that the public space lacks value, but that it lacks autonomous value in and of itself. The value accruing to the public space is a function of the universal value attributed to the social actors (those morally autonomous individuals) acting and interacting in the public realm. More than anywhere else, America is characterized by a community of absolute subjects, each "ontologically" self-contained, existing in a state of "metaphysical equality" and united only by the logic of rational exchange.

This, I realize, is a highly controversial statement, and the reader will immediately think of the abortion controversy as a negation of my claim. Yet the abortion controversy is in fact a foremost example of the private realm achieving a representative status as locus of public values. Moreover, it is precisely in the case of abortion that we can see the contemporary contradiction between the idea of civil society and the institutional premises of modern liberal-individual society. It is, not surprisingly, the pro-life activists who, in their critique of abortion, present something akin to the idea of civil society. Thus, in one of the very few studies carried out on the attitudes and agendas of pro-life activists, that done by the anthropologist Faye Ginsburg, three themes are seen to dominate:

1. Antagonism to "irresponsible sexual behavior," identified as natural to men and unnatural to women
2. A concern with the social and cultural devaluation of dependent people . . . those who because of disability, misfortune, or age cannot function independently or participate in productive activity
3. A critique of market rationality and instrumentality in human relations, which they see as growing and dangerous trends that must be reversed and which they see as "displacing nurturant ties of kin and community"[69]

From this we see that their positions can be characterized as (1) an attempt to protect the moral integrity of the individual (conceived albeit in totally different terms, but as a principled position, strikingly similar to that of the prochoice activists) and (2) an attempt to articulate a model of mutuality and communal responsibility not all that distant from that of the classic civil society tradition. This latter position stands in marked contrast to that of the pro-choice activists, who articulate a position of individual "rights" removed from the mutually validating realm of community.

In the conflict between the two camps we have a foremost example of how the premises of liberal-individualist society (based on the morally and economically autonomous and "rights"-bearing individual) stand in conflict with those of mutuality encompassed by the idea of civil society. We have, further, an example of how the personal realm is imbued with a public and ethical aura that makes of competing moral claims an irreconcilable conflict, not given to compromise. As John Gray recently pointed out,

> By treating the abortion issue . . . as a question of constitutional rights rather than of legislative policy, in which a balance can be found between competing interests and ideals, the dominant schools of American jurisprudence have made of the issue one which admits of no compromise and so cannot be moderated. They thereby deny the US that peaceful settlement of the abortion issue that has been achieved, not only in other English speaking countries such as New Zealand and the United Kingdom, but also in such predominantly Catholic countries as France and Italy.[70]

This is in fact the crux of the issue. For it is precisely the personal sphere that is viewed not in terms of interests (given to an instrumental mediation and so the province of that governmental sphere in which interests are represented, i.e., the legislature) but of public, moral principle (and so decided on within that institutional sphere which, in the United States, represents the "moral authority," the guardians as it were of Durkheim's precontractual, sacred principles of society: the Supreme Court). The case of abortion, then, does not prove that the public arena is not devoid of autonomous value, but only that the personal sphere that replaces it is not always trivial. That it often becomes trivial as the personal is continually projected into and conflated with the public realm is, however, often the case and will be dealt with again.

In the United States, more than elsewhere, we live in Weber's "iron cage," where, with the dissolution of the community of saints as the locus of moral authority, we are left as individuals pursuing individual interests devoid of a shared, public meaning. In Weber's words:

> Where the fulfillment of the calling cannot directly be related to the highest spiritual and cultural values, or when, on the other hand, it need not be felt simply as economic compulsion, the individual generally abandons the attempt to justify it at all. In the field of its highest development, in the United States, the pursuit of wealth, stripped of its religious and ethical meaning, tends to become associated with purely mundane passions, which often actually give it the character of sport.[71]

Weber's "iron cage" is not only the cloak of economic compulsion but its civic or civil corollary, that is, of the relations between these interest-motivated individuals, which can no longer be framed in terms other than a "Humean" calculus of interest, no longer in terms of a shared ethical space. In this sense, as John Dunn has pointedly reminded us, the

> . . . secular "Lockean" liberals of the contemporary United States are more intimately than they realize the heirs of the equalitarian promise of Calvinism. If the religious purpose and sanction of the calling were to be removed from Locke's theory, the purpose of individual human life and of social life would both be exhaustively defined by the goal of the maximalization of utility.[72]

This then is the other side of Weber's "iron cage." For it is only when each individual is him/herself defined in universal terms that the relations between them become utilitarian and interest-motivated, devoid of grounding in a shared ethical space. This process, which began with the ethical validation of individual conscience among ascetic-Protestants, eventually voided the (public) space between individuals of any autonomous value.[73] The mutual exclusion between these individuals is precisely what Weber found existing between social groups in the United States, though he nevertheless saw them as existing within an inclusive framework.[74] It is thus perhaps no wonder then that America, of all places, has been the most receptive to the postmodernist argument. Here, more than anywhere else, the fundamental premises of social existence are those of the apotheosis of the particular.

The elevation of the particular or private sphere to a status that is somehow representative of the social whole is but one aspect of the loss of a public sphere wherein individuality, as a component of ethical solidarity, is constituted. The "universal" subject is the counterpoint to a devalued public sphere within which society and its constitutive relations are presented. This phenomenon, or rather, one aspect of it, was noted more than 150 years ago by Tocqueville. The absence of a shared public space within which critical reason could exert its influence struck Tocqueville as one of the most dangerous aspects of American life. Thus he notes:

> The first thing that strikes the observation is an innumerable multitude of men all equal and alike, incessantly endeavouring to procure the petty and paltry pleasures with which they glut their lives. Each of them, living apart, is as a stranger to the fate of the rest—his children and his private friends constitute to him the whole of mankind; as for the rest of his fellow-citizens, he is close to them, but he sees them not; he touches them, but he feels them not; he exists but in himself and for himself alone; and if his kindred still remain to him, he may be said at any rate to have lost his country.[75]

The effect of this exaggerated privacy and concomitant loss of a shared public life is that "every day renders the exercise of the free agency of man less useful and less frequent; it circumscribes the will within a narrower range, and gradually robs a man of all the uses of himself."[76] Important to note, for the author, it "is the principle of equality [that] has prepared men for these things: it has predisposed men to endure them, and oftentimes to look on them as benefits." The final result of such a situation:

> In modern society everything threatens to become so much alike, that the peculiar characteristics of each individual will soon be entirely lost in the general aspect of the world.[77]

In America, that prototype of all modern societies, we thus see, in starkest light, the conflict we have traced above—that between

138

the equality of citizens and the logic of equality rooted in instrumental reason, which through its very progress undermines that public and ethical space on which it depends.

Thus far we have seen that the issue of how society is represented to and among its constitutive members turned on the proper way of conceiving and representing the increasingly distinct realms of the private and the public. In positing the relations between both, classical modernist political theory was caught in the contradictory demands of its own premises—founded on the unitary categories of reason and the equality of citizens. Every step in universalizing the premises of equality implied a progressive realization of reason. But at the same time it led to a loss of the representative qualities of the public sphere as such. This, for Tocqueville, was the inherent logic of America. As equality progresses the public sphere recedes as the arena where human will is actualized. That very public sphere, which for Kant was necessary for the continual workings of practical reason—and hence equality and freedom—was devalued by the very realization of equality.[78]

The result of this developmental dynamic is, as we have seen, twofold: on the one hand, the devolution of the public sphere—progressing together with the emergence of the private or particular as absolute locus of value; on the other hand, the attempt, most salient in America, to clothe the private realm with a public aura in an attempt to ensure the continued existence of some public presence. This is evident in the changing language of rights as well as in the changing loci of political thought and action, cast in increasingly personal terms and concerns. Thus, to take but one example of new attitudes toward what is seen as "political," a recent article in the *Duke Law Journal* claimed that the social acceptance of certain types of behavior on the part of males—such as belching, passing gas, and spitting in public—and the concomitant disapproval of this behavior on the part of females constitutes a subtle form of women's oppression and abuse.[79] Here too we see a pervasive concern to define as a public issue and so one resonant with the language of equality and rights (though one would hesitate to define exactly what "rights" are involved) an issue which, at best, would be regarded by John Stuart Mill as a "self-regarding act" (i.e., one that did not violate a "distinct and assignable obligation" to others).[80] Similarly, the positing of personal sexual practices in the public arena—not as a matter bearing on the integrity of individual choice or dignity but of public policy and social ordering—is a case in point. The radical feminist and lesbian attack on liberal humanism represents precisely such a projection of what had hitherto been conceived of as private issues into public concerns.[81] It is of some interest that here too the most vociferous proponents of this type of politics, as well as of a position of women's separation, are to be found in America.[82]

Here perhaps I should take the trouble to clarify that I view these developments not as political aberrations but as inherent to and consonant with the defining contradiction of modern civilization. Private and personal matters become public concerns precisely because it is the private individual who represents the universal category of the ethical. And it is this very autonomy of the private individual which belies any attempt, within the liberal-individualist tradition, to return to an idea of civil society based on natural sympathy and moral affections. A good example of this can be found in the public debate in England following the (1957) Report of the Wolfenden Committee on Homosexual Offenses and Prostitution, which recommended that "homosexual behaviour between consenting adults in private should no longer be a criminal offence." Arguments offered by the conservative jurist Lord Patrick Devlin against the principles (if not all the specific recommendations) of the report are, not surprisingly, posed in terms taken from the classical tradition of civil society and not from the liberal tenets of legal rights. He argued that public morality precedes (analytically) public law and that where the majority of the population view a (however personal) practice as "abhorrent . . . I do not see how society can be denied the right to eradicate it."[83] With arguments reminiscent of both Durkheim and the Scottish moralists, he draws on the social basis of any morality ("I do not think that one can talk sensibly of a public and private morality any more than one can talk of a public and private highway") which would of course logically proscribe actions that society viewed with sufficient disapprobation. (Devlin's actual word was "disgust").[84]

Lord Devlin's position goes a long way in clarifying how arguments based on a civil society tradition of shared mutual affections and mores would cut away the foundations of the principled individual rights on which modern society is conceived. More significantly it illustrates how, within this tradition, rights have to be abstract and general, and it shows that the Reason realized in the public sphere (through rights) has to be conceived of as an instrumental reason mediating the contracts between "ontologically" self-sufficient individuals (universals in themselves). For if Reason is conceived in any other terms—as ethical (what Weber termed *wertrationalität*)—we end up back with a (pre-Humean) conception of Reason embodying contrasting and irreconcilable sets of ultimate goods. That this is not so in the liberal-individualist model is, again, because Reason (in the public sphere) is seen as value-neutral and instrumental, value being the province of the transcendentally constituted individual and so of the private, not the public, sphere.

It is this insight which brings us back to the "apotheosis" of the particular and private in the contemporary debates around citizenship. Private concerns become public interests because that is the only possible safeguard of their existence in a society where the distinction between the two has been lost. As Reason loses its public character, through its own achievement in universal citizenship and equality (which, in turn, by recognizing the universality of each individual, make of the shared sphere of their interaction a solely instrumental realm), the private sphere is endowed with a new public importance as the repository of universal truths.

As we have seen, however, we are witness not solely to the de-structuring of both realms (which, as analyzed by Hannah Arendt, was inherent in modernity itself), but to a transformation of the terms of representation.[85] The transposition of public and private in contemporary America bears witness to more than the lost efficacy of both (or either); it indicates an attempt to reconstitute a public arena in light of contradictory tensions that informed its modernist articulation. On a more abstract and theoretical level, this is precisely what is attempted by the postmodernists, who, abjuring universals, posit the particular in their stead. The problem posed by this mode of representation, by the public representation of the private, is, however, as pointed out by Niklas Luhmann, that of any self-referential system, ultimately of the part supporting the whole.[86] This problem is indeed at the heart of the contemporary mode of representation, of which the case of the public and private spheres is the closest to our concerns.

The attempt to posit singular entities in lieu of universals or, in social terms, the private in place of the public bears, as we have attempted to show, a striking resemblance to the Weberian thesis of the loss of a public locus for charismatic action and meaning. This loss, rooted in the mutually negating dynamics of equality and reason analyzed above, results in the increasing difficulty of representing ultimate value positions in the public realm. In their stead the representation of the ethical, is relegated to the particular, the individual, and the private sphere of social life. The devolution of the public sphere as locus of ethical realization is thus concomitant with the failure of the former to provide an arena for the workings of critical reason. Aspects of this development, noted by Hannah Arendt and Jürgen Habermas, were already documented in the 1840s by Tocqueville in reference to American society. Similarly, the retreat of value commitments into the private sphere of particular lives is the social concomitant of the more abstract and philosophical project of the current proponents of postmodernity, who, in fact, attempt to legitimize this development.

However, as we have seen, some mode of representation is nevertheless posited in the contemporary world by the projection of the private into the public sphere. Society cannot do without the play of representation. Representation is not only crucial to the very workings of Reason, but fundamental to the existence of society.[87] Its centrality, and with it that of a public realm as necessary to the continued existence of even the private sphere, was eloquently attested to by Hannah Arendt, who reminded us that

> . . . since our feeling for reality depends utterly upon appearance and therefore upon the existence of a public realm into which things can appear out of the darkness of sheltered existence, even the twilight which illuminates our private and intimate lives is ultimately derived from the much harsher light of the public realm.[88]

Somewhat more prosaically, using Niklas Luhmann's terms, the "representation of society in society," of its constitutive relations posed in terms of some ultimate good, is, as argued most recently by Charles Taylor, necessary to our very existence as human agents in society.[89]

The problem with the contemporary mode of representing social life is, however, in the contradiction that inheres to it, that of the part supporting the whole. The question thus remains whether the current terms of representation, which abjure universal frameworks (of the good or the true), can nevertheless support a concept of society. The consistent refusal to articulate a universal standard of the good, together with the apotheosis of the particular, would seem, rather, to threaten the very ability to represent society at all. Such a failure carries with it, however, certain social consequences—those of a disenchanted and (as radical as it may seem) a fundamentally unrepresented world. It is perhaps in this context that we can understand somewhat more fully Weber's vision of an "iron cage." Deprived of a representation of society through the withdrawal of ethical value and its representative functions into the private realm, our individual and social existences are imprisoned by their own expressive muteness.

As human existence is itself dependent on the expressive capacity of humankind, alternative forms of representation will no doubt continue to appear, perhaps along the lines outlined above.[90] Whether they will further the course of the charisma of reason, or point perhaps to some new form of magical manipulation of a *weiderentzauberte* social cosmos, remains to be seen. In either case, what would seem to be precluded is a return to a mode of representing society on that interweaving of "reason" and "revelation," which played such a crucial role in the civil society tradition of the eighteenth century. An awareness of this problem has in fact informed current attempts to articulate a vision of civil society along somewhat different lines. These attempts, however, subsume the constitutive terms of individual and social existence not only in the West, but in East-Central Europe as well. In the following chapter we shall analyze some of the defining modes of civil existence in both societies, the better to appreciate the viability of current attempts to resurrect the idea of civil society in either place.

CHAPTER 4

Jerusalem, Budapest, Los Angeles

In Search of Civil Society

I

In the previous chapter we traced the contradictions that inhered to the eighteenth-century idea of civil society as they worked themselves out (and were transformed) in the nineteenth-century idea of citizenship. We noted how the problem of civil society—of maintaining solidarity among social actors conceived of as autonomous legal and (more importantly) moral agents—became the problem of defining the terms of citizenship in the modern nation-state. Concentrating on the West European and North American context, we arrived at one of the defining paradoxes of citizenship and so in essence of the idea of civil society as an institutionalized set of practices in the modern world. This, we recall, was the contradiction between equality and the very terms of equality in the modern world.

To recapitulate briefly: the institutionalization of civil society in

145

terms of citizenship implied the representation of society in terms of the workings of a universal-abstract reason, which, in the public realm, was embodied in the idea of universal citizenship. That is to say, membership and participation in society were defined not—as in the premodern era—in terms of ascriptive, kinship, territorial, or religious affiliations, but in terms of a shared ideological membership in the community of reason. Most salient in the United States of America (as we noted in our analysis of socialism), these new terms of collective membership (which can best be characterized as the "ideal-type" of modernity) were never fully recognized. They nevertheless represented a constant referent in contemporary society's representation of itself. (The very problematic nature of this model forms the core of the current chapter.) Within this model every extension of citizenship represents a more perfect realization of the "rights of Reason" within the public realm. This is true whether we think in terms of the extension of citizenship developed by Marshall, from civil to political to social citizenship (from legal and civil rights to political participation to welfare entitlements), or in terms of more contemporary issues that turn on the themes of race and gender.

The paradox or contradiction that inheres to this model is, however, that every further realization of the (perforce) universal and abstract definitions of citizenship undermines the ability to articulate the shared social or political space of citizenship in ethical terms. For the universal (i.e., ethical) solidarity of a community of citizens rests on the moral inviolability of each individual and not in the shared space of their interaction. Universal citizenship (based on the principles of reason) developed in the eighteenth and nineteenth centuries as a way of articulating a broader form of solidarity (within the confines of the nation-state) that cut across existing particular and often primordial criteria of trust and solidarity. In terms of civil society it represents an extension of the mutual solidarity of moral sentiments and natural affections that was first posed by the thinkers of the Scottish Enlightenment as the foundation of the social order. More importantly, it formalized these rather amorphous ideas within an institutional framework of rights (and later entitlements). Here we recall the substantial contribution made by Immanuel Kant in articulating a more rigorous model of civil society than that presented by the

146

Scottish Enlightenment. This very formalization gave civil, political, and social substance to the idea of civil society but, at the same time, undermined its foundations in the idea of a shared realm of sociability. For it was the autonomous individual and not—as in the Scottish Enlightenment—the shared realm of their sociability that came to represent the universal and ethical foundations of the social order.

The further consequences of this dynamic—in terms of the changing nature of the public and private realms in contemporary America (or rather the United States)—were explored at the end of the previous chapter. It might not be a bad idea, however, to change somewhat the level of analysis and view the contradictions of citizenship and of civil society in somewhat different terms. In the following we shall approach the problems of citizenship and civil society from a number of different perspectives. We shall first view how the story, as told thus far, holds true only for certain societies and not for others. The development of citizenship and civil society in Western Europe and North America will thus be contrasted with the situation in East-Central Europe (with a brief mention of Israel as well) and the abiding problems of constituting civil society in these lands will be explored in both its historical and more contemporary aspects. This analysis will lead us to a new appreciation of the concept of social trust as essential to any idea of civil society, in the West as in the East. The very different sets of problems faced by these different societies in reconstituting a sense of trust—as essential to the workings of civil society—will be explored.

As we shall see, the problems of social trust, its definitions, boundaries, and criteria and so also the problems of civil society are not the same in all societies. In some they stem not (or perhaps not yet) from those inherent contractions of citizenship in its liberal-individualist articulation but, rather, from the lack of any similar realization of the principles of citizenship and of reason itself. Hence the title of this chapter. The cities—Jerusalem, Budapest, Los Angeles—are used here more as metaphors than as indicators of place. They each represent the very different types of problems that face anyone attempting to use the concept of civil society in either its descriptive or its prescriptive guise in three contemporary settings. I shall begin with three stories, three

147

vignettes. All are true, all modest, pianissimo illustrations of three different realities, all of which pose serious questions to the idea of civil society.

II

Jerusalem. A hot summer day some six months before the outbreak of the Intifada (in December 1987).[1] The municipal bus no. 5 in Tel Aviv makes its way from the central bus station into town, taking on more and more passengers at every stop.* At one of the early stops a middle-aged Palestinian man, clearly a day laborer, gets on and sits at the window seat directly behind the rear door. He is poorly dressed and somewhat dirty. His clothes are torn, he is unshaven, his hair is uncombed and full of plaster. He carries a box of tools. As the bus fills up, the seat next to him remains empty. The passengers on the bus are mostly secular Jews, some young, most middle-aged. As time passes these passengers are pushed tighter and tighter together on a hot and overcrowded, beginning to be suffocating, bus ride. Still no one occupies the empty seat next to the day laborer. At the corner of King George and Dizengoff streets, an orthodox man wearing a gabardine coat and sidelocks enters the bus. On his way to the back of the bus he spies the empty seat and without further ado sits down.

Budapest. September 1990, a week or so into the beginning of the school year. A resident of Rózsadomb (a very exclusive residential district of Buda) whom we shall call Mrs. Kiss and who happens to be Jewish goes out for a walk one afternoon and meets her neighbor, whom we shall call Mrs. Szigetváry. Mrs. Szigetváry is an elderly lady, a grandmother whose grandchild has gone to kindergarten with Mrs. Kiss's young boy. Mrs. Szigetváry's grandson, János, is of mixed color. His mother is Hungarian, and his father an African. Mrs. Kiss inquires after János's health, as she had not seen him at school since the beginning of

* Though our story takes place in Tel Aviv, I have kept Jerusalem in the title of this chapter and as referent throughout because of its strong historical and metaphorical resonances and relevance to the problematic nature of civil society in contemporary Israel.

the school year. Mrs. Szigetváry replies that János is quite well, it is just that they are not sending him to the neighborhood school, but to a school rather far away, in town, in Pest. Mrs. Kiss asks the name of the school, and Mrs. Szigetváry replies that it is a new school, just opened this year on Lendrai Utca. Mrs. Kiss mentions that she was unaware of any school on that street. Mrs. Szigetváry answers that it is indeed a brand-new school and adds, somewhat hesitantly, that it is in fact a Jewish school. Since János was so different from other children, his parents thought it best that he be with other children who were also different. . . . A year later, I should add, János really is very happy at this new school and is more comfortable there than he was with his former classmates.

Los Angeles. Venice, California, one of the few places in L.A. where there is any public space to speak of. Here at least there is a boardwalk, the beach, and cafés and bookstores that can be approached by foot (and not solely by automobile). Our scene is the back alley behind Brooks Avenue just west of Main Street. Property here is at a premium, and homeowners often have to invest well over half a million dollars for small houses, some of them not much larger than bungalows. Late one morning in the fall of 1988 a homeowner is taking out his garbage and placing it in the trashcans in the alley when he meets a Mexican (or Mexican-American, I do not know) woman whose dress and overall demeanor mark her as a street person and homeless. She is going through the trash, collecting bottles and cans for the five-cent redemption value. Very politely the homeowner asks her what she is doing and if he can be of some help. He is the epitome of civility. His words to the street lady are in the same neutral— but respectful—manner a bank-clerk would use to greet a customer, or perhaps a waitress at Burger King take an order with the perennial smile and "have a nice day." The Mexican lady too explains her enterprise—looking for bottles—in the most neutral of terms, to which the homeowner remarks that the neighbor a few houses down had a party the other night and there are sure to be many bottles in his trash. They both part affably, and the whole interaction (at least to the observer) seemed about as meaningful as a supermarket clerk explaining to a customer where to find the ketchup.

*   *   *

What do these three stories illustrate, and how do they advance our understanding of the contemporary problems of civil society? Well, first of all, <u>what all stories have in common is a concern with the terms of solidarity and mutuality in society.</u> All point, in different ways, to the different ways solidarity or even, at a more fundamental level, basic interpersonal trust is constructed and conceived in the different societies. In these terms the perspectives from Jerusalem and Budapest have much in common, and both are seemingly at odds with the view from Los Angeles.

In both Jerusalem and Budapest we are witness to what we may conceive of as the limits of that civil component of civil society. There, in both societies, differences—crucially, ethnic, racial, and religious differences—are still important categories and criteria in society's representation of the most fundamental bonds of trust and mutuality between its members. Although anyone familiar with these three different societies will need little explanation of their importance, it would be best to lay bare the moral implications of each story.

The story of Mrs. Kiss and Mrs. Szigetváry is perhaps the simplest and most accessible. Here we see how Jews (and of course blacks) are seen as something less than full members of society. We see how both the mutuality of civil society and the universal membership in the community of reason (i.e., citizenship) are limited by the continued saliency of ethnic and national identities. Of course, it may be argued that the continuity of anti-Semitism in contemporary Hungary is a cultural phenomenon only and not expressed at the level of institutional practices—legal, political, or social. That may be true, but it would be wise to be cautious and to take the argument of those who claim that the resurgence of anti-Semitism in 1989 was simply "an election phenomenon and not rooted in social realities" with more than a grain of salt. Some thirty years ago too, in the 1958–59 period, there was also a feeling that anti-Semitism had been rooted out in the decade or so of state socialism (it certainly did not seem to exist publicly in the 1948–53 era). Yet in that period anti-Semitism began to surface again, and it became popular to say: "Although he is a communist, at least he is a decent people's cadre, not a Jew."[2]

More importantly, and to return to contemporary realities, we

150

should recall what is happening throughout Eastern and East-Central Europe today. We have only to turn to the ethnic conflicts, indeed wars, in Yugoslavia and the former Soviet Union; to the problem of Hungarian minorities in Romania, Slovakia, and Serbia, and of Russian minorities in the Baltic States; to the problematic nature of any future relations between an independent Moldavia and Romania (and the Hungarian reaction to such a move), as well as the emerging tensions between the Czech and Slovak components of the Federated Czech and Slovak Republics (not to mention the possibility of ethnic conflict breaking out in Bosnia-Herzogoniva or Macedonian independence from the Federated Yugoslav government and the Greek reaction to such a move), to realize how far the countries of Eastern and East-Central Europe are from an ability to institute fully the principles of universal citizenship that cut across and overcome ethnic particularities.

It would be well to remember that these problems emerged at the end of World War I, with the breakup of the Austro-Hungarian Empire. At that time it was established that about 30 percent of the roughly 100,000,000 inhabitants of the successor states were minorities whose national aspirations would not be fulfilled in the Versailles Peace Treaty.[3] More significantly, the National Minorities Treaty meant to guarantee the rights of these peoples implicitly recognized that the new states formed in Eastern Europe after World War I could not be relied upon to provide full protection under law, that is, full legal and civil citizenship, to those ethnic inhabitants who were not part of the national majority. The problem of citizenship in this part of Europe—the problem of formally instituting those principles of civil society in legal, civic, political, and social frameworks—that was first encountered in West European and American consciousness in June 1914 in Sarajevo is still with us. And it may yet find its (inherently uncivil) solution in Sarajevo.

From Budapest to Jerusalem, from East-Central Europe to the Middle East we encounter a similar set of problems. That is to say, a similar mediation of the universalistic terms of citizenship by particular, primordial criteria of membership, trust, and solidarity. Once again, we need not belabor the point, as any reasonably well-informed observer is familiar with the situation in the occu-

151

The Idea of Civil Society

pied territories (which Israel has held from more than half of its existence as a State) and with the realities of life on the "other" side of the green line (the old prewar 1967 borders): The move from a democratic state ruled by law to an area where more than 1,600,000 people are denied the most fundamental civil legal and political rights of citizenship and where the rule of law was replaced since June 1967 by the legislative powers of the military commander (that is, by military orders) and since 1981 by an Israeli "civilian administration." Our story, however, took place not in Ramallah or Gaza or Hebron but in Tel Aviv ("the first Hebrew city"). And of course Jews do sit next to Palestinians on municipal buses and often have close working relations with them. The point illustrated by our story, however, is that they inhabit—to a great extent—different civic, and indeed civil, universes. Insofar as Israel is a Jewish State (so defined by language, culture, educational curricula, and of course the allocation of resources and principles of public distribution of private goods), the Palestinian inhabitants of Israel proper (i.e., citizens of the State) are not full members of society. And while some would—correctly—argue that one must take into consideration the historical conflict (in the prestate period between ethnic groups, following 1948 between states, and once again threatening to deteriorate into one between ethnicities) before making any normative judgment with respect to the degree of democracy in Israel, that is precisely my point. Here (as in East-Central Europe) the continuing existence of national identities and loyalties undermines the ability to construct a model of citizenship and participation in the nation-state along principles of liberal-individualist ideology.

Moreover, and this is the subtlety of the "Jerusalem story," we are witness in Israel to a conflict not only between Jews and Arabs but within the Jewish majority, over a more secular-universalistic and a more religious-particularistic definition of the polity. The interesting place to view this conflict is, however, not necessarily in the extreme right-wing parties in Parliament, those like Tzomet or Moledet who advocate the transfer of the Palestinian inhabitants of "Greater Israel" across the Jordan River, nor in the extreme religious parties like Shas, for whom the Palestinians are identified with the religio-historical entity of Amalek—that nation which the bible commands the people of Israel to wipe off the face

152

of the earth, that nation which, in the historical consciousness of the Jewish people, has always been identified with an almost metahistorical enemy.[4] These positions are so far from what we (and it would seem a majority of Israeli citizens as well) consider to be the shared culture of a modern democratic polity that there is little point in explicating them. What is interesting to note in terms of the problem of civil society is how the increasing particular and religious definitions of politics in contemporary Israel inform even a liberal discourse.[5] Thus, for example, some liberal religious leaders, such as Rabbi Rifkin of Ephrat, have argued for the proper and civil treatment of the Palestinian people in terms taken not from a liberal discourse on citizens' rights but from the biblical injunctions to treat the "Ger," the stranger in our midst, in a proper fashion. The argument here, the legitimation for civility and civic culture here, is thus based not on the liberal tradition of citizen rights but on biblical, that is, Jewish religious injunctions on the ancient Israelites' responsibilities to the stranger or the Other.

And here we can return to our no. 5 bus and the contradictions of Israeli reality that it represents. The interpretation for the behavior of our commuters that I would like to offer is as follows: The secular Israeli has a problem with the Palestinian (individual or collective/national entity) that, in a paradoxical way, does not exist for the ultra-Orthodox resident of Israel. For the secular Israeli who, at least normatively, in principle if not always in practice, recognizes the universal principles of citizenship as the foundation of the polity, the Palestinian is a paradox (not to mention a potential physical threat). On the one hand he must, according to the above principles, be included in the ongoing definitions of participation and membership in the collectivity, in other words in civil society. On the other, by his language, culture, and religious, ethnic, and kinship loyalties and affiliations he is clearly a stranger, an Other who in the most fundamental sense does not belong.[6]

This as yet unresolved paradox faces all citizens of Israel, Palestinian and Jew alike. It is rooted in the attempt to wed universal Statlich criteria of membership with a particularistic, Jewish content of the State.[7] In a curious way this ambivalence is lacking in the world of the Orthodox Jew, who (and I do not mean to imply

153

that all do) rejects the universal pole of this conception of the State in favor of a particular (and in fact primordial) conception of the Jewish State. The Palestinian presents no problem for him in that he is so far from sharing a common public culture that he is seen no longer as an Other (with whom some communality must be shared, otherwise there is no meaning to the term) but simply as an alien, an inhabitant of a different world with whom relations are purely instrumental and logistical and with whom no trust, solidarity, or mutuality need be assumed. No paradox, no ambivalence, but also, in this reading, no membership, participation, or citizenship either. We see here not the breakdown of civil society on the shoals of national particularism, but an a priori indifference to the principles of civil society based on the decidedly premodern principle of religious legitimation.

And finally, Los Angeles. The story from Venice beach is perhaps the most opaque—at least for the American, if not the European, observer. Its meaning is hidden by its very "commonsensical" aura. After all, as one student asked me (totally misunderstanding the point), what did you expect—for him to invite her in for a cup of coffee, or a share in his bank account? The point, of course, has nothing to do with generosity or even with the principles of distributive justice. The point is the total lack of class identities illustrated by the protagonists in our story. They treated each other as equals, as, I noted earlier, "metaphysical equals." The differences between them were quantitative (a difference of money) and not qualitative. Every European (and not just East-Central European), upon hearing this story was impressed by its implications: the total lack of class solidarities and identities (and hence principles of exclusion) in the United States and the fact that such an interaction in Europe between one of great and one of little wealth and property would be characterized by myriad more or less subtle indicators of hate, envy, fear, jealousy, pride, humility, and so on. In the United States the interaction was totally smooth. Whatever the individuals may have felt inside, those feelings were not expressed in their interaction, in the shared space of their meeting. For here, as opposed to Europe (and most certainly those parts of East-Central Europe which carry with them the legacy of the Austro-Hungarian Monarchy), the status differences that supplement economic differ-

154

ences between social groups (and as we have seen were a crucial element in the construction of class identities and solidarities) have no place. They do not in fact exist. Status is a function of wealth and of consumption patterns.[8] It is not a function of the type of primordial variables of *Stände* that in Europe continued into the nineteenth century to define class differences (and so, as we have seen, the trajectory of the socialist movement). In Venice, California, as in most other parts of the United States, individuals confront one another in their individual identities and not as members of broader solidarities or groups. Here, more than elsewhere (and certainly more than in Jerusalem or Budapest), the universalism of citizenship based on the autonomous individual is the most fully instituted within society. Here too, however, the ability to articulate a sense of community between these autonomously conceived individual entities is most intractable.

To sum up: what we have in Los Angeles is one pole of that modern dialectic—an extreme individualism—an apotheosis of the particular, of the subject, freed from the validating claims of community. That public arena on which rationality depends has been voided of content through the very realization of the individual.

In Jerusalem and in Budapest we have the other pole. It is not the loss of a public space that threatens the existence of civil society, but the as-yet-to-be-constituted private subject. The subject whose identity and autonomy are guaranteed by law and are recognized both by other members of society and by the State. The subject, existing with other subjects in a state of "metaphysical equality," whose existence is constitutive of civil society—it is this subject, whose existence is not yet sufficiently established in the current realities of either East-Central Europe or Israeli society and politics, that threatens the basis of civil society.

The historical analysis of these different "cases" would of course require a separate study in itself. In a sense our own work here has been devoted—almost exclusively—to uncovering the historical and analytical conditions that resulted in that paradox of modern life illustrated by the story from Los Angeles. In Israel and East-Central Europe, the different situation is the result of a very different set of factors, for which we must nevertheless provide some historical background.

155

III

The differentiation of civic selfhood from communal or collective attributes was a process that, in Western Europe, took place over hundreds of years. It owed much to the religious doctrines of sectarian or ascetic-Puritanism, but also—as Stein Rokkan has showed us—to the unique process of nation formation and integration that took place from the period of absolutism to the early modern era.[9] The trajectory and timing of state-building in Western Europe; the different phases of elite integration, mass participation, and active membership (the franchise); and the establishment of redistributive agencies (the modern welfare state) all allowed the development of autonomous social bodies, independent of state power.

Building on the work of Stein Rokkan, Otto Hinze, and others, S. N. Eisenstadt has developed a topology of West European development that stresses the historical plurality of the corporate actors that characterized West European societies from the breakup of the Roman Empire. In Eisenstadt's topology the organizational heterogeneity of West European civilization, based on the multiplicity of sociopolitical centers, and status hierarchies, and the changing boundaries of collectivities is matched by a heterogeneity of symbolic orientations drawn from the cultural legacy of the Judeo-Christian religions and Greek and Roman civilization, which, together with the Germanic tribal legacy, contributed to the "very high degree of multiplicity and cross-cutting of cultural orientations and structural settings."[10] In highly schematic terms, Eisenstadt's topology includes the following components as characteristic of West European civilization: (1) a multiplicity of social and political centers, (2) a high degree of permeation of the territorial peripheries by these centers, but also of the impingement of the periphery on the centers, (3) a relatively small degree of overlapping of the boundaries of class, ethnic, religious, and political entities, (4) a relatively high degree of autonomy accorded the different groups and strata in terms of their access to the social center, (5) a multiplicity of different elite groups, each relatively autonomous of each other and of the social center, (6) the autonomy of the legal system, especially with respect to the

156

political and religious systems, and (7) the autonomy of the cit- ⎤
ies as centers of social and cultural life.[11] ⎦

In somewhat less schematic and more generally recognized terms, the importance of the Church as a social center independent of the Empire (Gelasian's doctrine of the "Two Swords"), the autonomy of cities, and the importance of an autonomous legal system (rooted in the legacy of Rome) all contributed to the differentiation of society from the State in the West European context. This later aspect, of an autonomous legal system, within which individuals were conceived of as "articulated wholes" and not as an "undifferentiated mass," was central to the development of both the idea of individual rights and the idea of representative institutions.[12] In the first instance it affirmed the individual's membership in a particular community (with its own communal rights) independent of any ties of feudal dependence.[13] In the second, it contributed through the *Law of Corporations* to the idea that "the right of the community will be exercised by means of an Assembly of Representatives."[14] Thus were the early corporate rights of community as autonomous societies given specific legal form as each represented (and representative) group was seen to be a *universitas* in itself. The "pluralism within unity" noted above as characteristic of medieval Christian civilization was thus extended beyond the competing claims of *Imperium* and *Sacerdotium* to include as well (by the thirteenth century) a *societas civilis*, a civil or political society (and the terms were interchangeable until the late eighteenth century) autonomous from the State. All these factors severely mediated the ability of royal authority to impose autocratic structures of rule even in the so-called period of absolutism.

In Eastern Europe—but also in East-Central Europe—the situation was markedly different. The countries of East-Central Europe did not, it is true, suffer the extreme absolutism of the "eastern model." This was characterized in Russia by the aborted development of free cities and of an independent nobility (under the state-building policies of Ivan III [1462–1505] and Ivan IV, "The Terrible" [1533–84] and later under Peter the Great [1682–1725] by the formal subjection of the Orthodox Church to the State. Together these led to the atomization and homogenization of society as "an amorphous mass of subjects" lacking the legal autonomy and articulated rights of the late medieval *societas civilis* in the West.[15] Rather, as Jeno Szücs has argued, East-Central Europe was caught between the Western and Eastern models.

While countries like Czechoslovakia, Poland, and Hungary all had certain features of the pluralist Western institutional (and symbolic) structure, the historical development of those countries was markedly different. Moreover, the role played by these structural factors—as well as their concrete characteristics—tended to be very different. A case in point is that of the medieval city. East-Central Europe was lacking in autonomous cities, or cities of comparative size to those of the West. The urban settlements that did exist there tended to be, in George Schöpflin's terms, "bureaucratic agglomerations—the seat of administration—or garrison towns or static, introverted settlements clinging to commercial privileges."[16] Rather than serve as independent loci of organized interests, towns tended to be dependent on the State and to serve its interests.

Similar divergence from the Western model was to be found in the autonomy of law and in the Western feudal principles of reciprocity. In the East, this autonomy was severely limited by the principle of the discretionary power of the State, which strengthened the autonomy of the State from a society too weak to regulate its activities and maintain its own independence. Traditions of reciprocity of rights were also severely limited (though existing in principle in Bohemia and Hungary) and often nonexistent. The results of this development were felt into modern times, when "political rights accorded to individuals were few" and "reciprocity of rights was largely limited to what the elite was prepared to concede."[17] What characterized East-Central European development was thus the lack of precisely those autonomous and plural spheres in society which in the different models of West European development were seen to be at the heart of its particular developmental path.

Caught on the one hand between the West and the East the societies of East-Central Europe had little room for expansion. Later the pressures of Ottoman expansion and the rise of the Hapsburgs prevented the development of independent representatives of rights and interests within what later became hegemonic State structures. Concurrently the emergence of a "second feudalism" at the end of the sixteenth century strengthened the local nobility and thwarted the development of an independent entrepreneurial class. It also extended the system of prebendal landholdings, which bound the peasant to the land in precisely the period when private peasant landholdings were increasing in the West. Of equal if not greater importance, the "second feudalism" and the lack of bourgeois development led to the later integration of the landed aristocracy into the State administrative machinery. This "neofeudal" class of administrative elites was one of the crucial factors in the unique path of the Eastern counties to modernity, of the principles of "modernization from above" and the inherently contradictory task of creating a civil society from above at the hands of a political elite who had no interest in reform and who "legitimized its attitudes by arguing that the state was the source of modernity and progress, whilst society was backward."[18]

The derivatives of this development in ideological terms was the peculiar manner in which Western "liberal" ideology was appropriated by the ruling elites of the European periphery. Rather than an ideology of personal freedom and individual emancipation, it was used to strengthen the power of the State, the last preserve of a class "seeking alternatives to entrepreneurship."[19] All of these factors contributed in different ways in different cases to the peculiarities of modernization in East-Central Europe and the lack of independent structures of national rule (the dismemberment of Poland by Prussia, Austria, and Russia, the subjugation of the southern and western parts of the region to the house of the Hapsburgs)—that is, to the organization of these societies under Imperial regimes where older, corporate forms of social organization prevailed into the nineteenth century and beyond (we shall return to this issue shortly).[20]

Our concern here, however, is neither with the variations within the countries of East-Central Europe nor with presenting the general path of their historical development from medieval to modern times.[21] We are interested, rather, in one specific aspect of this historical dynamic—the one most relevant to the contemporary problems of civil society. As is well known, the social and political history of East-Central Europe has often been used to explain their peculiar paths to modernity, the saliency of the State apparatus, and the lack of distinction between State and society, or civil society, in these countries. In this reading—as we have intimated in previous chapters—the demand for civil society in East-Central Europe is really for those types of democratic structures and institutions (the legally free individual, the rights of free expression, the right to organize interest groups and political parties, and more recently "real" participation in the decision-making process) which we identify with West European and North American democracies and which, we might add, are seen to be rooted in the historical conditions of State-building in those countries. What is of great importance for our own argument is a fact less universally remarked upon—though crucial for any understanding of the individual "pole" or component of the civil society tradition—namely, the effect of East-Central European historical development on national identities and, more importantly, on the relationship between ethnicity and nationalism within the nation-state formation.

The distinction of national from ethnic identities, which characterized West European development, was central in the above-mentioned separation of national identity, and later of civic selfhood, from the local, ethnic, and particular solidarities from which the European nation-state emerged.[22] The long-drawn-out process of State-making and nation-building in western Europe was characterized by the only gradual integration of different *ethnie* into one national identity (characterized by its own territory; economy; legal, educational, and cultural systems; and historical memories). Central to this process were the different features of linguistic assimilation, social mobilization, and, at a much later date, mass education and the effects of mass media. In this process, as Daniel Lerner noted more than thirty years ago, the formation of "psychologically mobile personalities" enabled the establishment of "empathy" between individuals of different ethnic and religious traditions.[23] In terms of our analysis, this empathy rested on the replacement of traditional criteria of solidarity and collective membership and participation with the "modern" values of individual rights, universal citizenship and the idea of the morally autonomous person.

What took place, to different extents in the different countries of Western Europe, was (1) the crystallization of a national identity out of different ethnic groups (sometimes, as in England, France, and Spain, around an ethnic core group, and sometimes, as for example in Greece or Switzerland, without such core groups), and (2) the formalization and universalization of the criteria for membership and participation within this national entity on the principles of citizenship and mass participation in the social and political life of the nation.[24] The early modern idea of civil society emerged, we recall, as the first stage of this process was coming to completion (in England and the United Kingdom) and the second stage just beginning. It thus reflects in its naïve assumptions of the complementarity of communal and individual attributes that historical moment where the thrust of the second process had not yet vitiated the terms of mutual solidarity contained in the first.

In Western Europe, especially in those older states consolidated prior to the Peace of Westphalia (1648) and through the achievement of political, economic, and cultural unification at the elite level and the formation of institutional structures "for the extraction of resources . . . the maintenance of internal order . . . the adjudication of disputes . . . and the protection of established rights and privileges," national identity was the outcome of a prior consolidation of administrative, legal, and cultural institutions, which unified multiple ethnic groups into one common nation.[25] In Eastern and East-Central Europe the situation was very different.

There, in marked reversal of the historical development of Western societies, the nation-state (or, more precisely, the administrative-bureaucratic structures of State rule) emerged (after World War I) before the nation itself. Contributing to this was the aforementioned "gentry" character of political elites, who (in the nineteenth century), while leading the nationalist movements in East-Central Europe, did not identify national independence with more than their own corporate interests. Social reforms were minimal, and the democratic component of national movements was submerged in the corporate interests of the political elite. Indeed, the very ethnic fragmentation of these societies led to the view that the State itself produces national sentiment and not the other way around. By the mid-nineteenth century all of the ruling elites agreed that the nation stemmed from the state, and the sole question was the State's role as a cultural, administrative, or coercive producer of nationalism.[26] Thus, the type of mass mobilization around social reforms that characterized Western nationalism and indeed united diverse communities into one national identity did not eventuate.

Without any prior crystallization of national identities, the period of nation-state formation proper (following World War I) saw the establishment of new states that either were multinational or had significant national minorities. The disastrous results of this situation were complicated by the appeal of ruling elites in the interwar years to an ideology of national exclusion in a bid to retain legitimacy. (Even in Czechoslovakia, non-Czechs were not fully integrated into the civil polity and consequently viewed it with suspicion.)[27]

Consequently, to quote György Csepeli, one of the foremost Hungarian analysts of the problems of nationalism and ethnicity in East-Central Europe, "the concept of the nation came before the establishment of the proper national institutions and the emerging national ideology therefore had to refer more actively to elements of the ethnocentric heritage such as decent, cultural values and norms."[28] In East-Central Europe (as in Russia), the "prisonhouse of nations"—or rather of ethnic groups—caught first under protracted absolutist regimes and then under semi-autocratic or dictatorial regimes rooted in one ethnic majority, never emerged in national frameworks of freely associating citizens. What emerged in their stead was the continuity of ethnic identities and solidarities into the twentieth century, outlasting not only the Hapsburgs, Romanovs, and Hohenzollerns, but state socialism as well.

The implications of this pattern of development for the issues of civil society in contemporary East-Central Europe (for which the story from Budapest was of course but a metaphor) should be clear. For while civil society as "democracy" does provide an alternative to state socialism, the existence of the necessary preconditions for civil society—based on the autonomous individual (freed from communal identities) as moral agent—cannot be taken for granted. If what is necessary for the existence of civil society is some synthesis of the public and the private, the social and the individual, and, if, as we have argued throughout, the

162

basis for this synthesis in contemporary Western democracies (and especially in the United States) is no longer possible (the previously noted paradox of equality), the situation in East-Central Europe (and in Jerusalem) is very different. There it is not the apotheosis of the individual that vitiates the civil (and communal) pole of civil society but the continued existence of strong ethnic and group solidarities, which have continually thwarted the very emergence of those legal, economic, and moral individual identities upon which civil society is envisioned.

To reiterate, the existence of the individual—freed from ascriptive identities—was itself based on the twofold historical moment of (1) national integration and (2) the universalization of citizenship within the nation-state. The first process took place in an only partial and mediated manner (especially in those parts of East-Central Europe under the Hapsburg Monarchy). The second process—of universal citizenship—was never realized (not even in Czechoslovakia, where formally it was the most developed, but where minorities were not perceived as full members of the national community) and achieved only a caricature of itself under state socialism, which, appropriately enough, has been termed by Elemér Hankiss as "negative modernity." Indeed, Ivo Banac has argued, as the crises of state socialist ideology deepened, as "negative modernity" turned in on itself, the "bureaucratic nationalism" of state socialist regimes was transformed as the older national identities and solidarities reemerged, with a saliency we are only now beginning to appreciate.[29]

Before proceeding further, an important distinction must be made. I am not arguing here that the existence of group identities as such militates against the existence of civil society. Clearly the very existence of voluntary associations, political parties, and interest and corporate groups (such as those that characterized Western democracies) is the very stuff of civil society, as has been argued from Hegel through Durkheim and down to such contemporary thinkers as Charles Taylor and Michael Waltzer. The distinction between such groups and the type of group identities and loyalties that characterized the ethnic identities of East-Central Europe is precisely in the nature and definition of the relation between groups and between members within a group. In the West the voluntary associations of civil society are interest groups;

163

they are organized for the pursuit of mutual interest on the institutional level (of what Habermas would call strategic action). Their interaction with other groups (and with the State) is defined by this instrumental rational orientation (and the terms of membership within the group are likewise so defined). They do not posit (or indeed represent) an alternative moral vision to that of society at large. They do not as such undermine or threaten the overriding definitions of membership and participation in collective life. They are themselves predicated on the definition of public space as one of instrumental interaction between autonomously constituted individual moral agents.

While the practice of corporatism differs greatly within different West European polities, the distinction between the organized institutions of the State—the executive, legislature, and judiciary—and broader corporate interests nevertheless remains a fundamental fact of political life. Indeed, to quote Colin Crouch, "Civil society enters these institutions only through its members adopting formal, specialized, political roles, whether as a member of one of these institutions or as individual citizen-electors. Functional and other specifically denominated social interests may approach the political institutions as external lobbies and pressure groups, but their entry within them is regarded as a form of corruption."[30]

This distinction between the organs of State rule and the representation of functional interests in society in Western democracies is critical to understanding the difference between these polities and those of East-Central Europe. In the latter case the historical legacy of a relatively unmodernized and organic State never accepted the principle of individual autonomy and equality as the basis of the polity, upon which this type of organization of corporate interests (and, more centrally, the autonomy of the democratic State) rests. We may add that such attempts as Charles Taylor's recent argument for civil society in terms of the existence of corporate group interests in society miss this crucial underlying feature of the action and definition of corporate groups in Western democracies.[31]

In East-Central Europe (as in the East proper), the establishment of civil society is, however, threatened by precisely the continued existence of ethnic solidarities whose terms of individual membership and relations to society at large as well as to the State are not defined solely by such interests and instrumental-rational modes of behavior. Quite the opposite. The continuity of ethnic loyalties and solidarities (and so also the potential for ethnic exclusion) within groups undercuts the very definition of universal citizenship within the nation-state upon which the former (Western) type of interest group is based.

This is true not only for ethnic or national groups but for other corporate interests as well. For, again, the corporatism of East-Central Europe is different from that of the West. It is, in fact—especially where the Church is concerned—much more akin to the original corporate ideology as originating within French Catholicism, with its claims to social hegemony (which of course in the latter case were never realized). In East-Central Europe, corporate (national or other) groups represent not only different interests but, often (to borrow the term used by Vincent Wright to characterize the different worlds of late-nineteenth-century French society) different "metaphysical universes."[32] The parallel, by the way, is far from facile, especially in terms of the conflict between secular and religious groups in contemporary Poland. For the corporate interests of the Church in the West and the East cannot be judged in the same light.

The public role of the Church in East-Central Europe is very different from that of the Church in the West. It represents not simply one interest group among many, but an alternative moral universe of values or norms, an image of the public good with claims to overall legitimacy that the Church in West has more or less renounced. Religion in East-Central Europe is not a private matter, as the mandatory religious instruction in public schools or the canceling of funds and equipment for hospitals performing abortions in Poland today attest.

Even in Hungary, where the Church is much less identified with national virtues and never played the oppositional role to the State that it played in Poland (and so lacks the same support), the official reception granted the reinterment of Cardinal Mindszenty's remains illustrates the strong symbolic role of the Church in the emergent society. Mindszenty, we recall, was a royalist, a vehement anti-Semite, antiliberal clergyman, and the State honor bestowed upon him at the reinterment contrasts sharply with the paucity of government members who attended the reinterment of the well-known Hungarian democrat Oscar Jaszi, which took place that same summer, in 1991.

What the future role of the Church will be we cannot, of course, know. José Casanova, for one, has argued, in the Polish case, for the possibilities of either consociational pluralism, privatized religion, or Catholic hegemony.[33] The failure in Hungary to pass draconian abortion legislation supported by the Church and the current debates over abortion in Poland and the Church's role in this debate (and this is what is important and not the debate itself) illustrate how open history is, but also what is important to bear in mind, the unique nature of those (in this case corporate) actors acting on the historical stage. We should bear in mind, however, Colin Crouch's dictum that

> . . . the longer the interval, or sharper the breach between the destruction of ancient guild and Standestaat institutions, and the construction of typically modern interest organizations, the more likely committed did the state become to liberal modes of interest representation, and the less likely to tolerate sharing public space, the less likely were modern organizations to target their ambitions on participation of that kind.[34]

As we have seen, the countries on the European periphery never really experienced the "liberal-parliamentary parenthesis" of late-nineteenth-century West European polities—semifeudal forms of corporatism continued to define political life, under the Hapsburgs (in Hungary for instance under the Tisza regimes) throughout the nineteenth century.[35] East-Central Europe thus presents an extreme case of the continuity of decidedly illiberal forms of corporate representation into the twentieth century, certainly up to World War II. We would do well to bear this in mind and to heed the warning of those who, like George Schöpflin, see this heritage as a major obstacle to the establishment of liberalism in postcommunist societies.[36]

Indeed, to return to the national or ethnic issue, we can turn again to the West, to view how in Crown Heights (Brooklyn) or Brixton (London) or in Hoyerswerda (Sachsen-Germany) the organization of interest groups on racial (i.e., ethnic-particular lines) is—when it transcends the institutional channels of interest-

166

motivated action—seen as a breakdown of civil society and not as its realization. What such types of solidarities threaten is precisely the fundamental models of modern national identity, based on the ideology of the individual, upon which modern democratic society rests. What is played out *in minora* in Crown Heights (between blacks and orthodox Jews) or among the Neo-Nazis in Hoyerswerda is, more fundamentally, what is currently threatening the transition to democracy in East-Central Europe.

In Israel (to which we shall devote less space because of the idiosyncrasy of its historical development), the situation is similar, though posited in sightly different terms. There it is not the existence of distinct *ethnie* whose allegiance to (and protection by) the State threatens the idea of civil society. Rather it is the idea of the State as moral community—defined in terms of the Jewish people—that poses seemingly insurmountable challenges to the existence of civil society. The reason why such a definition of the State in terms of the Jewish people causes different resonances from the definition of the French, English, or Swedish State, and most especially that in the United States, is of course rooted in the complexities of Jewish historical development: the colonial nature of the Zionist enterprise, the continuity of strong collectivist definitions of state and society within the Jewish tradition (perpetrated by both internal factors, such as the overriding religio-cultural definition of Judaism, which has always stressed collective redemption rather than individual salvation as at the core of its soteriological doctrines, and external pressures and threats—from the "failure of emancipation" to the horrors of the Holocaust), and of course the very raison d'être of Zionism itself as an attempt to provide for the physical security, economic well-being, and cultural integrity of the Jewish individual through the reconstruction of the Jewish nation as an independent people with its own political and territorial integrity. In this process, civil selfhood (as well as state structures) became identified with and oriented toward particular-collectivist rather than universalist-individual definitions of the nation-state.

Complicating this ever further is the continual struggle between religious and secular definitions of the polity and of public life and space. (This latter is, in the context of Israel, meant most literally, as the physical violence that attends conflicts over the opening of moviehouses on Friday night in Jerusalem or over the inauguration of new roads in Orthodox sections of the city attests). The political saliency of orthodoxy in Israel rests, however, less on the contingency of party politics than on the strong religious component that defines Jewish tradition (especially after the destruction of European Jewry), upon which the legitimacy of the State rests.

All this is of course but one aspect of contemporary Israel and its historical development. Zionism also contained strong universal assumptions, rooted in its very real emancipatory claim for a new model of Jewish existence in the modern world. The strong socialist orientations of much of prestate Zionism bears eloquent witness to this pole of civil culture in Israel. The tragedy and pathos of contemporary Israel is of course that it is but one side of a seemingly intractable dilemma. For since 1967 and the continued occupation of the West Bank and the Gaza Strip, and more especially since the rise of the Likud in 1977, the early universalist assumptions that defined public life (however mediated they were in practice) have increasingly given way to an ethno-religious definition of political life and practice. These two elements stand in continual tension in contemporary Israel, and an argument can be made for either their inevitability (given the strong collectivist premises of Zionism from its inception, as illustrated for example in the notion of "Hagshama," individual realization through collective participation), or their contingent-historical nature (ensuing from the realities of the extended conflict, the occupation, and so on).

Neither argument is our task here. Our concern is, given the present realities of East-Central Europe or of the Middle East (and I have taken Israel as an example precisely because it, of all countries in the region, contains the most Western-individual-universal definitions of public life), can the idea of civil society play, in Charles Taylor's terms, a role in the "future defense of freedom".[37]

I think it should be clear by now that however admirable the idea of civil society is as a political slogan, we should have serious doubts as to its efficacy as a concrete model for social and political practice. These doubts arise both from the inadequacy of the idea itself, along with the contradictions that inhere to it, and from the

168

fact that it reflects not only a particular stage of historical development in the West but the particular conditions that obtained there and not necessarily in other parts of the world. Clearly the first objection pertains mainly (but not solely) to the use of civil society in approaching the contemporary situation in Western Europe and the United States, and the second to its relevance to other societies, most especially contemporary East-Central Europe, where the term in its contemporary articulation first emerged.

We shall begin by transposing somewhat the terms of our analysis to clarify what I mean by the inadequacy of civil society in facing the conflicts and problems of contemporary existence. Having presented these conflicts in the form of both illustrative vignettes and an (all too brief) historical sketch, I would like to approach it from a more accepted social-scientific vantage point, that of trust. If, as I have argued, the problem of civil society is one of a synthesis between collective solidarity and individualism and of the reigning definitions of each, then the notion of trust, in institutions and interpersonally, would seem a good place to begin. What I wish to do is thus to rephrase the continuing problems of civil society in the United States and Western Europe as well as in East-Central Europe in terms of the problem of trust. Such a perspective will, I hope, provide us with yet another vantage point from which to view the problems attendant on any vision of social life predicated on the idea of civil society.

The existence of trust is an essential component of all human relationships. As such it has also found its place as one of the fundamental concepts of sociology and sociological analysis. Indeed, since the nineteenth century and the theoretical insights of Emile Durkheim on the existence of a "pre-contractual" element in all social arrangements, the importance of trust to the existence of society has been recognized by all students of social life.

On the most general and abstract level it can be stated that the need for perduring, stable, and universally recognized structures of trust is rooted in the fundamental indeterminacy of social interaction. This indeterminacy, between social actors, between social actors and their goals, and between social actors and resources, results in a basic unpredictability in social life notwithstanding the universality of human interdependence. In Anthony

169

Giddens's words, "Trust brackets distance in time and space and so blocks off existential anxieties which, if they were allowed to concretise, might become a source of continuing emotional and behavioral anguish in life."[38] This is true not only on the personal level, in the period of early, infant socialization, but on the broader societal level as well. Consequently, any long-range attempt at constructing a social order with continuity of social frameworks of interaction must be predicated on the development of stable relations of mutual trust between social actors. Clearly, however, different forms of organizing society (on the macrosociological level) will bring in their wake different forms of establishing trust in society.

In this context one of the major arenas where the study of trust—on the interpersonal as well as the institutional level—has been central has been in the study of modernization. Here, studies in the 1950s and 1960s concentrated on the establishment of new bases of trust in society centering on new terms of solidarity and of citizenship, and on what were in fact new parameters defining the boundaries of trust in modernizing social structures.[39]

This focus on the changing nature of trust in modernizing societies is not surprising given the extraordinary importance of a universal basis of trust in modern democratic societies. The emphasis in modern societies on consensus, the ideology of pragmatism, problem-solving, and technocratic expertise, as well as conflict management (as opposed to ideological fission), are all founded on an image of society based on interconnected networks of trust—between citizens, families, voluntary organizations, religious denominations, civic associations, and the like. Similarly the very "legitimation" of modern societies is founded on the "trust" of authority and of governments as generalizations of trust on the primary, interpersonal level. In fact the primary venues of socialization, whether they be the educational system or the mass media, are oriented to the continuing inculcation of this value and what is in fact an "ideology" of trust in society.

Various thinkers have of course posited the basic characteristics of trust in the social order in different terms. For Giddens, it is the extension of that "ontological security" of early trusting relations between ego and alter to the external world, whether through

170

more particular, primordial relations of kin, territory, or religious affiliation, or through more modern beliefs in "abstract systems."[40] Indeed, in Giddens's reading, in modern democratic societies trust in individuals is increasingly relegated to the private realms of friendship or intimacy, and in the public sphere it is replaced by a more diffuse and abstract form of trust. For Luhmann, the distinction between trust as a function of risk and confidence as a sense of familiarity (whose opposite is not risk but danger) is central to understanding the dynamics of modern, highly differentiated societies.[41] In a more classical model, harking back to Durkheim's notions of the pre-contractual elements of social life (i.e., the necessity of rules regulating the market and governing contracts that are themselves not the subject of contract), is the use of the term made by S. N. Eisenstadt and Luis Roniger.[42] They define the workings of trust in society as those limitations placed on the free exchange of resources—such limitations as the very definition of public goods (those that if provided to one member of the collective must be provided to all), or the public distribution of private goods. In this reading such phenomena as welfare entitlements or the progressive income tax are limitations placed on the free exchange of goods based on the overall definitions of trust and solidarity in society—definitions which, in modern societies, as Durkheim noted close to one hundred years ago, are based on the idea of autonomous individual as the center and moral foundation of the social order. The derivatives of this idea in terms of the equality of citizens and the extension of this equality in different realms which require such limitation should be clear from our discussion in previous chapters.

In the context of East-Central Europe the problem of trust takes on a special dimension. Here, as we have seen, the reigning definitions of individual identity are still to a large extent collective and rooted in the solidarity of particular ethnic groups. What is lacking, in this sense, is that individual pole of the civil society synthesis upon which civic selfhood and citizenship in their formal, institutional, and universal guise are seen to rest.

In this context interpersonal trust, as well as trust in the formal institutional structures of society, is still characterized by markedly "premodern" (what can be most generally characterized as *gemeinschaft*) criteria. The basic networks of trust are woven

171

around ethnic relations, local communities, shared religious faith, and of course the continuing saliency of given traditions. Not surprisingly, it has often been remarked that in East-Central Europe the dividing line between private and public life is more salient than in the West. This insight—into what is essentially the status of civility in East-Central Europe—is directly connected to the foundations of trust in society, to the most basic terms of interpersonal solidarity and communicative modes. Civility, the mutual recognition of each individual's innate human dignity and membership in the political community is, as Edward Shils has argued, at the heart of civil society and, in his words, "at bottom the collective consciousness of civil society."[43] This very Durkheimian formula, however, presumes the (equally Durkheimian) idea of pre-contractual trust, which, we recall, in modern democratic societies is based on the liberal idea of the moral individual freed from particular, communal identities and what we may term ethical solidarities.

The contemporary problem, however, is the very existence of such an idea in East-Central Europe. It would be best perhaps at this point to inject some "hard" social-scientific evidence into our discussion. Though difficult to isolate in concrete terms, one possible source of information on such ideas and on the existence of trust beyond the local, private, and particular realm is in the European Value Survey research conducted in 1982 and 1990 among twelve European countries. Unfortunately, we have only one representative sample from East-Central Europe—Hungary—which, though limited, is interesting. Moreover, Hungary is seen as the most Western, market-orientated of the East-Central European countries, both today and over the past two decades, as a result of the legacy of Kadar's "goulash communism" and the workings of the "second economy." It should thus offer (theoretically at least) the closest case to that of the West. From close to eight hundred questions I have chosen the most relevant to the issue of trust and its generalization and abstraction.[44] These are presented in the three accompanying tables. The first provides data collected in Hungary in a 1990 Survey on the existence of "trust" toward various ethnic and national minorities (comparative data here are missing). The second provides an important longitudinal view (from 1982 to 1990) of trust (in fact in the de-

172

Table 1

European Value Survey 1990: Data Set of the Hungarian Academy of Sciences' Institute of Sociology (in percentages)

Trust in	1 very much	2 a little	3 both yes and no	4 not very much	5 not at all	9 do not know	0
Church	23.0	—	(26.2)*	29.2	17.4	3.3	0.8
Romanians	3.9	10.8	26.1	23.2	22.2	13.3	0.5
Jews	13.9	23.6	31.1	11.3	7.7	12.0	0.5
Gypsies	2.3	10.8	14.6	28.3	42.4	1.1	0.5
Slovaks	6.2	14.9	30.5	18.3	11.3	18.4	0.5
Own family	89.5	5.6	2.8	0.5	0.4	0.6	0.6
Hungarian indiv.	23.0	45.8	20.4	8.7	1.1	0.5	0.5
German minority in Hungary	11.8	22.7	32.2	10.5	7.4	14.7	0.8

Sample: N = 1301–1314

* This percentage chose the response "rather" and not "both yes and no."

173

Table 2
European Value Surveys 1982 and 1990: Data Set of the Hungarian Academy of Sciences'
Institute of Sociology (*percentages*)

Trust in	1 very much		2 rather much		3 not very much		4 not at all		9 do not know		0	
	1982	1990	1982	1990	1982	1990	1982	1990	1982	1990	1982	1990
Trade union	20.1	6.0	36.1	22.3	19.7	38.4	7.8	25.6		6.7	16.3	1.1
Parliament	49.0	8.3	35.4	35.9	6.1	36.5	1.2	13.5		4.8	8.3	0.9
Legal system	39.4	13.6	44.9	40.3	9.0	32.0	1.8	8.9		4.3	4.8	0.9
Press, mass media	28.5	6.8	50.5	35.6	16.3	42.3	1.9	10.4		3.6	2.8	1.1
Church	14.8	23.0	22.0	26.2	25.9	29.2	33.9	17.4		3.3	3.3	0.8
Public administration	27.6	8.5	42.3	38.7	19.7	38.4	4.8	8.0		5.2	5.5	1.2
Educational system	28.9	13.5	48.9	41.0	14.2	32.7	2.1	7.7		4.1	5.9	1.0

Sample sizes: 1982, N = 1226–1423
1996, N = 1301–1314

Table 3

Individualism and Privatism in Ten European Countries, 1982
(*percentages*)

	England	Ireland	France	Belgium	Ger-many	Nether-lands	Spain	Den-mark	Italy	Hun-gary
You may trust people	43	40	22	25	26	38	32	46	25	32
Is there anything you would sacrifice yourself for, outside your family? NO!	60	55	64	61	53	54	38	49	45	85
Parents have their own lives; they should not sacrifice themselves for their children	18	15	17	21	28	15	13	39	27	44
Childrearing principles: respect for other people	62	56	59	45	52	53	44	58	43	31
loyalty, faithfulness	36	19	36	23	22	24	29	24	43	10
With whom do you prefer to spend your leisure time? alone	11	12	10	9	8	12	7	8	20	10
with your family	48	39	47	51	52	49	53	53	36	72
with friends	27	27	22	18	27	15	23	12	29	10
going out, seeing people	11	12	8	7	5	12	4	4	8	3

Note: All samples were representative national samples.
SOURCE: European Value Systems Study 1982.

The Idea of Civil Society

cline of trust) in precisely those civic institutions—trade unions, media, even parliament—that are necessary for the establishment of civil society. We see here that the most "trusted" institutions of national life are the Church and the family.[45] The third table presents comparative results on the 1982 Survey on trust in different countries.[46]

What we see from all three sets of data, in both absolute and, more importantly, comparative terms is a failure of extended—abstract or generalized—trust in society and its institutions. Rather, we find the continuing articulation of trust along more private and restricted venues.[47]

These findings in the case of Hungary can be supplemented by the social-psychological research carried out by György Csepeli on the terms and definitions of Hungarian national identity. Csepeli distinguished between what he termed *Gesellschaft* and *Gemeinschaft* types of national identity. In the *Gesellschaft* pattern national identity is perceived as membership in a democratic political community, and in the *Gemeinschaft* pattern by the presence of attitudes and beliefs turning on the idea of ethnic purity and distinctiveness, folklore, and cultural traditions.[48] These categories are supplemented by others, the most important for our purposes being what Csepeli terms "low profile national consciousness," where "the nation is conceived as a social psychological community united by a cultural tradition that facilitates communication among people who consider themselves to be members of that community."[49] When correlated across religious affiliations the results are interesting:

	Jewish	Protestant	Catholic
Gesellschaft	45	23	32
Low profile	11	38	51
Gemeinschaft	19	41	44

SOURCE: György Csepeli, "Competing Patterns of National Identity in Post-Communist Hungary," *Media, Culture and Society*, vol. 13 (1991), p. 337.

Here we see the existence of "modern," or at least liberal, definitions of the political community and the nation articulated by a culturally salient minority while members of other religious

176

groups maintain more *Gemeinschaftlich*, or premodern, but not liberal-individualist, definitions of the political community.

These survey results and the corresponding questions they raise as to the existence of those necessary preconditions for any civil society are further strengthened by the research carried out by Andras Sajo on rights-awareness in Hungary.[50] What Sajo found, in a study of 1,650 respondents carried out between December 1986 and January 1987, was a very "limited, accidental, cursory, and contradictory" awareness of rights. That awareness, moreover, interpreted rights in a pragmatic manner, where "arguments on human dignity are scarce and because of prejudice some people are not willing to extend human dignity to all members of the society," where "submissiveness and primitive rebellion work hand in hand without questioning seriously the authoritarian legitimation of public administration," and where "there is little respect among the citizens towards each other."[51] What is lacking here is again the existence of precisely those universal notions of human dignity and moral individualism (rooted in the natural law tradition) which serve as the inclusive basis of citizenship, of membership and participation in the national community, without which the idea of civil society makes little sense.

If we put all three surveys—on values, national identity, and rights—together, we find a perhaps unfortunate but perfectly consistent correlation of restricted definitions of trust with restricted definitions of membership in the political community and the lack of any universal recognition of individual integrity (at least in its legal sense). All raise serious questions as to the viability of any idea of civil society founded on the moral individualism of liberal democratic ideology.

Argument can of course be made that the historical traditions of Hungary (if not of East-Central Europe) were reinforced rather than obliterated by the false universalism of state socialism. The basic divisions of "we" and "them" that had defined ethnic particularisms became transformed into a similar dichotomy of State and society (with different social groups and elites on either side of the divide). The content of particular definitions may have changed, but the pattern remained the same.

This may well be so, but the corresponding argument, or rather, its utilitarian, free-market extension—that given the play of mar-

ket forces these particularities will break down in the face of a
new individualist orientation—is open to serious question. Here
too I would like to rely on the set of survey data collected by
Csepeli and Örkney on the relation of market activities and political values. Their findings are again of interest. For what they
found was the lack of any correlation between entrepreneurial
activity and "liberal" political or economic orientations. To quote
their findings:

> Even the idea of privatization, the key market-economy notion,
> which in principle belongs integrally to the entrepreneur's posi-
> tion, is absent. Nor do liberal political and economic attitudes as a
> whole fare better, with the single exception of ideological rejection
> of socialism, for which there is a mild sympathy. This situation
> amounts to far more than a simple paradox. A class has emerged
> which in its state *per se* lacks an adequate consciousness of its own
> existence.[52]

The existence of liberal political and economic orientation were
thus not the result of market position but the function of social
origins and "cultural capital" irrespective of market affiliation. In
fact, as they note, it was only among certain social groups (originating in the intelligentsia with high cultural capital and experience of oppositional activity) that liberal ideas could be found.

While these findings are highly tentative and are the results of
research carried out during the process of transition itself, they do
correlate with the other research findings noted above as well as
with the preliminary research being conducted into the workings
of the second economy and of the "socialist entrepreneurs." The
fact that no correlation between entrepreneurial activity and liberal political values was found is not at all surprising given the
social and political history of Hungarian society. Whatever else
they are, the workings of a free-market are not in themselves a
guarantee of a liberal society and are not sufficient preconditions
for the existence of civil society.[53] Indeed, argument has been
made that the very organizational networks of current entrepreneurial activity characterized by low density, lack of cohesion,
and, crucially, the lack of trust all militate against the establishment of true "marketization."[54] In destroying whatever elements
of civil society did exist, state socialism destroyed as well the basic

trust necessary for the establishment of a market economy.[55] Interestingly, this insight is from economic observers of contemporary Hungary and not from sociological or political theorists. They too realize that, as I have attempted to argue throughout, civil society rests first of all on the idea of the autonomous individual and the terms of association, trust, and mutuality between these individuals articulated on general, universal principles (principles whose first stage of realization must be in the classical idea of citizenship—whatever the contradictions that inhere to this idea in the West today).

Of course, it is still too early to know what the long-term effects of a market economy will be on the societies of East-Central Europe. At present it has engendered a deep moral crisis as people are caught between conflicting modes of action. This may yet change. The reason we have entered into this analysis here, however, has less to do with market rationality than with the terms of trust in society, which, as we have seen, continue to be of a restricted and private nature.

To say that civil society calls for the generalization and universalization of trust is of course correct. To say that the idea of civil society also provides the way to establish such a system of trust, especially in the historical and social conditions of East-Central Europe, is, however, another matter. This is the problem. For while civil society certainly assumes a modern articulation of trust in society, founded on the notion of legal and ethical personhood, it does not provide us with any blueprint for the establishment of relations between social actors where such a notion does not fully exist. These relations are the nuts and bolts of citizenship and of civil society, if you will. Any approach to the problem of civil society based on a pluralism of motives and interests is thus insufficient in those societies where pluralism is not solely of interests, but of affective ideological universes as well.

To concretize this issue, we may look at the very process of transition in East-Central Europe. This transition, as is often noted, effects all elements of social life, not least the nature of trust, both between individuals themselves and between individuals and the major institutions in society. The transition to a market economy implies a fundamental reorientation of those structural arenas where trust is essential for the workings of the

179

social order. One of the primary areas where this can be seen is the reorganization of the public and private realms. The emergence of a market economy implies a redefinition of the terms of public and private realms and of the relative role of each in the constitution of new "ground rules" for social interaction (as, for instance, in the agreed rules of distributive justice). On an abstract and institutional level these can be subsumed under three central headings:

1. The restructuring of access to major markets in society
2. The construction of new definitions of public goods
3. New rules and definitions for the public redistribution of private goods

A reorientation of the nature of trust in society must be a central component of the restructuring of these spheres in line with the workings of a market economy, especially when we recall that under state socialism there existed a historically unique configuration of trust characterized by:

1. An almost total lack of trust on the general societal (that is to say, institutional) level concomitant with closely articulated networks of trust on the interpersonal level (in more formal terms, there was a failure to generalize trust from the particular to the social level.)
2. The continuation of structures of trust based on premodern, particular, and often primordial criteria
3. The existence of an almost schizophrenic situation in times of shortages, where conflicting interests (the need to maximize resources but also the need for others to accomplish this) led to a constantly unfolding dialectic of trust and mistrust (Here the best example is perhaps the perennial housing shortage and the strategies of what were called in Hungarian "death contracts" where trust and mistrust were interwoven on a personal and pathological level.)[56]
4. A basic grid through which interpersonal trust could be articulated based on the absolute dichotomy of we and them (i.e., the citizens of the country on the one hand and the party bureaucracy on the other)

180

The politically central question remains, What will happen now? How will the generalization of trust on the societal level progress, and what forms will trust, on the interpersonal level, take in postcommunist societies? An interesting example of the problems involved is that presented by the Hungarian taxi and truck drivers' strike of October 26–28, 1990. In this case we witnessed, on the one hand, the continuity of distrust of institutional government (not only by the strikers but indeed, in the early hours of the strike, by society at large, who feared military intervention and, in the popular phrase, a "repeat of 1956"). On the other hand, there did evolve over a three-day period an institutional framework for presenting and discussing grievances, a consensual agreement, and, crucially, through televised arbitration (one of the strikers' chief demands), a new form of mutuality, participation, and trust, not only among the actors, but of society at large.

In this context, it may be noted that in the pretransition era there already existed some degree of generalized trust (on the societal level) that took different forms in different East Central European countries. It would be useful to think of the role of the media in Hungary, of the Catholic Church in Poland, and of outstanding cultural elites or charismatic personalities in Czechoslovakia. All cases present examples of the continuity of culturally traditional forms of generalized trust that were not totally destroyed during the period of state socialism. In all three cases, during the mid-1980s culturally specific and politically autonomous modes of generalized trust, rooted in the (pre–state socialist) political culture of the countries, reemerged with a new saliency and came to play a critical role in the transition to a democratic polity and market-oriented economy. How these forms of trust can be institutionalized into the political structures of a working civil polity remains a question. In all cases it is clear that a number of crucial changes must evolve in the present configuration of trust for a democratic and market-oriented society to be viable.

First, there must be an almost quantum leap in the extension of trust to the institutional level for the progressive realization of market economics.

Second, there will, of necessity, be a reorientation of the almost

181

"feudal" nature of interpersonal trust based on strong nonmarket ties of reciprocity and mutuality. What form this will take is, however, an open question.

Third, the basic grid of "we" and "them," which had defined social solidarity and the boundaries of trust within state socialist societies, has already been dismantled. What is taking its place at present is thus a redefinition of the basic terms of social solidarity, of "we-ness" in society. We are witness to this process in a number of different areas, primarily in the rising ethnic and national consciousness of East European societies. This "revival" (if that is what it is) of primordial and ethnocentric bases of trust is of course fraught with danger for the emergence of a true civic polity. It does not, however, in itself rule out the establishment of mutual cooperation between different social groups. Whether that will be the rule or, in contrast, a heightening of intergroup tensions and mistrust will take place depends precisely on the new definitions of trust evolving in society.

From the above it is clear that whatever the nature of trust in the West European and North Atlantic societies, in East-Central Europe it cannot be taken for granted. Its fundamental structures, values, boundaries, and venues are changing drastically. How they are changing and what the potential social and political consequences of this change will be will determine the nature of society—its inherent civility or lack thereof.

In brief, our argument thus far has been that not only is trust necessary for the workings of society, but a specific form of generalized trust—rooted in modern individualist norms—is necessary for the workings of civil society. To call for the establishment of civil society without taking into consideration the fundamental terms of trust in society is but an empty rhetorical exercise. Of course, we have not been able to present a precise and rigorous study of trust in the East-Central European context, but I hope we have raised enough questions as to its difference from the accepted structure of trust in the Western democratic polities to "distrust" any naïve belief in the hasty or automatic establishment of civil society in those societies with the advent of the free market and democratically elected governments.

Trust, as the anthropologist Keith Hart explains, stands somewhere between "faith" and "confidence," between "status" and "contract," between "nation/descent" and "market/state," between "community" and "individual," between "custom" and "law."[57] In social structures lacking market rationality, with "no ground for confidence in the outcomes established by contract," trust as "the negotiation of risk occasioned by the freedom of others" is the *sine qua non* of social life. In the previously noted dichotomies, Hart is concerned to posit "ideal-type" distinctions between societies where trust (as association) exists between kinship and civil society. These distinctions are based on his study of the Frafras in Ghana, caught, as he so brilliantly shows, between traditional and market economies, between kinship and contract. He of course realizes that these are just ideal types, and every society, even the most modern, continues to have elements of associational life, of trust, which coexist with and, à la Durkheim, define the very terms of contract.

Our own discussion thus far has been an exercise in illustrating how the general usage of civil society, whether in the Scottish Enlightenment or among contemporary thinkers, is predicated on precisely this aspect of trust and association between legally constituted individuals involved in market transactions.

Before turning to the issue of civil society in the West, one final caveat with regard to civil society in East-Central Europe is appropriate, especially as it draws directly on Hart's anthropological work. For there are—certainly surprising—parallels between the Frafras in northeast Ghana and the popular idea of civil society as a description of those more or less mass political movements of citizens in East-Central Europe. The Frafras were, as we noted, caught between different social structures, having no recourse to either established (traditional) certainties of kinship or the legal (modern) certainties of contract. They evolved associational networks of mutual trust as the basis of their social and economic interaction.

Similarly, the failure of state socialism, both as an economic control system providing basic goods and, more importantly, as an ideological system of legitimation, allowed for the evolution of civil society (in its generally accepted sense, not as one pole of Hart's dichotomy) at the point of breakdown. Indeed, the same can be said of social movements in the West. Only there, it is not the general breakdown of the social order but a circumscribed area of contested claims and interests that social movements address in lieu of adequate State provisions. The problem with this reading of civil society, as social movements in the East and the West, is the problem of institutionalization, of the principles and practices of establishing long-term confidence and trust. Just how severe these problems are in contemporary East-Central Europe—how they are related to the problem of constructing trust in society and to the historical development of these societies, we have already seen. We must turn now to the West and the problem of civil society there.

V

To a great extent this whole essay has been an attempt to provide the necessary background for understanding the interaction of our citizens from Los Angeles—and, by implication, the problematic meaning of civil society in all liberal individualist societies, the United States being in effect the extreme example of such societies. An extended exercise on this point now is not really called for. Rather, it would be useful to open some new perspectives and pose some questions about the current attempts to argue the case for the idea of civil society in Western democratic settings.

In one sense, positing the problem of civil society in terms of trust—in Western as in Eastern Europe—is but an extension of our whole preceding argument. In the West, however, it is not the continued existence of particular venues of interpersonal and institutional trust that threatens the existence of civil society, but the very opposite. The very abstraction of trust, in its universal form, is itself the core problem for those who claim a lack of civil society in the West. Here too, such claims as Charles Taylor's to "disengage the individual from the State" and for political decentralization are basically rooted in the need to concretize that mutuality upon which all trust must be based.[58] Here, then, we have a rephrasing of the modern paradox. The very universalization of trust through, as Anthony Giddens points out, abstract systems (of political legitimation or money) vitiates the mutuality and communality upon which trust must be based.[59] What Giddens terms the "disembedment" of social systems in modern societies is but the result of abstracted systems of trust that, at every moment, must be re-validated or reembedded in what he calls, following Goffman, the rituals of civil inattention (or facework). In a sense the interaction of our two citizens in the alley behind Brooks Avenue was an exercise in just such a ritual, if not of inattention then of studied civility. The general result of this dynamic, however, has been both the oft-noted "deinstitutionalization" of the private sphere and the "overinstitutionalization" of the public sphere.[60] In our terms, it is the breakdown of that synthesis of public and private upon which the idea of civil society was seen to rest.

Less concerned with the overall dynamic of modernity than is Giddens, and with its particular implications for the structuring of self-identity, we are nevertheless interested in the implications of his insights for the problems of civil society in liberal-individualist societies. We can spell out these implications in terms of the problem of rights and trust or, to borrow a phrase from Jürgen Habermas, of justice and solidarity.[61]

Interestingly enough, the idea of rights, so central to the political program of liberal-individualism, can be seen as resting on the prior existence of trust. From the writings of Puffendorf on, rights have been seen to be rooted in the notion of moral personhood (Puffendorf's *entia moralia*), which is what imposes an inner "bond" on the will of another person.[62] The moral component of right, however, brings us back to that trust and mutuality existing between moral agents without which this "right" would have no force (especially when the transcendent dimension, the Will of God, is removed from the formula). One good way to get a purchase on this is to consider the case of the promise (the declaration of will, *declaratio* or *signum voluntatis*), itself central to political theorizing since Grotius, for whom the obligation to fulfill promises was an element of natural law. The obligation to fulfill promises arises from the moral agency and autonomy, from the freedom and responsibility, of the participants. Without the prior existence of these conditions, really rights to freedom, autonomy, and responsibility, the moral dimension of promise-keeping cannot be adequately explained. It is, in A. I. Meldon's terms, the conferring of these prior rights that "provides a warrant for the promise-keeping act."[63]

185

Here we can see, once again, why the United States has served for so many as the paradigm not only of modernity in general but of a truly "civil society." For it was (as analyzed in Chapter 2) here more than elsewhere that the idea of moral personhood, of the autonomous and agentic individual as the locus of the political community, emerged with greatest saliency. We are also in a better position to appreciate why the discourse of individual rights is so central in the United States (as we saw in the abortion issue), rooted as it is in the very constitutive principles of social life. Here too, however, we begin to see the emergent tension that inheres to this vision of society as compact, as constituted, if you will, by the promises of contracting parties, and that turns on the element of trust.

For the promise (and its derivatives in terms of the contract) rests also on the prior existence of trust and has been indeed used by philosophers, sociologists, and anthropologists as the primary heuristic device to illustrate the existence of trust in society. For the "perfect duty" (Kant) of promise keeping is what units us in a moral community, is itself warp and the woof of those "bonds of mutual respect between members of a moral community."[64] Without the moral community of mutually respecting individuals, there is no moral personhood and so no agentic individual upon which the obligations of promise-keeping can be based. This situation can be schematized as in the accompanying diagram.

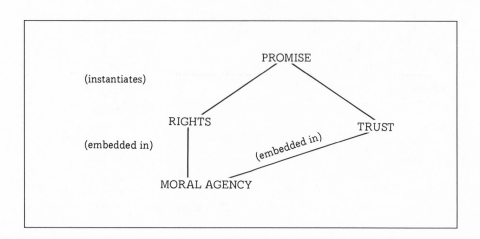

Here we see again the paradox of modern society, rooted in abstract and generalized trust, which in the political sphere is represented by the universalization of citizenship (that guarantee of moral agency in the public arena secured by the State). The very universalization of trust in citizenship, however, undermines that concrete mutuality and shared components of the moral community upon which trust is based. Hence the call for a return to civil society.

The problem is that the idea of civil society—what in fact kept society civil—implied, in its classical reading, a small society. This was true for Ferguson as for Montesquieu. The mutual trust upon which civil society was based (for the classical theorists) was guaranteed by personal acquaintance. As Leo Strauss reminded us, "only a society small enough to permit trust is small enough to permit mutual responsibility. . . . Just as man's natural power of firsthand knowledge, so his power of love or of active concern, is by nature limited; the limits of the city coincide with the range of man's active concern for nonanonymous individuals."[65] Strauss was discussing ancient philosophical visions of the "good," of the synthesis of public and private concerns that is at the heart of civil society, and the same insight was shared by Adam Ferguson. Indeed, Ferguson clearly saw the dangers presented by what we would today call a highly differentiated society to the existence of civility and trust. Thus he notes:

> Under the distinction of callings, by which the members of polished society are separated from each other, every individual is supposed to possess his species of talent, or his peculiar skill, in which the others are confessedly ignorant; and society is made to consist of parts, of which none is animated with the spirit that ought to prevail in the conduct of nations.[66]

In developing this point, Ferguson goes on to note:

> In proportion as territory is extended, its parts lose their relative importance to the whole. Its inhabitants cease to perceive their connection with the state and are seldom united in the execution of any national, or of any sactious designs. . . . It is even remarkable, that enlargement of territory, by rendering the individual of less consequence to the public, and less able to intrude with his coun-

187

cel, actually tends to reduce national affairs within a narrow compass, as well as to diminish the numbers who are consulted in legislation or in other matters of government.[67]

As we can see, the classic model of civil society rested on a vision of shared mutuality (and so an assumed homogeneity) between citizens. That is what assured the shared trust upon which civil society rested.

In this context, to recall for a moment our prior discussion of corporatism (and the distinction between corporate groups as interest groups and as conflicting metaphysical universes), it is not surprising to find that the most homogeneous of modern democratic polities, such as Sweden, have the fewest problems in dealing with severe conflicts between interest groups in society.[68] Moreover, it is precisely these countries where pluralism in the public sphere, as an aspect of civil society, can be most fully institutionalized (as for instance in the educational sphere), rooted as it is in the shared culture of prior solidarity and trust. Contrast this to the struggles in France over the wearing of the "foulard" or "hejab" by female students or the separation of boys from girls in English state schools serving Muslim communities—or indeed over language in the United States.[69] In these latter cases, the very heterogeneity of society leads to those types of problems the idea of civil society as pluralism is meant to solve. That it cannot serve this role results not only from its naïve sociological presuppositions but, as we have attempted to argue, from the contradictions that inhere to the idea itself.

Thus we see that if in East-Central Europe the problem of civil society is the failure to generalize trust in all the meanings of citizenship; in the West, it is the very generalization or abstraction of trust that militates against the idea of civil society as a normative program. Rights and trust thus stand in a complimentary tension the one with the other, where the latter is articulated on general or universal principles. The inadequacy of the classical civil society idea in overcoming this tension is of course rooted in its own assumptions on the nature of trust and solidarity.

We would do well to continue this line of argument beyond the classics and into the more contemporary arguments over civil society. These have been advanced most rigorously by Andrew

Arato and Jean Cohen in terms of the phenomenon of the New Social Movements.[70] The fundamental problem with this reading of civil society as the existence of the New Social Movements is not solely that of institutionalizing the new social demands for identity, autonomy, and recognition articulated by these movements. This argument, as we have suggested, would be along the lines that any perduring institutional arrangement would, at the end, bring us back to the problem of abstract trust and the attenuated terms of mutuality it implies. Indeed, it is perhaps a realization of this problem that has led some theorists of the New Social Movements–Civil Society argument to turn increasingly to Habermas and discourse ethics in an attempt to ground their argument for civil society on firmer foundations.[71] And it is here that we might most fruitfully engage with this most developed contemporary argument for the revival of any idea of civil society in today's world. We cannot reproduce here the rich literature (mostly of a highly abstract nature) that attends this debate. We must, however, take note of some of its dimensions, as they present, so we will argue, yet another "reworking" of the tensions and contradictions in the idea of civil society, contradictions centering on the ideas of rights and trust or, as mentioned, of justice and solidarity.

In the "civil society as new social movements" argument, as most rigorously developed by Jean Cohen, the specific features of the New Social Movements—their unique social base, the nature of their social and political impingement, and the very nature of their demands—present something akin to a practical illustration of a type of democratic action, based on "communicative interaction," which is the hallmark of Habermas's theory. Through the action and interaction of these groups a "plurality of democratic forms" could emerge that would exemplify the workings of civil society in something close to its original, ethical formulation. In Cohen's argument, a structural plurality in the public sphere of civil society (in this case of social movements) ensures the possibility of defining social life "in terms of participation and publicity."[72] Such participation and publicity ensure in turn the rights of communication, of discourse, and would seem to revitalize the public sphere and renew a public life now dominated by large-scale organizations that have "have attained a quasi-political character and [take on] tasks of economic and political steering."[73]

As can be seen, one central element of this equation is the notion of communication and, as proposed by Habermas, the idea of communicative validity, which is central to his attempt to ground ethnical action in a communicative rationality. There are thus two poles to this argument. The first centers on Habermas's own theory of communicative rationality as a (possible) set of legitimizing practices (in fact, and in light of the dissolution of natural law theory, perhaps the only alternative to that type of legitimation based on a transcendent [Locke] or transcendental [Kant] ethics that was once at the heart of political theory).[74] The second centers on the practical application of this theory, in general and in terms of new social movements in particular. At both poles there are serious questions that can be raised about this attempt to posit civil society as a realm of communicative action in the Habermasian sense. We shall begin with the second pole, the practical one, which will lead us, in short order, to the greater, more theoretical problem of interpreting civil society in terms of discourse ethics.

Most generally, discourse ethics posits a set of criteria, a guide or standard, for distinguishing legitimate from illegitimate norms. These criteria, of rational and universal consensus, are, it is argued, the sole possibility of arriving at said consensus in the relativistic world of plural values that we all inhabit (the result of the previously noted dissolution of natural law theory and of any possibility of grounding ethics in an ontological or transcendent vision). Without entering into a detailed analysis of this theory, one core component is worthy of our attention in approaching the civil society as discourse ethics formula. This is the tenet or, more properly, the metanorm which specifies that a norm is justified only when "the consequences and side-effects for the satisfaction of the interests of every individual which are expected to result for the general conformance to that norm can be accepted without compulsion by all."[75] All who would be affected by the implementation of a given norm must thus have the right and the ability to participate in the debate over it, a debate which is public and participatory (and not, as with Kant, one that takes place within the workings of an individual mind).

190

There are two major problems with practical implications of this idea. One, perhaps as Seyla Benhabib has noted, is trivial, the second, less so. The first problem rests on the assumption that all participants in the debate are "modern," that is, they all share this universal rational orientation to action and toward the ethical validation of action. It assumes, in Benhabib's words "the willingness and capacity of individuals and the culture at large to adopt such an ethical standpoint in the first place."[76] That this is not so in today's world is clear and, yes, perhaps trivial as well. The second problem with any practical application of this formula is, however, a bit less trivial. Let us assume that all people in the world are "modern" and rational, and that the force of transcendent or ontological arguments no longer holds, not in Croatia, not in Gaza, nor even in Crown Heights. The world is nonetheless still organized into nation-states, and people are citizens of such states and not of the world at large. However, the economic, legal, and political relations among states do leave us living in a world where major decisions in one state (however, let us assume hypothetically, rationally, publicly, and universally arrived at) effect the life, liberty, and happiness of those living in other states. Take as an example the current review of immigration policy in the EEC, most especially in France and Germany. Even if we assume free public and participatory debate over this matter, even if we assume that such civic organizations as SOS RACISME have as much impact on these debates as more institutionalized, formal political structures, the results of these debates, restricting or opening the gates of immigration, affect not only the residents (citizens or others) of France and Germany, but hundreds of thousands of people in Turkey, Pakistan, North Africa, and so on. Given the interconnected nature of today's world economies, for civil society to attain the validity mandated by discourse ethics, it would have to include all of humanity and not just the citizens (or residents) of a given state. Social movements and the institutional arena of their interaction would have to be of an international scope and not limited to the confines of a particular nation-state.[77]

The utopian aspects of such a situation should be clear and need not detain us. Habermas himself has made no political or indeed normative claims for the theory of discourse ethics. How-

191

ever, the example of immigration policy brings us to the second set of problems with the civil society as discourse ethics argument. For the problem with this interpretation of civil society is not solely at the practical level, but at the theoretical level as well. And this problem turns on squaring the old circle of justice and solidary, legality and morality, or, as we discussed earlier, rights and trust.

It is surely no mere coincidence that current debates in ethical theory turn precisely on these issues, which, as we have seen, have been central to Western political theory at least since the early seventeenth century (though an argument can be made, following Castoriadis, that they are constitutive of the whole Western political tradition from its origins in Greek philosophy).[78] The distinction between "communitarians" (of however diverse political position, and we may take as an example either Alasdair MacIntyre or Charles Taylor) and "universalists" (whether of a liberal, Rawlsian variety or Habermas himself) is essentially over the priority of a collectively articulated social good over the idea of universal (individual or not) rights. The communitarian position, which roots the social good in the traditions of a particular human community, posits this good over against a universal idea of rights (or justice) not so embedded. Again, here, in philosophy, some notion of solidarity is posited over against a notion of abstract justice. The latter is, in the communitarian position, always seen to be rooted in the former, and in fact inexplicable without such communal grounding. The universalist position does not so much argue for the priority of justice over solidarity, of (abstract) rights over socially defined (and hence perforce relativistic) good, as it attempts, most especially in Habermas's recent work, to overcome this very dichotomy.[79] Here, of course, is the relevance of this debate to our own subject of civil society. For if in some way the internal contradictions (however defined) contained in the idea of civil society can be overcome or synthesized, a way would seem to be open to imbue the older idea of civil society with concrete contemporary meanings—at least at the theoretical level. It is this belief that sustains the civil society as new social movements argument. Thus the major question for us is whether or not the idea of discourse ethics, of communicative rationality, manages to overcome the universalist–communitarian debate and to

192

synthesize the hitherto conflicting meanings attributed to justice and solidarity. (Here too we see the relevance of the immigration example. For even if communicative rationality can be assumed among citizens in the nation-state participating in the debate, it is still bounded, and, more pointedly, the argument to restrict immigration is defined, by solidaristic criteria, i.e., of what is good for members of the given national community.)

Habermas, it must be noted, is well aware of this problem, of the need in essence to synthesize universalistic and communitarian positions in order to constitute a new system of "postconventional" ethical validity. His recent argument with Kohlberg on the terms of joining "justice" and "benevolence" turns on precisely this issue.[80] It would be best here to quote Habermas at length, in a passage that, however abstract, resonated with the themes we have been discussing throughout this whole chapter:

> As a component of a universalistic morality, of course, solidarity loses its merely particular meaning, in which it is limited to the internal relationships of a collectivity that is ethnocentrically isolated from other groups. . . . Justice conceived in postconventional terms can converge with solidarity as its reverse side only when solidarity has been transformed in the light of the idea of a general discursive will formation. To be sure, the fundamental notions of equal treatment, solidarity and the general welfare, which are central to all moralities, are (even in premodern societies) built into the conditions of symmetry and the expectations of reciprocity characteristic of every ordinary communicative practice, and indeed, in the form of universal and necessary pragmatic presuppositions of communicative action. . . . The ideas of justice and solidarity are present above all in the mutual recognition of responsible subjects who orient their actions to validity claims. But of themselves these normative obligations do not extend beyond the boundaries of a concrete lifeworld of family, tribe, city or nation. These limits can be broken through only in discourse, to the extent that the latter is institutionalized in modern societies. Arguments extend *per se* beyond particular lifeworlds, for in the pragmatic presuppositions of argumentation, the normative content of the presuppositions of communicative action is extended—in universalized, abstract form and without limitations—to an ideal communication community . . . that includes all subjects capable of speech and action.[81]

193

As we can see, Habermas posits solidarity not in opposition to a universal morality but as a component of it (in modern societies—and we need not enter here into the problem of the descriptive versus prescriptive elements of this theory). To do this, the very terms of solidarity have to be generalized, universalized, and reformulated beyond the particular definitions of membership in a circumscribed human community. Though the concrete mechanisms of this transformation remain, in the above formulae, something of a "black box," the potential for such transformation is posited as inherent in the very logic of language and linguistic competence (or universal-pragmatics). Here then a new (theoretical) basis for ethical action is posited. It can be schematized as:

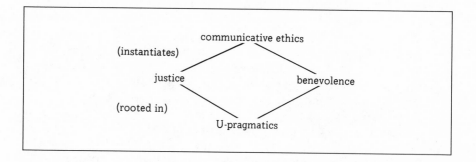

If we recall our earlier diagram, we can see that the teleology of trust has been replaced by a teleology of rationality.

The question remains, however, is this universalization of solidarity, via communicative rationality, more than a *trompe-l'oeil*? Does it not redefine solidarity in such a way as to void it of any meaning? The very word solidarity implies "solidarity with," and solidarity with something or someone implies solidarity over against, in distinction from some other. Does not the very notion of a universal solidarity contradict itself?

The notion of community of need and solidarity implies, in a very real sense, as Seyla Benhabib has argued, solidarity with concrete individuals.[82] The concrete other (or at the very least that other who can be "concretized" though mutual ties of history, ideas, love, care, and friendship) has always provided the locus of solidarity (rooted perhaps in the very psychosocial development of the infant ego). Trust, as we have seen, arises from precisely those shared affective aspects of the social world which cannot, it would seem, be totally subsumed into the workings of a rational formula of linguistic pragmatics. <u>Trust and communal mutuality in some sense always contain an exclusionary (if not particularistic) component</u> for them to have any meaning.

It is, I submit, this fact more than any other that poses serious problems for the attempt to reconstitute the idea of civil society upon the basis of discourse ethics. The conflicting character of justice and solidarity cannot be overcome simply by positing their unity. It was, we recall, the very universalization of the principles of solidarity (through citizenship and the idea of the morally autonomous individual at its core) that defined justice in the modern world but at the same time undermined that solidarity upon which justice itself was based. The reworking of this classical Durkheimian problem in terms of communicative rationality does not, however, seem to solve this fundamental problem of modern social life.

The practical obstacles of realizing civil society in the theory of the New Social Movements are thus, as we see, complemented by theoretical problems that cut to the core of any idea of civil society as a workable synthesis of conflicting claims (of interest) and (moral) desiderata. The anthropological fiat of the Scottish Enlightenment synthesis of the public and the private has been replaced by a philosophical fiat, synthesizing abstract justice and shared communal norms. In both cases, however, the constitutive problems of (ethically) integrating individual and social life are elided, not solved.

Finally, I "trust" the reader will forgive this rather long (if severely abbreviated) excursus into ethical theory. It was deemed necessary only in light of the current attempts to resurrect the idea of civil society by grounding it in the principles of discourse ethics. If, as I have attempted to argue, serious inadequacies remain in the latter (especially when removed from the purely abstract philosophical realm and placed in a more sociological context), this attempt will ultimately leave us empty-handed. Such is my fear. For if <u>in East-Central Europe</u> the particular, cir-

195

cumscribed channels of trust are what preclude any meaningful theory (or practice) of civil society, in the West it is the very abstract and generalized nature of trust that militates against that solidarity upon which civil society must also stand. The "solution" of discourse ethics to this problem, in essence defining solidarity (as the concrete needs of mutuality) out of the equation, is no solution.

The philosophical aspects of the contradictory demands of justice and solidarity are, however, much less our concern than the problem of civil society. And the thrust of our whole argument has been to warn against any uncritical "return" to this concept as a solution to these problems. Among sociologists, this attempt is especially ironic once we recognize that the above-noted contradiction is essentially the same as that which plagued Talcott Parsons's structural-functional model of systems integration once it was realized that such functional systems as Integration (i.e., solidarity) often stand in tension (and not in Parsons's assumed harmony) with the functions of Pattern Maintenance (those definitions of individual motives, needs, goals, etc., which can be seen as the normative, value premises of the social order, i.e., its principles of justice).[83] The current fragmentation of the social sciences and the heterogeneity of their conceptual scheme cannot be rectified by a return to what is in essence a presociological concept. And the idea of civil society is presociological precisely because it assumes as unproblematic what, as we have seen, are the fundamental and constitutive problems of modern existence.

The squaring of justice and solidarity, of private interest and public good, remains the problem of civil society and of citizenship in the modern world. That the very idea of citizenship is the necessary first stage toward resolving these problems should be clear, especially when we view those societies not yet so constituted. That there is no easy road to the type of citizenship we identify with the West European and North Atlantic polities should also be clear—if not from the foregoing historical analysis, then at least from each morning's headlines. That this idea of citizenship as that of autonomous rights-bearing individuals united in a community of Reason is itself only a partial solution to the problem of civil society is however also clear, as the very demand for a return to civil society indicates.

196

However, and once again, any attempt to return to an ethical solidarity *not* based on the idea of the individual as autonomous moral agent leads nowhere (or rather has led to some of the most horrible murders of this murderous century). We need only recall the type of ethical nationalism that has been tearing the towns and villages of Yugoslavia (and parts of the former Soviet Union) apart; or the fascist ideology of the "ethical state," Giovanni Gentile's concept of the "state within," to recoil from this alternative.

The problem then is clear. The solution less so. For while the idea of civil society is offered as a solution, the concrete implications of this idea are often left unstated. If it means solely the "disengagement of the individual from the State" and the principle of decentralization (as it seems to be for Charles Taylor and Michael Waltzer), this is not sufficient, not in a unified world economy and not when it comes together with demands "to socialize the economy so that there is greater diversity of market agents, communal as well as private."[84] For how can the economy be efficiently socialized with a decentralized state? What, in such a situation, would limit or mediate the workings of "pure" market forces? All attempts to spell out the concrete implications of the idea of civil society run into similar problems. For example, to call on the one hand for the plurality and "domestication" of nationalism as an element of civil society assumes a Western model of historical development, where national particularisms are to some degree already mediated by the universalistic assumptions of citizenship. On the other hand, to identify the workings of civil society with the "shaping of a co-op budget" rather than "decisions on national fiscal policy," or with "voluntary work in a hospital" rather than "joining a political party" (which could present a National Health Insurance program on its platform) is more an attempt to elude the problems of civil society than to provide for their solution.[85] And while it is fashionable these days to talk of "associational life," such talk begs the question. For when these associations are ethically construed as different "metaphysical" or normative universes (as is often the case in East-Central Europe and other countries), they represent not the realization but the destruction of civil life. On the other hand, when these associations are built around the principle of interest, they cannot as such mediate or mitigate interest-motivated action in the name of some other or higher ethical unity. The idea of civil society itself was able to play this role when, as we have seen, the foundations of moral action were constructed in terms not only of the transcendental principle of Reason but of a transcendent morality as well. (Again, recall how the transcendent principle of grace was, in late-seventeenth-century New England, internalized and transformed into the idea of the transcendental moral individual governed by reason.) With the loss of these foundations in Reason and Revelation, the idea of civil society itself becomes the problem rather than the solution of modern existence. And while it is certainly true that this realization would seem to leave us less than sanguine about the possibility of reconstructing civil society, as idea or ideal, it will, I would hope, make any move in this direction more realistic.

Concluding
Remarks on Civil
Society

❦

Sometime in the late 1960s the mathematician, satirist, and folk-singer Tom Lehrer poked well-meaning fun at folksingers and songs of protest by noting how difficult it was "to get up in a coffeehouse or college auditorium and come out in favor of all those things that everyone else in audience is against, like peace and justice and brotherhood and so on."

Here I find myself in a very different situation and fear that I will be understood as coming out against all those things that every well-meaning reader is for, such as peace and justice and brotherhood and so on. I trust, however, that this fear is mis-placed and that the circumscribed nature of my argument is clear. That is, I am not saying that there is no theoretical, or indeed practical, solution to contemporary dilemmas in the East or the West. But neither am I positing a solution to these dilemmas. That would presume much too much. I am simply presenting an ar-gument on the inadequacy of the idea of civil society as a solution to those contemporary impasses that in fact, turn, if you will, on

199

the specific definitions of justice and brotherhood in both East European and Western societies. In the East, the (practical) conditions for the emergence of the classical Western liberal-individualist model of civil society do not fully exist, and in the West we must seriously question the (theoretical) possibility of their reemergence (given our analysis of trust, solidarity, and the contradictions of modern civilization).

Surely the qualms expressed here on the idea of civil society sound not only heretical but also somewhat strange. Allow me then to develop, one last time, a few of the strains of thought that led me to such an unpopular position. Perhaps I should add here, in passing, that the very unpopularity of such a position is more marked today among West European and American academics than among those of Eastern and East-Central Europe. This contrasts with the situation a few short years ago, when such a statement east of the Elbe would have branded one a supporter of the incumbent regimes, whereas in the West most academics would have looked at one blankly without comprehending what one was talking about—except, that is, for a few more left-leaning colleagues who, like Andrew Arato, Jean Cohen, and John Keane, were using the idea of civil society as a tool to critique both Western capitalist and Eastern communist (or, rather, state socialist) societies. This situation has changed radically as the idea of civil society has been taken up by mainstream Western intellectuals as the new *cause célèbre*, the new analytic key that will unlock the mysteries of the social order. Thus, and again ironically, as the idea of civil society is being promulgated in international scholarly conferences, as learned as well as more popular journals are devoting issues and articles to the idea of civil society, at the same time some thinkers in East-Central Europe are beginning to doubt the efficacy of the whole notion in dealing with the problems facing society in the midst of the transition to a capitalist, free-market economy.

Not that the idea of civil society does not continue to find important resonances in East-Central European societies, not that it is not the theme of conferences and articles here, and not that it does not continue to be used as a political slogan—often by the parties holding power. All this continues to be the case, and it is precisely here, in the different uses of the idea of civil society, that

200

it is best to begin, to recall the reasons for my own profound suspicion of this idea.

We can begin by noting three somewhat overlapping but nevertheless distinct uses of the idea of civil society, both in the East and in the West. The first is the more direct and concrete political use of civil society as a slogan of different movements and parties, as well as, in the West, individual thinkers who may use it to critique certain government policies. The second use of the term is by social scientists as an analytic concept, that is, a quasi-scientific term to describe (or even perhaps explain) certain forms of social phenomena, of social organization on the macro-level, or even perhaps as a possible venue to link micro- and macro-levels of social analysis. In its new popularity the idea of civil society is being used more and more to describe certain forms of social organization that once were associated with the ideas of democracy and citizenship—a point we shall return to in a moment. The third use, which somewhat infuses the first two, is as a philosophically normative concept, that is—putting it in somewhat grandiose terms—as an ethical ideal, a vision of the social order that is not only descriptive, but prescriptive, providing us with a vision of the good life.

The idea of civil society as a political slogan should not detain us too long. Many ideas have been used as political slogans, from "no taxation without representation" to "a society of free producers," "soldiers' and sailors' soviets," and so on. Any party or movement is free to use any politically efficient slogan it sees fit, but that in itself does not make it a sociological concept. We would, however, do well to recall the different resonances of civil society and of its components in the East and the West. For they have led to much confusion and misunderstanding across societies and cultural traditions. Recall, for example, the very different role of the Church (one of the important components of those voluntary organizations of civil society in the West) in Western and Eastern Europe.

It is one thing to assign to the Church a role as a political actor within a pluralist civil society, a role akin to that of any other interest group, and quite another thing to identify the Church with the very essence of that national entity which, supposedly, finds expression in the workings of civil society. In fact in Poland,

201

where the idea of civil society has a markedly Polish national cast to it, where it resonates strongly with Polish peoplehood, with national independence and with national, even *Statlich* institutions, the role of the Church as a prime political actor is very different from its role in the West. The increasing strength of the Church as a political actor as well as the equally increasing resentment against that strength, a resentment manifest recently in the failure to push through the Parliament a draconian abortion bill that the Church advocated, betray just how insufficient the idea of civil society, as Westerners conceive it, is—even as a political slogan, even in Poland. And, as long as we are noting the problems of civil society as a political slogan, we should also recall the ethnic divisions of East-Central European societies, which pose serious questions about the viability of the idea of civil society in a political sense, at least in societies characterized by ethnic and national heterogeneity (as opposed to the homogeneity of certain Scandinavian countries) or in societies whose terms of collective membership and solidarity are not those of an ideology of individualism (as in the United States).

In fact the ethnic and religious divisions of East-Central Europe bring us back to the above-mentioned difference in the meaning of the term "civil society" in the East and the West. In the East civil society evokes a strong communal attribute that, while apart from the State, is also equally distant from the idea of the autonomous and agentic individual upon which the idea of civil society rests in the West. The very pluralism that so many in the West identify with the idea of civil society rests on an almost Durkheimian idea of the individual as infused with moral and transcendental attributes, which is lacking in the East. In Hungary, for example, where there is no word for civil society—where its nearest approximation means the burghers of Debrecen, not of Pecs or Szeged, or Budapest, nor presumably of Los Angeles or Jerusalem, but solely of Debrecen—the idea of civil society resonates first with that which is not of the State. Something akin to the English word civilian (but while civilian in English is distinguished primarily from the military, here it is distinguished from all occupants of State office). The individual actor within civil society is seen in the East, however, as firmly embedded within communal, mostly primordial attributes that define the individual in his or her opposition to the State.

It is thus a point of no little interest that while in the West the idea of civil society is used as a political slogan to advance the cause of community, to mediate somewhat the adverse effects of the ideology of individualism, at least in the United States, in the East the idea of civil society, if it is to have any meaning beyond that of either support for existing governments or a nostalgia for the days of samizdat, that is, the days of a relatively uncomplicated solidarity among would-be reformers and beyond the contemporary pettiness and politicking of party politics (and I may add, beyond the deep political and social divisions that now exist between individuals who were once united in an uncomplicated rejection of the regime)—if the idea is to have any further meaning here, it must be to advance an idea of the individual as an autonomous social actor and as an ethical and moral entity, an idea that is in a sense foreign to the political traditions of this area.

In the last few sentences I see that I have begun to slip a bit from the political into the normative attributes of the idea of civil society—a common but nonetheless dangerous tendency—and it would be best to halt this slide by turning for a moment to the analytic aspects of civil society as a sociological concept. Here there are two broad uses of the term. The first is on the institutional or organization level of a type of political sociology, and the second makes it a phenomenon in the realm of values and beliefs. As the second will bring us back in short order to the normative aspect of the idea of civil society, I suggest we begin with the first, the idea of civil society as an expression of a type of institutional order. Here, as I have attempted to argue, the concept of civil society seems to add little to existing ideas of democracy or of citizenship, especially as developed by T. H. Marshall. Let us briefly recall some of the characteristics of democracies posited by such thinkers as Robert Dahl and Arend Lijphart: (1) the freedom to form and join organizations, (2) freedom of expression, (3) the right to vote, (4) eligibility for public office, (5) the right of political leaders to compete for support and votes, (6) alternative sources of information (what we would call a free press), (7) free and fair elections, and (8) institutions for making government policies depend on votes and other expressions of preference.[1] This list, taken from Robert Dahl's *Polyarchy*, published in 1971 and used by many social scientists in the intervening decades, seems to me to contain but few additions (and some deletions) from Marshall's famous development of the three forms of citizenship (civil, political, and social) and, more importantly, to contain the essence of what is meant in East-Central Europe by the idea of civil society.

Indeed, I would hazard the guess that the use of the term civil society instead of democracy in Eastern Europe to describe the above organizational features of social life is to be explained less by any additional analytic weight carried by the idea of civil society than simply by the fact that civil society as a term was neutral and uncorrupted by forty years of State propaganda, whereas the term democracy—as in People's Democracy—was heavily tainted by the past and as a political slogan not as unencumbered as civil society.

The second—and again very general—use of civil society in the social scientific literature is as pertaining to a phenomenon in the realm of values, beliefs, or symbolic action. Here civil society is identified with some more or less universalistic mode of orientation on the part of social actors, and with the definition of citizenship in terms of universalistic, highly generalized moral bonds. This reading of civil society combines a Durkheimian emphasis on moral individualism as the basis of solidarity within modern, *gesellschaftlich* societies with a Weberian emphasis on the increased rationality of modern forms of social organization as the embodiment of universalist values. This is fine as far as it goes and as long as one accepts a Parsonian synthesis between Weberian notions of charisma (as for instance the apotheosis of the Charisma of Reason in the 1794 *Declération de la droits de l'homme et du citoyen*) and Durkheimian notions as to the basis of the sacred in modern societies—both rooted in the idea of the individual as the center of the moral order.[2]

The problem with this reading, however, lies in what it ignores, and what it ignores is precisely the problem of liberal-individualist ideology, that is, how to constitute a sense of community among and between social actors who are conceived of in terms of autonomous individuals. In slightly different but similar terms, it

204

ignores Weber's problem of the iron cage of increasing rationality, which, while furthering the workings of a universal Reason, also cuts at the basis of a shared communality. Community or communality is always particular, Durkheim's universal individualism (and Habermas's ideas of communicative validity) notwithstanding. And not surprisingly, most of the more popular cries for a reconstituted sense of civil society in the West stress precisely this need to reassert a sense of shared communality in the face of what is perceived as an individualism defined in terms of self-interest.

It is moreover precisely this tension between individualism and community, between particular and universal interests, that brings us back to the idea of civil society as a normative concept. We must, however, recall that the modern—and I stress modern—idea of civil society as developed from the end of the seventeenth century (in the writings of John Locke) through the Scottish Enlightenment and into the nineteenth-century writings of Hegel and the Marxian critique of Hegel, all turned around this tension and dichotomy. It was in the modern era, with the nascent capitalist economy and the freeing of the individual from traditional communal and often primordial ties, that the problem of squaring individual and social goods and desiderata achieved a new saliency. The modern ideas of civil society developed by Locke, Ferguson, Smith, and Hutcheson (and, to some extent, Shaftesbury) were all attempts to posit a solution to the new problem of the social order that emerged at the end of the seventeenth century.

We certainly have not had the space here to review the writings of the eighteenth and nineteenth centuries on the idea of civil society in anything close to their entirety. Yet our own limited exercise should have had some value in elucidating just how fragile an edifice the idea of civil society is, especially in today's world. Our reading of John Locke revealed just how important the transcendental dimension, the belief in men as Godly subjects, was to Locke's image of civil society. Similarly, our reading of the Scottish Enlightenment texts made clear the naïve anthropology of moral sentiments and natural sympathy—of a Reason in step with the passions—upon which the idea of civil society as an ethical ideal rests. These beliefs, in Godly benevolence and in natural sympathy, are no longer ours to share, and we can no longer use them to construct our models of the social order. After Hume's attack on the Scottish Enlightenment view of Reason, and after Hegel's (and, following him, Marx's) attack on the "naturalist" premises of eighteenth-century thought, we are left with the problems but not with the solutions.

The assumed synthesis of public and private, individual and social concerns and desiderata, upon which the idea of civil society rests, no longer holds. The social as well as the philosophical conditions for this synthesis have changed drastically, and a return to more classical formulations will not suffice, not in East-Central Europe and not in Western democratic societies. The very different resonances contained in the idea of civil society, in Ferguson and Smith, Hegel and Marx, or indeed in contemporary thinkers from Budapest to Princeton, reflect the contradictions of modern existence—in the seventeenth century and today. Whether the concept of civil society itself as either analytic idea or normative ideal brings us any farther toward their resolution is, however, open to serious question.

And finally, a word on civil society as a political slogan. I can but recall the words of William Morris's *A Dream of John Ball*: "I ponder all these things, how men fight and lose the battle and the thing that they fought for comes about in spite of their defeat and when it comes turns out not to be what they meant and other men have to fight for what they meant under another name."[3] To accept this truth with stoicism, equanimity, and no loss of hope is the greatest contribution we all can make to the future establishment of, if not *civil* society, then at least a more civil one.

Notes

Introduction

1. Charles Taylor, "Modes of Civil Society," *Public Culture*, vol. 3, no. 1 (Fall 1990), pp. 95–118; Edward Shils, "The Virtues of Civil Society," *Government and Opposition*, vol. 26, no. 2. (Winter 1991), pp. 3–20; Edward Shils, "Was ist eine Civil Society?" in K. Michelski (ed.), *Europa und die Civil Society* (Stuttgart: Kult-Cota, 1991), pp. 13–52; Michael Walzzer, "The Idea of Civil Society," *Dissent*, Spring 1991, pp. 293–304; Daniel Bell, "American Exceptionalism Revisited: The Role of Civil Society," *The Public Interest*, no. 95 (1989), pp. 38–56.

2. Bell, "American Exceptionalism Revisited," p. 56.

3. Vladimir Tismaneanu, *Reinventing Politics: Eastern Europe After Communism* (New York: Free Press, 1992).

4. The most complete explication of John Keane's own views on the idea of civil society is to be found in his volume of essays, *Democracy and Civil Society* (London: Verso, 1988).

5. Karl Marx, "On the Jewish Question" *Collected Works*, vol. 3 (Moscow: Progress Publishers, 1975), p. 154.

6. See John Keane, "Despotism and Democracy," in his *Civil Society and the State* (London: Verso, 1988), pp. 35–72, as well as Norberto Bobbio, "Gramsci and the Concept of Civil Society," pp. 73–100 in the same volume. See also Bell, "American Exceptionalism Revisited."

7. Marcel Mauss, "A Category of the Human Mind: The Notion of Person, the Notion of 'Self'," In Marcel Mauss, *Sociology and Philosophy* (London: Rout-

ledge & Kegal Paul, 1979), pp. 85–89; Max Weber, *Economy and Society*, vol. 2 (Berkeley: University of California Press, 1978), p. 1209.

8. Richard Sennett, *The Fall of Public Man* (New York: Knopf, 1977).

9. For only one of the more recent examples of this popularity, see *Proceedings of the 1991 Annual Convention of the Hungarian Sociological Association*, June 24–28, "Magyarország A Világban" (Hungary in the World) in which 42 of the participants presented papers on the idea of civil society.

10. Many of these themes are addressed in the essays compiled by Charles Maier (ed.), *Changing Boundaries of the Political* (Cambridge: Cambridge University Press, 1987).

11. Carole Pateman, "The Fraternal Social Contract," in Keane, *Civil Society*, pp. 101–28.

12. Peter Singer, *Animal Liberation* (New York: Avon Books, 1975); T. Reagan, *The Case for Animal Rights* (Berkeley: University of California Press, 1983).

13. Max Weber, "Social Psychology of World Religions," in H. H. Gerth and C. W. Mills (eds.) *From Max Weber: Essays in Sociology* (Oxford University Press, 1958), p. 281.

CHAPTER 1   The Modern Idea of Civil Society

1. A good comparative analysis of contract theories in this period can be found in Hermann Klenner, "Social Contract Theories in a Comparative Perspective," *Law and Society* (Tokyo: Wasada University Press, 1988), pp. 49–68.

2. By referring to the idea of civil society as an ethical representation of society, I mean something very much along the same lines as Eric Voeglin's "self-illumination of society," through which society is represented to its constitutive members as an expression of their "human essence." On this concept see Eric Voeglin, *The New Science of Politics* (Chicago: University of Chicago Press, 1952), esp.. ch. 1.

3. *The Defensor Pacis of Marsilius of Padua*, ed. C.W. Previte-Orton (Cambridge, 1928).

4. George Sabine, *A History of Political Thought* (New York: Rinehart & Winston, 1950), pp. 141–51.

5. Sheldon Wohlin, *Politics and Vision* (Boston: Little, Brown & Co., 1960), pp. 69–82.

6. P. Stein, "Roman Law," in J. H. Burns (ed.), *The Cambridge History of Medieval Political Thought c. 350–1450* (Cambridge: Cambridge University Press, 1988), pp. 37–50; C. McIlwain, *The Growth of Political Thought in the West* (New York: Macmillan, 1932).

7. Cicero, *The Republic*, III, 2, cited in Sabine, *History of Political Thought*, p. 164.

8. R. Markus, "The Latin Fathers," pp. 92–122 in Burns (ed.), *Cambridge History*, esp. pp. 97, 99–100, 111.

9. R. Carlyle, *A History of Medieval Political Theory in the West*, 6 vol. (Edinburgh: Blackwood, 1936), vol. 2, 102–13.

10. Ernst Troeltsch, *The Social Teachings of the Christian Churches*, 2 vols. (New York: Macmillan, 1931), vol. 1, pp. 150–58.

11. Cited in Jaroslav Pelikan, *The Christian Tradition: A History of the Development of Dogma*, 4 vols. (Chicago: University of Chicago Press, 1971), vol. 3, p. 74.

12. Troeltsch, *Social Teachings*, vol. 1, p. 262.

13. *Ibid.*, pp. 260–61.

14. *Ibid.*, p. 266.

15. Richard Tuck, *Natural Rights Theories* (Cambridge: Cambridge University Press, 1979), pp. 32–44.

16. Quentin Skinner, *The Foundations of Modern Political Thought*, 2 vols. (Cambridge: Cambridge University Press, 1978), vol. 2, pp. 339–42.

17. Tuck, *Natural Rights*, p. 42.

18. See Otto Gierke, *Natural Law and the Theory of Society 500–1800* (Cambridge, 1934).

19. Hugo Grotius, *De Jui belli ai pacis*, Book I, ch. 1, Section X, p. 1.

20. *Ibid.*, p. 5.

21. Duncan Forber, *Hume's Philosophical Politics* (Cambridge: Cambridge University Press, 1975), p. 17.

22. See for example, John Rawls, *A Theory of Justice* (Cambridge, MA: Cambridge University Press, 1971), p. 11.

23. Tuck, *Natural Rights*, pp. 3, 5, 79, 172–73; John Dunn, *The Political Theory of John Locke* (Cambridge: Harvard University Press, 1969).

24. Book VII, sct. 89. The authoritative text of Locke's Treatises is John Locke, *Two Treatises of Government*, ed. Peter Laslett (Cambridge: Cambridge University Press, 1960). This text was not available to me in Budapest while writing this book. Consequently I have identified references by the Book and Section numbers, a practice followed in other cases where the authoritative versions of texts were lacking. In all cases references are to the second treatise.

25. *Ibid.*, Book, VIII, sct. 101.

26. *Ibid.*, Book VII, sct. 87.

27. *Ibid.*, Book II, sct. 4.

28. *Ibid.*, Book II, sct. 6.

29. Dunn, *Political Theory*, p. 106.

30. Locke, *Two Treatises*, Book VII, sct. 87.

31. Dunn, *Political Theory*, p. 127.

32. Locke, *Two Treatises*, Book XI, sct. 135.

33. *Ibid.*, Book XI, sct. 135.

34. Dunn, *Political Theory*, p. 103.

35. *Ibid.*, p. 260.

Notes

36. Charles Taylor, *Sources of the Self: The Making of Modern Identity* (Cambridge: Harvard University Press, 1989).

37. Alasdair MacIntyre, *Whose Justice, Which Rationality* (Notre Dame, IN: University of Notre Dame Press, 1988), p. 268.

38. Adam Ferguson, *An Essay on the History of Civil Society*, 5th ed. (London, 1782), p. 57.

39. Adam Smith, *Theory of Moral Sentiments* (Indianapolis: Liberty Classics, 1982), p. 50.

40. Albert Hirschman, *The Passions and the Interests* (Princeton, NJ: Princeton University Press, 1979), p. 109. See also Nicholas Phillipson, "Adam Smith as Civil Moralist," in I. Hont and M. Ignatieff (eds.), *Wealth and Virtue: The Shaping of Political Economy in the Scottish Enlightenment* (Cambridge: Cambridge University Press, 1985, pp. 179–202.

41. Smith, *Moral Sentiments*, p. 50.

42. Ferguson, *Civil Society*, p. 52.

43. *Ibid.*, p. 53.

44. Emile Durkheim, "The Dualism of Human Nature and Its Social Condition," in R. Bellah (ed.), *Emile Durkheim on Morality and Society* (Chicago: University of Chicago Press, 1973), pp. 149–68.

45. MacIntyre, *Whose Justice*, pp. 241–80.

46. Ferguson, *Civil Society*, p. 95.

47. I. Hont and M. Ignatieff, "Needs and Justice in the Wealth of Nations: An Introductory Essay," pp. 1–44 in Hont and Ignatieff, *Wealth and Virtue*, p. 11.

48. Jacob Viner, *The Role of Providence in the Social Order* (Princeton, NJ: Princeton University Press,1972), pp. 55–85.

49. Ferguson, *Civil Society*, p. 365.

50. Anthony Third Earl of Shaftesbury, *Characteristics of Men, Manners, Opinions and Times* (New York: Bobbs-Merrill, 1964).

51. Ferguson, *Civil Society*, p. 58.

52. *Ibid.*, p. 45.

53. *Ibid.*, p. 44.

54. MacIntyre, *Whose Justice*, pp. 218–325.

55. David Hume, *A Treatise of Human Nature*, ed. H. D. Aiken (New York: Macmillan, 1948), Book III, Pt. I, section 1, p. 185.

56. David Hume, *An Enquiry Concerning the Principles of Morals*, in A. MacIntyre (ed.), *Hume's Ethical Writings* (Notre Dame, IN: Notre Dame University Press, 1965), appendix I, p. 131.

57. Hume, *Treatise*, Book III, Pt. II, section 2, pp. 69–82.

58. *Ibid.*, p. 225.

59. *Ibid.*, Book III, Pt. II, section 3, p. 63.

60. *Ibid.*, p. 65.

61. *Ibid.*, section 2, p. 63. I believe this point is central and, I would hesitatingly add, slightly obfuscated in MacIntyre's claim that Hume failed to follow his own strictures in clearly distinguishing "ought" from "is." See A. MacIntyre, "Hume on 'Is' and 'Ought,' " in V. C. Chappell (ed.), *Hume* (New York: Anchor Books, 1959), pp. 245–64. MacIntyre claims that Hume does indeed derive moral predicates (ought) from universally valid rules of conduct (is) through the individual obligation to follow such rule. However, as Hume makes clear (and MacIntyre admits), the necessity to follow these rules is in the individual's self-interest. The threat of universal savagery that would follow the dissolution of society and of the universal rules of justice is what makes every individual person "a gainer" in following such rules. Following the rules of justice and property is, as Hume never tires of emphasizing, founded on men's cognizance of their own interests. Following this they become a convention and are assimilated into social morality as a virtue. MacIntyre, of course, bases his claim of Hume's lapse on this introjection of reason (and hence appreciation of what is) into an analysis of "ought." The more crucial point, I believe, is that the "ought" is not articulated in terms of a universal or constitutive good, but is itself posited in terms of particular interests. Whatever the logical status of this "ought," it is sociologically distinct from an "ought" founded on universal principles of morality or of the good. It cannot therefore be thought of in the same terms as justice or the moral good which characterized philosophical theory (including that of the Scottish Enlightenment) prior to Hume. With this break any attempt to posit society as a normative order (as opposed to simply the interlocking of mutual and particular interests) becomes impossible.
62. Hume, *Treatise*, Book III, Pt. II, section 2, p. 64.
63. *Ibid.*
64. Ferguson, *Civil Society* (*supra*, n. 38), pp. 364–367.
65. Hume, *Treatise*, Book III, Pt. II, section 2, pp. 61–62.
66. *Ibid.*, section 4, p. 86.
67. See Immanuel Kant, *The Metaphysical Elements of Justice*, Pt. I of *The Metaphysics of Morals* (1794), trans. J. Ladd (New York: Bobbs-Merrill, 1965).
68. Susan Meld Shell, *The Rights of Reason* (Toronto: University of Toronto Press, 1980), p. 83.
69. Immanuel Kant, *Critique of Practical Reason*, trans. L. W. Beck (New York: Macmillan, 1985), p. 90.
70. Immanuel Kant, "Idea for a Universal History from a Cosmopolitan Point of View (1784), trans L. Beck, pp. 11–16 in L. Beck (ed.), *Immanuel Kant on History* (New York: Bobbs-Merrill, 1963).
71. Immanuel Kant, *Anthropology From a Pragmatic Point of View*, (1797), trans. M. Gregor, (The Hague: Nijoff, 1974), para. 325; *idem*, "Conjectural beginnings of Human History (1786), trans. E. Fackenheim, pp. 53–68 in Beck, *Kant*, para. 115–17; *idem*, *On the Old Saw: That What May Be Right in Theory Wont Work in Practice*, trans. E. B. Ashton (Philadelphia: University of Pennsylvania Press, 1974).

72. John Laursen, "The Subversive Kant: The Vocabulary of Public and Publicity," *Political Theory*, vol. 14, no. 4 (November 1986), pp. 584–603.

73. Hannah Arendt, *Lectures on Kant's Political Philosophy* Chicago: University of Chicago Press, 1982), p. 60.

74. Immanuel Kant, "What Is Enlightenment" (1784), trans. L. Beck, pp. 3–10 in Beck, *Kant*, 1963.

75. John Rundell, *Origins of Modernity* (Madison: University of Wisconsin Press, 1987), p. 28.

76. Kant, *Metaphysical Elements of Justice*, para. 230–32.

77. *Ibid.*, para. 237–38.

78. Shell, *Rights of Reason*, p. 123.

79. Kant, *Metaphysical Elements of Justice*, para. 217–28.

80. Rundell, *Origins*, p. 35–55.

81. On this aspect of Rousseau's thought, see Robert Shaver, "Rousseau and Recognition," *Social Theory and Practice*, vol. 15, no. 3 (Fall 1989), pp. 26–28.

82. G. W. F. Hegel, *The Philosophy of Right*, (1821), trans. T. Knox (Oxford: Oxford University Press, 1952), pp. 4–57.

83. *Ibid.*, pp. 105–55; G. W. F. Hegel, *Hegel and the Human Spirit: A Translation of the Jena Lectures on Philosophy of Spirit (1805–1806) with Commentary*, trans. L. Rauch (Detroit: Wayne State University Press, 1983), pp. 99–118.

84. Hegel, *Human Spirit*, p. 118.

85. J. M. Bernstein, "From Self-consciousness to Community: Act and Recognition in the Master–Slave Relationship," pp. 14–39 in Z. A. Pelczynski (ed.), *The State and Civil Society: Studies in Hegel's Political Philosopohy* (Cambridge: Cambridge University Press), 1984.

86. Hegel, *Philosophy of Right*, para. 4, pg. 20.

87. Joachim Ritter, *Hegel and the French Revolution* (Cambridge, MA: MIT Press, 1984), p. 158.

88. Hegel, *Philosophy of Right*, para. 7, p. 23.

89. *Ibid.*, para. 182, pp. 122–23.

90. *Ibid.*, para. 184, p. 123.

91. *Ibid.*

92. *Ibid.*, para 185, p. 123.

93. *Ibid.*, para. 238, p. 148; para 225, p. 154.

94. *Ibid.*, para. 255, p. 154.

95. *Ibid.*, para. 288, p. 189.

96. In this context it is interesting to see how Hegel ascribes to the civil servant a type of inner motivation that we have become familiar with through Weber's analysis of the Protestant Ethic. Take the following quote for example: "The state does not count on the optional, discretionary, services (e.g. on justice administered by knights errant). It is just because such services are

optional and discretionary that the state cannot rely on them, for casual servants may fail for private reasons to fulfil their duties completely, or they may arbitrarily decide not to fulfil them at all but pursue their private ends instead. What the service of the state really requires is that men shall forgo the selfish and capricious satisfaction of their subjective ends; by this very sacrifice they acquire the right to find their satisfaction in, but only in, the dutiful discharge of their public function. . . . It follows that a man's tenure of his civil service post is not contractual though his appointment involves a consent and an undertaking on both sides. A civil servant is not appointed, like an agent, to perform a single casual act of service; on the contrary, he concentrates his main interests (not only his particular interests, but his mental interests also) on his relation to his work. Similarly, the work imposed upon him and entrusted to him is not merely a particular thing, external in character. . . . The work of a civil servant . . . is as such a value in and for itself. . . . Those who are entrusted with affairs of state find in its universal power the protection they need against another subjective phenomenon, namely the personal passions of the governed, whose private interests, &c., suffer injury as the interest of the state is made to prevail against them." Ibid., Zusatz 294, pp. 191–92. Here we see not only some familiar elements from Weber's analysis of bureaucracy (continuity of administrative business, separation of incumbent from office) but, more central, a highly complex psychologically determined theory of motivation toward a model of rational activity. In Weber's case this dealt with economic activity, in Hegel's writings with State administration. Common to both is an attempt to conceptualize different types of social action that emerged with the modern nation-state and bearing on the workings of civil society. The market, and with it rational-interest-motivated economic action, is, after all, as we have seen, paradigmatic of the type of individual exchange (and recognition) typified by civil society. In curious ways the Hegelian and Weberian perspectives complement each other, dealing as they do with a psychological theory of inner motivation as a central determining element in the workings of civil society (or, more properly in respect to Hegel, of its final aufhebung). We must bear in mind, however, that while both are attempts to understand crucial aspects of the modern world, the difference between them is still Weber's value-neutral science as opposed to Hegel's positive and normative evaluation of the class of civil servants as embodying universal interests.

97. Karl Marx, Preface and Introduction to A Contribution to The Critique of Political Economy (Peking: Foreign Languages Press, 1976), p. 10.
98. Ibid., p. 9. Emphasis added.
99. Friedrich Engels, "Karl Marx: A Contribution to the Critique of Political Economy," in Marx, Critique, p. 54.
100. Karl Marx, "Contribution to the Critique of Hegel's Philosophy of Law," in K. Marx and F. Engels, Collected Works, (New York: International Publishers, 1975), vol. 3, p. 8.

101. Jean Cohen, *Class and Civil Society* (Cambridge, MA: MIT Press, 1982), pp. 29–36.

102. Karl Marx, "On the Jewish Question," in K. Marx and F. Engels, *Collected Works* (Moscow: Progress Publishers, 1975), vol. 3, pg. 153.

103. *Ibid.* Emphasis in original.

104. *Ibid.*, p. 162.

105. *Ibid.*, p. 164.

106. *Ibid.*, p. 165.

107. *Ibid.*, p. 166.

108. *Ibid.*

109. *Ibid.*

110. *Ibid.*

111. *Ibid.*, p. 168.

112. Lesek Kolakowski, "The Myth of Human Self-Identity," in L. Kolakowski and Hampshire (eds.), *The Socialist Idea* (New York: Basic Books, 1975).

113. *Times Literary Supplement* (London), June 21, 1991, p. 22.

CHAPTER 2   Sources of Civil Society: Reason and the Individual

1. Giambattista Vico, *The New Science of Politics*, trans. Bergin and Fisch (Ithaca, NY, 1948); I. Berlin, *Vico and Herder* (London, 1946); A. R. Caponigri, *Time and Idea: The Theory of History of Giambattista Vico* (London, 1953). On civic humanism, see J. G. A. Pocock, *The Machiavellian Moment* (Princeton, NJ: Princeton University Press, 1975); Felix Rabb, *The English Face of Machiavelli* (London, 1964); Caroline Robbins, *The Eighteenth Century Commonwealthmen* (Cambridge, 1959).

2. On Burke's traditionalism, see G. Sabine. *A History of Political Theory* (New York: Rinhart & Winston, 1961), pp. 607–19. For a different interpretation, see J. G. A. Pocock, "Burke and the Ancient Constitution: A Problem in the History of Ideas," pp. 203–32 in J. G. A. Pocock, *Politics, Language and Time* (New York, 1973). For Hegel's concept of World Spirit see G. W. F. Hegel, *The Philosophy of History* (New York, 1956). On the "moral" aspects of Marx's thought, see Istvan Meszaros, *Marx's Theory of Alienation* (London, 1970). For a good recent synthesis of Marx's conception of history, see G. A. Cohen, *Karl Marx's Theory of History: A Defense* (Oxford, 1978).

3. Knud Haakonssen, "Hugo Grotius and the History of Political Thought," *Political Theory*, vol. 13, no. 2 (May 1985), p. 248.

4. Otto Gierke, *Political Theory of the Middle Ages* (Boston: Beacon, 1958), p. 75.

5. Wolfgang Schluchter, *The Rise of Western Rationalism* (Berkeley: University of California Press, 1981), p. 104.

6. S. N. Eisenstadt, "The Axial Age: The Emergence of Transcendental Visions and the Rise of the Clerics," *European Journal of Sociology*, no. 23, 1982, pp. 294–314.

7. Eric Voeglin, *Order and History*, vol. 1 (Baton Rouge: Louisiana State University Press, 1954).

8. Benjamin Schwartz (ed.), "Wisdom, Revelation and Doubt: Perspectives on the First Millennium BC," *Daedalus*, Spring 1975.

9. Eisenstadt, "Axial Age," p. 300.

10. Robert Bellah, "Religious Evolution," *American Sociological Review*, vol. 29 (1964), pp. 358–74.

11. Max Weber, "Social Psychology of World Religions," in H. Gerth and C. W. Mills (eds.), *From Max Weber: Essays in Sociology* (New York: Oxford University Press, 1958). pp. 44–45.

12. Wolfgang Schluchter, "The Paradox of Rationalization," in W. Schluchter and G. Roth, *Max Weber's Vision of History* (Berkeley: University of California Press, 1979), p. 23.

13. S. N. Eisenstadt, "Heterodoxy and the Dynamics of Civilizations," *Proceedings of the American Philosophical Society*, vol. 128 (1984), pp. 105–6; Schluchter, *Rise of Western Rationalizm*, p. 43; R. Lovin and F. Reynolds (eds.), *Cosmogony and Ethical Order* (Chicago, 1985).

14. Schluchter, *Rise of Western Rationalism*, pp. 44–48; D. A. Knight, "Cosmogony and Order in the Hebrew Tradition," pp. 133–57 in Lovin and Reynolds, *Cosmogony*; Hans Betz, "Cosmology and Ethics in in the Sermon on the Mount," pp. 158–76 in Lovin and Reynolds, *Cosmogony*.

15. S. N. Eisenstadt, "This Worldly Transcendentalism and the Structuring of the World: Weber's Religion of China and the Format of Chinese History and Civilization," *Journal of Development Studies*, vol. 1 (1985), pp. 168–86; Schluchter, *Rise of Western Rationalism*, pp. 47, 67; Benjamin Schwartz, "Transcendence in Ancient China," *Daedalus*, 1975, pp. 57–69; *idem, The World of Thought in Ancient China* (Cambridge, 1985), pp. 56–134; John Smith, "The Individual in the Judeo-Christian Tradition," pp. 251–67 in C. Moore (ed.), *The Status of the Individual in East and West* (Honolulu, 1968).

16. Marcel Mauss, "A Category of the Human Mind: The Notion of Person, the Notion of 'Self,' " in Marcel Mauss, *Sociology and Philosophy* (London: Routledge & Kegan Paul, 1979), pp. 85–89.

17. Louis Dumont, "A Modified View of Our Origins: The Christian Beginning of Modern Individualism," *Religion*, vol. 12 (1982), pp. 1–27.

18. Ernst Troeltsch, *The Social Teachings of the Christian Churches*, 2 vols. (New York: Macmillan, 1931), vol. 1 pp. 110–11; Adolf Harnack, *History of Dogma*, (New York: Dover, 1961), vol. 1, pp. 203–22; Jaroslav Pelikan, *The Christian Tradition: A History of the Development of Dogma*, 4 vols. (Chicago: University of Chicago Press, 1971), vol. 1 pp. 278–331.

19. On the Eucharist community, see Rudolf Bultman, *Primitive Christianity* (Philadelphia, 1956), p. 187.

20. For discussion of the different views on the "real presence" in the Eucharist among the English reformers, see Francis Clark, *Eucharist Sacrifice and the Reformation* (London, 1960), pp. 127–76.

215

Notes

21. See David Little, *Religion, Order and Law* (Chicago: University of Chicago Press, 1984), p. 41.

22. Troeltsch, *Social Teachings*, vol. 2, pp. 590–92.

23. John Calvin, *Institutes of the Christian Religion*, ed. John McNeill (Philadelphia, 1960), vol. 4, I, p. 5.

24. E. Troeltsch, *Social Teachings*, vol. 2, pp. 596–97. In Calvin's thought, the freedom within which the true body of believers lived must be differentiated from the state of existing political society and from the unregenerate, among whom the command of God had to be enforced by coercion until the coming of the Kingdom of God. At its coming, according to Calvin, the separation between those "in Christ" participating in the world of freedom and those still subject to coercion would be dissolved.

25. Donald Kelly, *The Beginning of Ideology* (London, 1981), p. 80.

26. Richard Rogers, *Seven Treatises . . . Called the Practice of Christianitie*, 2d ed. (London, 1605), pp. 497–98.

27. It must be noted that when approaching the realm of political society Calvin realized the inability of identifying the Church visible with the invisible Church of the elect and therefore accepted the necessity of ministerial prerogative and power. These formed the basis of the particular notion of Calvinist "theocracy" in which the powers of Church and State were to work together toward the establishment of God's Kingdom on earth. And, in fact, the different forms of national covenants, whether the Geneva Confession of Faith (1536), the Scottish National Covenant (1638), the English Solemn League and Covenant (1643), or those of the New England town churches, effectively attempted just such a total reformulation of collective life.

28. Talcott Parsons, "Christianity and Modern Industrial Society," in E. Tiryakian (ed.), *Sociological Theory* (New York: Harper & Row, 1967), p. 51.

29. Max Weber, *The Protestant Ethic and the Theory of Capitalism* (New York: Charles Scribner's Sons, 1958). For one of the most significant and recent criticism of the Weberian thesis, see M. MacKinnon, "Calvinism and the Infallibility of Grace" and "Weber's Explanation of Calvinism," *British Journal of Sociology*, vol. XXXIX, no. 2 (June 1988), pp. 143–210.

30. Benjamin Nelson, *The Idea of Usury: From Tribal Brotherhood to Universal Otherhood* (Chicago: University of Chicago Press, 1969), p. 241.

31. Benjamin Nelson, "Self-Images and Systems of Spiritual Direction in the History of European Civilization," in S. Klausner (ed.), *The Quest for Self-Control: Classical Philosophies and Scientific Research* (New York: Free Press, 1965), p. 71.

32. *Ibid.*

33. Benjamin Nelson, "Conscience and the Making of Early Modern Culture: The Protestant Ethic Beyond Max Weber," *Social Research*, vol. 36 (1969), pp. 16–17.

34. Pocock, *Machiavellian Moment* (*supra*, n. 1), p. 396; W. Hunt, *The Puritan*

Moment: The Coming of Revolution in an English County (Cambridge: Cambridge University Press, 1985), pp. 90–91, 131–35; M. Watts, *The Dissenters* (Oxford: Clarendon Press, 1978), pp. 30, 31, 41, 42, 55, 56; J. McGee, *The Godly Man in Stuart England* (New Haven: Yale University Press, 1976).

35. On the restructuring of the political order in Calvinism, see Little, *Religion, Order and Law* (*supra*, n. 1), pp. 62–80; Michael Waltzer, *The Revolution of the Saints* (Cambridge: Cambridge University Press, 1965), pp. 30–57; Troeltsch, *Social Teachings* (*supra*, no. 18), vol. 2, pp. 617–25.

36. Dumont, "Modified View of Our Origins" (*supra*, no. 17).

37. John Winthrop, *Winthrop Papers* (Boston: Massachusetts Historical Society, 1931), vol. 2, p. 283.

38. John Winthrop, "A Reply to an Answer Made to a Declaration . . ." (1637), in Thomas Hutchinson (ed.), *A Collection of Original Papers Relative to the History of the Colony of Massachusetts Bay* (Boston, 1764), pp. 100–101.

39. John Cotton, "Copy of a Letter to Lord Say and Seale in the Year 1636," in Hutchinson, *Original Papers*, pp. 414–15.

40. Quoted in Kenneth Lockridge, *A New England Town: The First Hundred Years* (New York: Norton, 1970), pp. 4–5.

41. John Davenport, *A Discourse About Civil Government in a New Plantation Whose Design is Religion* (Cambridge, 1663), pp. 14–15, 45.

42. Edward Johnson, *Wonder Working Providence of Sions Saviour in Neew England* [1654] (New York: Delmar, 1974), p. 46.

43. On the relation of biblical law to English law among the New England Puritans, see George Haskins, *Law and Authority in Early Massachusetts* (Hamden, CT: Archon Book, 1960), pp. 17–32.

44. *The Book of General Lauues and Libertyes Concerning the Inhabitants of Massachussets* (Boston, 1648), p. A2.

45. *Ibid.*

46. *Ibid.*

47. *Ibid.*

48. On these distinctions, see Haskins, *Law and Authority*, pp. 158–62.

49. Thomas Sheppard and John Allin, *A Defense of an Answer. . . .* (London, 1648), p. 86.

50. This expression is of course taken from Perry Miller's collection of essays, *Errand into the Wilderness* (New York: Harper & Row, 1964), which supplemented his two-volume magisterial study of New England Puritanism, *The New England Mind: The Seventeenth Century* and *The New England Mind: From Colony to Province* (Boston: Belknap Press, 1953).

51. J. Bossy, *Christianity in the West 1400–1700* (Oxford: Oxford University Press, 1985), p. 108; E. Battis, *Saints and Sectaries: Anne Hutchinson and the Antinomian Controversy* (Chapel Hill: University of North Carolina Press, 1963), pp. 330–44; D. Hall, *The Antinomian Controversy: A Documentary History* (Middletown, CT: Wesleyan University Press, 1968), p. 95.

52. On the process of economic change, see Bernard Bailyn, *The New England Merchants in the Seventeenth Century* (Cambridge: Harvard University Press, 1955).

53. The changes of midcentury, revolving around the Half-Way Covenant, the neglect of the test of relation, the Stoddard–Mather debates, the increasing sacramentalism of Church practice, the doctrine of preparationism (for the Lord's Supper), the "new Baptismal Piety," and the practice of covenant ownings, have been studied by generations of New England historians. For their role in the development of new terms of individual identities and values, see Adam Seligman, "Inner Worldly Individualism and the Institutionalization of Puritanism in late 17th century New England, *British Journal of Sociology*, vol. 41, no. 1 (1990), pp. 537–57.

54. On the increasing sacramental character of the New England Congregational Churches, see E. B. Holifield, *The Covenant Sealed: The Development of Puritan Sacramental Theology in Old and New England 1570–1720* (New Haven: Yale University Press, 1974), esp. ch. 8. Illustrative of this process was the acceptance of the Saybrook Platform of 1705, which is discussed by D. Hall, *The Faithful Shepherd* (New York: Norton, 1972), p. 274; R. Bushman, *From Puritan to Yankee* (Cambridge: Harvard University Press, 1967), p. 151.

55. On the Awakening, see Bushman, *From Puritan to Yankee.*

56. It should be noted that Weber himself noted the "loss of the sect character" among Independents in New England through such compromises as the Half Way Covenant, which made membership a birthright. My claim here is that this sect character or elements of it were not so much lost as transferred from the realm of the Church to that of the civil polity. Max Weber, *Economy and Society* (Berkeley: University of California Press, 1978), p. 208.

57. See Paul Lucas, *Valley of Discord: Church and Society Along the Connecticut River, 1636–1662* (Middletown, CT: Wesleyan University Press, 1968), pp. 126, 242, 244.

58. John Wise, *Vindication of the Government of New England Churches* (Boston, 1717), pp. 32–47.

59. Carl Becker, *The Declaration of Independence* (New York: Vintage Press, 1958), p. 78.

60. John Adams, *The Papers of John Adams,* 4 vols. ed. R. Taylor, (Cambridge: Belknap Press, 1977), vol. 4, pp. 291–93.

61. *Ibid.,* p. 230.

62. James Wilson, *The Works of James Wilson,* ed. B. Wilson, (Philadelphia: Bronson & Channing, 1804), vol. 3, p. 205.

63. *Ibid.,* vol. 1, p. 124.

64. E. L. Tuveson, *Redeemer Nation: The Idea of America's Millennial Role* Chicago: University of Chicago Press, 1968).

65. Alan Heimart, *Religion and the American Mind,* Cambridge: Harvard University Press, 1966), p. 61.

66. Tuveson, *Redeemer Nation*, p. 23.

67. Heimart, *American Mind*; N. O. Hatch, *The Sacred Cause of Liberty: Republican Thought and the Millennium in Revolutionary New England* (New Haven: Yale University Press, 1977); Ruth Bloch, *Visionary Republic: Millennial Themes in American Thought 1765–1800* (London: Cambridge University Press, 1985).

68. Pocock, *Machiavellian Moment* (*supra*, no. 1).

69. John Adams, *Dissertation on Cannon and Feudal Law* (Boston, 1765), p. 126.

70. David Lovejoy, *Religious Enthusiasm in the New World* (Cambridge: Harvard University Press, 1985), p. 227.

71. Tuveson, *Redeemer Nation*, p. 24.

72. Pocock, *Machiavellian Moment*, p. 512.

73. Adams, *Papers* (*supra*, n. 60), vol. 2.

74. *Ibid.*, pp. 230, 291–93, 311–12.

75. Robert Bellah, "Civil Religion in America," *Daedalus*, vol. 96 (Winter 1967), pp. 1–21.

76. Wilson, *Papers* (*supra*, n. 62), vol. 1, p. 106.

77. Robert Bellah, *The Broken Covenant* (New York: Seabury Press, 1975).

78. R. W. B. Lewis, *The American Adam* (Chicago: University of Chicago Press, 1958).

79. F. McDonald, *Novus Ordo Seclorum* (Chapel Hill: University of North Carolina Press, 1978), p. 58.

80. Bernard Bailyn, *Pamphlets of the American Revolution 1740–1776.* (Cambridge: Belknap Press, 1965), p. 27.

81. *Ibid.*, p. 559.

82. *Ibid.*, pp. 426, 441.

83. Adams, *Papers*, vol. 2, p. 140.

84. *Ibid.*, vol. 1, pp. 333–53, 344.

85. Some aspects of this are dealt with in Adam Seligman, "Charisma and the Transformation of Grace in the Early Modern Era," *Social Research*, vol. 58, no. 3 (1991), pp. 591–620.

86. Yehoshua Arieli, *Individualism and Nationalism in American Life* (Cambridge: Harvard University Press, 1964), p. 83.

87. *Ibid.*

88. Georg Jellinek, *The Declaration of the Rights of Man and of Citizens: A Contribution to Modern Constitutional History* (Westport, CT: Hyperion Press, 1979), p. 48.

89. *Ibid.*, p. 53.

90. *Ibid.*, p. 80.

91. *Ibid.*, p. 62.

92. *Ibid.*, p. 61.

93. *Ibid.*, p. 92.

94. *Ibid.*, p. 9.

95. Arieli, *Individualism and Nationalism.*

96. This aspect of Kant's thought and the interrelated nature of personhood and conscience and moral action are discussed in Ludwig Siep, "Person and Law in Kant and Hegel," in R. Shurmann (ed.), *The Public Realm* (Albany: SUNY Press, 1989), pp. 82–104, from which the following quotation is taken (p. 84).

97. Emile Durkheim. *Sociology and Philosophy* (New York: Free Press, 1974), p. 54.

98. Benjamin Whichcote, "The Uses of Reason in Matters of Religion," pp. 42–61 in C. A. Patrides (ed.), *The Cambridge Platonists* (Cambridge: Cambridge University Press, 1969), p. 46.

99. Mauss, "Category of Human Mind" (*supra*, n. 16).

100. Otto Gierke, *Natural Law and the Theory of Society 500–1800* (Cambridge, 1934).

101. I Corinthians 12:12,13.

102. Sheldon Wohlin, *Politics and Vision* (Boston: Little, Brown & Co., 1960), p. 101.

103. Gierke, *Political Theories of Middle Ages* (*supra*, n. 4), p. 10.

104. This is essentially the same argument offered by Hegel in the *Philosophy of Right*, where he defines modern existence in civil society in terms of the "ego coming to be apprehended as a universal person." Para. 209, p. 134.

105. Max Weber, *Economy and Society*, vol. 2 (Berkeley: University of California Press, 1978), p. 556.

106. Nelson, *Idea of Usury* (*supra*, n. 30).

107. Jürgen Habermas, *Theory and Practice* (Boston: Beacon Press, 1974), pp. 132–33.

108. *Ibid.*

109. Gierke, *Natural Law*, p. 40. Emphasis added.

110. G. W. F. Hegel, *The Philosophy of Right* (1821), trans. T. Knox (Oxford: Oxford University Press, 1962), p. 134.

111. Albrecht Wellmer, "Models of Freedom in the Modern World," pp. 227–252 in M. Kelly (ed.), *Hermeneutics and Critical Theory in Ethics and Politics* (Cambridge: MIT Press, 1990), p. 238.

112. Jellinek, *Declaration of Rights of Man* (*supra*, n. 88), pp. 74–75.

CHAPTER 3   Civil Society, Citizenship, and the Representation of Society

1. Adam Przeworski, *Capitalism and Social Democracy* Cambridge: Cambridge University Press, 1985), p. 32.

2. S. M. Lipset, "Radicalism or Reformism: The Sources of Working Class Politics," *The American Political Science Review*, vol. 77 (1983), p. 6.

3. H. F. Moorhouse, "The Political Incorporation of the British Working Class: An Interpretation," *Sociology*, vol. 7, no. 3 (1973), p. 345; J. M. Barbalet, *Citizenship* (Minneapolis: University of Minnesota Press, 1988), pp. 83–84.

4. These figures and the relative proportion of the electorate that increased after each reform bill are disputed among historians. For different figures, even more limited, see Samuel Bowles and Herbert Gintis, *Democracy and Capitalism: Property, Community and the Contradictions of Modern Social Thought* (New York: Basic Books, 1987), p. 43.

5. The classic query into this exceptionalism was made by Werner Sombart in *Why There is No Socialism in the USA* (London: Macmillan, 1975). The theoretical challenge of this problem has been taken up on numerous occasions by Lipset. For some of his contributions to this debate, see Seymour Martin Lipset, "American Exceptionalism in the North American Perspective: Why the United States Has Withstood the World Socialist Movement," in G. Adams (ed.), *The Idea of America* (Cambridge: Harvard University Press, 1977); *idem*, "American Exceptionalism," in M. Novak (ed.), *Capitalism and Socialism: A Theological Inquiry* (Washington, DC: AE. 1, 1979), pp. 34–60. For a somewhat different argument, see Aristide Zolberg, "How Many Exceptionalisms," in I. Katznelson and A. Zolberg (eds.), *Working Class Formation: 19th Century Patterns in Western Europe and the United States* (Princeton, NJ: Princeton University Press, 1986), pp. 397–455.

6. Lipset, "Radicalism or Reformism," p. 2.

7. Selig Perlman. *A Theory of the Labor Movement* (New York: A. M. Kelly, 1928), p. 167.

8. Arnold Mayer, *The Persistence of the Old Regimes: Europe to the Great War* (New York: Pantheon Books, 1981), p. 135.

9. Lipset, "Radicalism or Reformism," p. 2.

10. Paul Jacobs, "What Can We Expect from the Unions?" in I. Howe (ed.), *The Radical Papers* (New York: Doubleday, 1966), pp. 262–64.

11. Rienhart Bendix, *National-Building and Citizenship* (Berkeley: University of California Press, 1977), p. 96.

12. Leo Sampson, "Americanism as Surrogate socialism," in J. Laslett and S. M. Lipset, (eds.), *Failure of a Dream*, 1st ed. (New York: Anchor Books, 1974), p. 426.

13. The following argument is developed in much greater length in Adam Seligman, "The Failure of Socialism in the United States: A Reconsideration," in S. N. Eisenstadt *et al.*, *Center Formation: Protest Movements and Class Structure in Europe and the United States* (London: Pinter Press, 1987), pp. 90–117.

14. See, for example, F. Alexander, *Moving Frontiers: An American Theme and Its Application to Australian History* (Melbourne: Melbourne University Press, 1947); P. A. Sharp, "Three Frontiers: Some Comparative Studies of Canadian, American and Australian Settlement," *Pacific Historical Review*, vol. 24

(1955); P. J. Coleman, "The New Zealand Frontier and the Turner Thesis," *Pacific Historical Review,* vol. 27 (1958), pp. 221–37.

15. Stephan Thernstrom, "Socialism and Social Mobility," in Laslett and Lipset, *Failure of a Dream,* p. 550.

16. Sampson, "Americanism as Surrogate socialism," p. 426.

17. Bendix, *Nation-Building,* p. 115.

18. Lipset, "American Exceptionalism in North American Perspective" (*supra,* n. 5).

19. Samuel Huntington, *American Politics: The Promise of Disharmony* (Cambridge, MA: Belknap Press, 1981).

20. T. H. Marshall, *Class, Citizenship and Social Development* (Westport, CT: Greenwood Press, 1973), pp. 71–72.

21. See Massimo Paci, "Long Waves in the Development of Welfare Systems," in Charles Maier (ed.), *Changing Boundaries of the Political* (Cambridge: Cambridge University Press, 1987), pp. 179–99.

22. Michael Walzer, *Spheres of Justice* (New York: Basic Books, 1983), provides one of the foremost examples of just such an argument over the nuts and bolts of the contemporary meaning of citizenship.

23. See Paul Starr and Ellen Immergut, "Health Care and the Boundaries of Politics," in Maier, *Changing Boundaries,* pp. 221–54.

24. For example, in Hungary the Alliance of Young Democrats (FIDESZ), the most modern and Western-oriented of Hungarian political parties, has no principled defense of welfare entitlements (or of health care either) in its party platform.

25. The Speenhamland system was ultimately a total failure, leading to the pauperization of whole strata of rural men and women. The failure of this system and its replacement by the Poor Law Amendment of 1834 as integral to the building of a capitalist economy in England has been notably analyzed by Karl Polanyi in *The Great Transformation: The Political and Economic Origins of Our Times,* (Boston: Beacon Press, 1957), pp. 77–110. One of the many important points made by Polanyi turns on the inherent contradiction of administering poor relief on the principles of local solidarity and mutuality in an economic system no longer defined by traditional norms and obligations but by capitalist market relations. That this later principle carries its own set of contradictions is of course the point we wish to emphasize here.

26. Marshall, *Class, Citizenship,* p. 80.

27. Emile Durkheim, "The Dualism of Human Nature and Its Social Condition," in R. Bellah (ed.), *Emile Durkheim on Morality and Society* (Chicago: University of Chicago Press, 1973), pp. 161–62.

28. Emile Durkheim, "Individualism and the Intellectuals," in Bellah, *Durkheim on Morality,* p. 44.

29. See, for example, Emile Durkheim, *The Division of Labor in Society* (New York: Free Press, 1964), pp. 200–229.

30. Steven Lukes, *Emile Durkheim: His Life and Work* (Stanford, CA: Stanford University Press, 1985), pp. 320–60.

31. This position is explicated in Talcott Parsons, *The Structure of Social Action* (New York: Free Press, 1968), pp. 315–16.

32. *Ibid.*, p. 333.

33. Durkheim, "Individualism and Intellectuals," p. 52.

34. Lukes, *Emile Durkheim*, pp. 337–39.

35. Durkheim, "Individualism and Intellectuals," p. 45.

36. Lukes, *Emile Durkheim*, pp. 540–41.

37. Emile Durkheim, *Socialism* (New York: Collier Books, 1962), pp. 245–46.

38. Emile Durkheim, *Professional Ethics and Civic Morals* (Westport, CT: Greenwood Press, 1958), p. 69.

39. *Ibid.*, p. 65.

40. *Ibid.*

41. *Ibid.*

42. Durkheim, *Socialism*, pp. 34–35.

43. *Ibid.*, p. 247.

44. On socialism as a way of introducing morality into the economic sphere, see Lukes, *Emile Durkheim*, p. 246.

45. Durkheim, *Socialism*, p. 48.

46. *Ibid.*, p. 285.

47. Durkheim, *Professional Ethics*, p. 64.

48. *Ibid.*, pp. 64, 68.

49. *Ibid.*, p. 68.

50. Emile Durkheim, *Moral Education: A Study of the Theory and Application of the Sociology of Education* (New York: Free Press, 1961), p. 122.

51. Parsons, *Structure*, (*supra*, n. 31), p. 389.

52. Emile Durkheim, *Sociology and Philosophy* (New York: Free Press, 1974); Talcott Parsons, "Durkheim on Religion Revisited," in Talcott Parsons, *Action Theory and the Human Condition* (New York: Free Press, 1978), pp. 213–32.

53. Durkheim, "Individualism and Intellectuals" (*supra*, no. 28), p. 46.

54. Reference is here being made to Durkheim's analysis of modern societies, which is what is of interest to us. The above interpretation is not meant to reflect on Durkheim's analysis of conditions of "mechanical solidarity."

55. Durkheim, *Moral Education*, p. 19.

56. Thus, "if society is to be considered as the normal government of moral conduct then it must be possible to see in it something other than the sum of individuals, it must constitute a being sui-generis." *Ibid.*, p. 60.

57. Durkheim, *Sociology and Philosophy*, p. 54.

58. Max Weber, *Economy and Society* (Berkeley: University of California Press, 1978), 1209.

223

59. Max Weber, "Science as a Vocation," in H. H. Gerth and C. W. Mills (eds.), *From Max Weber: Essays in Sociology* (New York: Oxford, 1958), p. 155.

60. Jean-François Lyotard, *The Differend* (Minneapolis: University of Minnesota Press, 1988), p. 37.

61. Michel Foucault, *The Order of Things* (New York: Vintage Press, 1973), p. 387.

62. Weber, *Economy and Society,* p. 1209.

63. Jürgen Habermas, *The Structural Transformation of the Public Sphere* trans. Thomas Burger (Cambridge: MIT Press), ms. p. 72.

64. An especially enlightening historical analysis of this process, where the individual was endowed with universal significance and the public culture of citizenry united with a new idea of the individual and the role of this transformation in laying the groundwork for revolutionary practice and the emergence of modern politics, can be found in Roger Chartier, *The Cultural Origins of the French Revolution* (Durham, NC: Duke University Press, 1991), pp. 196, 334–37.

65. When the issue of "rights" was phrased in the seventeenth century (and before Hobbes) in terms of human rights, this referred back to their grounding in the classic natural law tradition, which rested on the notion of transcendental matrix. On this tradition, see the illuminating work of Richard Tuck, *Natural Rights Theories* (Cambridge: Cambridge University Press, 1979). In the transformation of natural rights theories from Hobbes via Rousseau, Kant, and Fichte to Hegel, the "natural" grounding of rights was transformed, and the term, while remaining in use, was voided of its previous philosophic content. Manfred Reidel, "Nature and Freedom in Hegel's Philosophy of Right," in Z. A. Pelczynski (ed.), *Hegel's Political Philosophy* (Cambridge: Cambridge University Press, 1971), p. 146.

66. See, for instance, Keith Tester, *Animals and Society: The Humanity of Animal Rights* (London: Routledge, 1991). For a more philosophical background to the discussion of animal rights, see James Sheehan and Morton Sosna (eds.), *The Boundaries of Humanity: Humans, Animals and Machines* (Berkeley: University of California Press, 1991), and for a controversial argument against "animal rights," see Michael Leahy, *Against Liberation: Putting Animals in Perspective* (London, Routledge, 1991).

67. Again, such a conception stood at the root of one tradition of classical natural law with its notions of *ius naturale* bound to a transcendental referent. Without such a generalized and universal other, however, any similarity with the contemporary status of the individual is lacking.

68. The use of the title of A. O. Hirshman's famous study *The Passions and the Interests* in this sentence is intentional. The inclusion of women's reproductive rights in the above category is not meant to establish a normative judgment, only to reflect the current state of polemics on this issue. For women's reproductive rights are framed, politically, not in terms of citizen's rights but in terms of the individual *qua* individual ownership of her own body. The limits of this mode of conceptualization are becoming increasingly clear with

224

the problems arising from biotechnology (IVF-GIFT of donated ova, surrogate motherhood, and artificial insemination), all of which have brought the realm of reproduction squarely into the public and civil realm. Similarly, the current controversy over clitoridectomy in France (*Revue de MAUSS*, no. 4, Deuxième trimestre 1989) indicates the futility of arguing rights in terms of personal or individual predilections. Finally, and as a good illustration of the argument I am advancing here, one may look to recent feminist attempts to articulate a "feminist theory" of "animal rights" based on affective sympathy and sentiments. Josephine Donovan, "Animal Rights and Feminist Theory," *Signs*, vol. 15, no. 2 (1990), pp. 350–75.

69. Faye Ginsburg, *Contested Lives: The Abortion Debate in an American Community* (Berkeley: University of California Press, 1989), p. 9.

70. John Gray, in *Times Literary Supplement* (London), February 1, 1991, p. 7.

71. Max Weber, *The Protestant Ethic and the Spirit of Capitalism* (New York: Scribner's, 1958), p. 182.

72. John Dunn, *The Political Theory of John Locke*, Cambridge: Harvard University Press, 1969), p. 250.

73. Interesting to note is that even in the seventeenth century New England was an extremely litigious society—one in which social conflicts were resolved by an appeal to abstract, legal formulae as opposed to the less formal, more community-oriented means. This mode of adjudicating personal disputes however, has not been characteristic of all of American society and does not hold in every place even today. We may recall here John Reed's characterization of Southerners for whom communal norms and mores maintain their saliency in the face of more abstract notions of justice represented by the State. Thus he notes: "To concede all legitimate coercion to the State would be repugnant to many Southerners, if not to most. Ultimately, individuals must have the ability—indeed may have the obligation—to settle such matters for themselves. A closer look at the South's homicide rates, perennially twice as high as the rest of the country's, bears this out. The sort of murders the South specialized in are not assaults on innocent and inoffensive citizens going about their business; they are, rather, responses to attacks on someone's person, honor, or self-esteem. They are in fact private attempts, however excessive or misguided, to redress grievances. Collective violence followed much the same pattern." This should suffice as warning to any uncritical attempts to return to principles of "community" in opposition to abstract justice as a model for the social order. For what it illustrates is the resistance of certain principles, such as honor, to abstraction and universalization (and so of their redress by the abstraction of money). As Reed goes on to stress, "when a Southerner says 'No one messes with me and gets away with it'. . . what is threatened is clearly not a lawsuit." John Reed, *One South: An Ethnic Approach to Regional Culture* (Baton Rouge: Louisiana State University Press, 1982), p. 173.

This refusal to refer certain personal matters to universal abstract principles of adjudication represents the continuing saliency of communal forms of identity, of an individualism which, however intense, is still rooted in community. For better or worse (and probably both) the face of the South has been changing over the past twenty years, as is its economic and political postion in the overall structure of American Society. As we shall see, however, in the following chapter, the types of identity that define (or defined) individual and collective existence in the American South continue to be salient in other societies, presenting very different challenges to the idea of civil society from those based on the universalism of reason studied here.

74. Max Weber, "Churches and Sects in North America," trans. and introduced by C. Loader and J. Alexander, *Sociological Theory*, vol. 1, no. 3 (1985), pp. 1–12.

75. Alexis de Tocqueville, *Democracy in America*, 2 vols. (1860, rev.) (New York: Vintage, 1945), vol. 2, p. 338.

76. *Ibid.*, p. 339.

77. *Ibid.*, p. 350.

78. Tocqueville's concern with the loss of critical reason, with the increasing identity of men "all equal and alike," was not his alone. It was a major theme throughout the nineteenth century and expressed in the fear of the "tyranny of the majority." It may be recalled that John Stuart Mill's famous tract "On Liberty" (1859) was addressed to this problem.

Of equal significance is the later, twentieth-century articulation of a similar concern with the loss of the public character of reason in the German conservative legal philosopher Carl Schmitt. Schmitt wrote *The Crises of Parliamentary Democracy* (Cambridge: MIT Press, 1988) amid the crises of the Weimar Republic (1926). In that work he was concerned with analyzing the increasing loss of the institutionalized public space (of parliament) where the workings of reason were to be actualized in classic liberal theory. His explanation of this phenomenon rested on what he saw as the abiding contradiction between liberalism and democracy. According to Schmitt, in modern mass democracies parliament had lost this representative function as the real work of legislation has moved from the public arena of public debate to the back rooms and secret chambers of committees—a modern-day reinstitution of that "Arcana rei publicie" that the original idea of parliament had sought to contain. For Schmitt the logic of this development was the contradiction between the "substantive equality" of liberalism and the "indifferent equality" of modern mass democracies based on the principle of homogeneity and identity. With the triumph of "universal [and hence indifferent] equality," the substantive inequalities of society do not disappear but simply remove to another sphere. And so, in Schmitt's analysis, the economic realm (of substantive inequality) is seen to dominate the political, which is itself devalued through the indifferent equality of mass democracy.

Though we cannot enter here into an anlaysis of Schmitt's politics, it is interesting to note that Schmitt too saw in mass democracy a threat to the principles of reason. And lest we see this as simply the thought of an ultra-conservative, we should recall that his analysis was in fact not that

226

different from that of Hannah Arendt in *The Origins of Totalitarianism*. What nevertheless distinguishes the above argument from both Schmitt and Arendt is the notion that it is less a contradiction between political principles (of liberalism and democracy) than the very progress of reason in the public sphere that brings about the devaluation of the latter.

79. Katharine Bartlett and Jean O'Barr, "The Chilly Climate on College Campuses: An Expansion of the Hate Speech Debate," *Duke Law Journal*, vol. 1990, no. 3, pp. 574–86, esp. pp. 580–81.

80. C. L. Ten, "Mill on Self-Regarding Actions," *Philosophy*, vol. 43 (1968), pp. 29–37.

81. I. Young, "Impartiality and the Civil Public," in S. Benhabib and D. Cornell (eds.), *Feminism as Critique* (Oxford: Basil Blackwell, 1987), pp. 57–76; C. Kitzinger, "The Regulation of Lesbian Identities: Liberal Humanism as an Ideology of Social Contol," in J. Shotter and K. Green (eds.), *Text of Identity* (London: Sage Publications, 1989), pp. 82–98.

82. M. Daly, *Gyn/Ecology: The Metaethics of Radical Feminism* (Boston: Beacon Press, 1978); A. Dworkin, *Intercourse* (New York: Free Press, 1987).

83. Patrick Devlin, "Morals and the Criminal Law," in D. Spitz (ed.), *On Liberty: John Stuart Mill. Annotated text. Sources and Background Criticism* (New York: Norton, 1975), p. 187.

84. *Ibid.*, p. 183.

85. Hannah Arendt. "The Public and the Private Realm," in Hannah Arendt, *The Human Condition* (Chicago: University of Chicago Press, 1958), pp. 22–78.

86. Niklas Luhmann, "The Representation of Society Within Society," *Current Sociology*, vol. 35, no. 2 (1987), pp. 101–8.

87. Stanley Rosen, *Nihilism* (New Haven: Yale University Press, 1978), pp. 206–13.

88. Arendt, "Public and Private Realm," p. 51.

89. Niklas Luhmann, "Tautology and Paradox in the Self-representation of Society," *Sociological Inquiry*, vol. 6, no. 1 (1988), pp. 226–37). The later argument is that made by Taylor in Charles Taylor, *Sources of the Self: The Making of Modern Identity* (Cambridge: Harvard University Press, 1989).

90. This theme has been taken up, in different ways by both Gunther Roth, "Charisma and the Counterculture," in G. Roth and W. Schulchter, *Max Weber's Vision of History* (Berkeley: University of California Press, 1979), pp. 119–43, and by Luhmann, "Tautology and Paradox," in the context of alternative social movements.

CHAPTER 4 Jerusalem, Budapest, Los Angeles: In Search of Civil Society

1. For a good and relatively balanced account of the Intifada, see Ze'ev Schiff and Ehud Ya'ari, *Intifada, the Palestinian Uprising: Israel's Third Front* (New York: Simon & Schuster, 1989).

Notes

2. Miklós Szabó, "Problems of Hungarian National Consciousness in the Second Half of the Twentieth Century," *Social Research*, vol. 55, no. 4 (1988), p. 699.

3. Hannah Arendt, *Origins of Totalitarianism* (New York: Harcourt Brace Jovanovich, 1973), pp. 269–79.

4. On these and similar political positions, see "Ha-Tehiya Platform: Israel Will Encourage the Emigration of Arabs from Judea, Samaria and Gaza," *Ha-Aretz*, August 31, 1988 (Hebrew); "Ha-Tehiya and Tzomet: Find the Difference," *Ha-Aretz*, September 2, 1988 (Hebrew); Kach, "A manifesto from the Kach Movement and Rabbi Meir Kahana," Jerusalem (n.d.), 1988, (Hebrew); *Moledet*, "Information Sheet #1," *Ramat HaSharon* (n.d.), 1988, (Hebrew); *Tzomet*, "Platform Principles" (n.d.), 1988 (n.p.) (Hebrew); E. Sprinzak, "Kach and Kahana: The Emergence of Jewish Quasi-Fascism," in A. Arian and M. Shamir (eds.), *The Elections in Israel* (Tel-Aviv: Ramot, 1984).

5. Important insights into this growing discourse of particularism in contemporary Israel can be found in Erik Cohen, "Ethnicity and Legitimation in Contemporary Israel," *Jerusalem Quarterly*, no. 28 (1983), pp. 111–24.

6. For more empirical and less impressionistic studies of attitudes of Jews and Arabs toward each other in contemporary Israel, see Sami Samoocha, "Minority Status and Ethnic Democracy," *Ethnic and Racial Studies*, 1990, and S. Samoocha, *Arabs and Jews in Israel*, vol. 1 (Boulder, CO: Westview Press, 1989). Vol. 2 is forthcoming, 1992.

7. A somewhat different view of political legitimation in Israel is presented by Charles Liebman and Eliezer Dov-Yehiya, "Israel's Civil Religion," *Jerusalem Quarterly*, no. 23 (1982), pp. 37–69.

8. This point has been explored by R. Coleman and L. Rainwater, *Social Standing in America: New Dimensions* (New York: Basic Books, 1978).

9. Stein Rokkan, "Dimensions of State-Formation and Nation-Building: A Possible Paradigm for Research on Variations Within Western Europe," in C. Tilly (ed.), *The Formation of Nation-States in Western Europe* (Princeton, NJ: Princeton University Press), 1975.

10. S. N. Eisenstad *et al.*, *Center Formation: Protest Movements and Class Structure in Europe and the United States* (London: Pinter Press, 1987), p. 11.

11. *Ibid.*, p. 15.

12. Otto Gierke, *Political Theory of the Middle Ages* (Boston: Beacon, 1958), p. 63.

13. Jeno Szücs, "Three Historical Regions of Europe," in Keane ed., *Civil Society and the State*, p. 307.

14. Gierke, *Political Theory*, p. 64.

15. Szücs, "Three Historical Regions," p. 319.

16. George Schöpflin, "The Political Traditions of Eastern Europe," in *Daedalus* special issue, *Eastern Europe, Central Europe, Europe*, Winter, 1990, p. 68. The following discussion owes much to Schöpflin's analysis.

17. *Ibid.*, p. 63.

18. *Ibid.*, p. 66.

19. Andrew Janos, *The Politics of Backwardness in Hungary 1825–1945* (Princeton, NJ: Princeton University Press, 1982), pp. 65–66.

20. *Ibid.*

21. Important comparative aspects of this process are explored in Perry Anderson, *Lineages of the Absolutist State* (London: New Left Books, 1974).

22. On various aspects of the state–nation relation, see L. Tivey (ed.), *The Nation-State* (Oxford: Robertson, 1980); B. Anderson, *Imagined Communities* (London: Verso, 1983); J. Breuilly, *Nationalism and the State* (Manchester: Manchester University Press, 1982).

23. Daniel Lerner, *The Passing of Traditional Societies* (New York: Free Press, 1985).

24. Anthony Smith, "State Making and Nation Building," in J. Hall (ed.), *States in History* (Oxford: Basil Blackwell, 1986), pp. 228–63.

25. Rokkan, "Dimensions of State-Formation" (*supra*, n. 9), p. 572.

26. Janos, *Politics of Backwardness*, p. 69.

27. Schöpflin, "Political Traditions," p. 71.

28. György Csepeli, "Competing Patterns of National Identity in Post-Communist Hungary," *Media, Culture and Society*, vol. 13 (1991), p. 328.

29. Ivo Banac, "Political Change and National Diversity," *Daedalus, Eastern Europe . . .* (*supra*, n. 16), pp. 141–60.

30. Colin Crouch, "Sharing Public Space: States and Organized Interests in Western Europe," in Hall, *States in History*, p. 180.

31. Charles Taylor, "Modes of Civil Society," *Public Culture*, vol. 3, no. 1 (Fall 1990), pp. 95–118.

32. Vincent Wright, "Fragmentation and Cohesion in the Nation-State, France 1870–1871," paper presented at the European Science Foundation Seminar on "The Construction and Reconstructing of Centre–Periphery Relation in Europe," Jerusalem, June 1984. See also his *The Government and Politics of France* (New York: Holmes & Meier, 1978).

33. José Casanova, "Church, State, Nation and Civil Society in Spain and Poland," in S. Arjoumand (ed.), *The Political Dimensions of Religion* (Berkeley: University of California Press, forthcoming). See also *idem*, "The Deprivatization of Catholicism: Church, Nation, Civil Society and the State in Poland," paper presented at a conference on "Religion and Marxism in Eastern Europe," University of Michigan, Ann Arbor, October 1988.

34. Crouch, "Sharing Public Space," p. 182.

35. On the use of this term, see Charles Maier, " 'Fictitious bonds . . . of Wealth and Law' on the Theory and Practice of Interest Representation," in S. Berger (ed.), *Organizing Interests in Western Europe* (Cambridge: Cambridge University Press, 1981).

36. George Schöpflin,"Obstacles to Liberalism in Post-Communist Polities," *Eastern Europe Politics and Society*, vol. 5, no. 1 (1991), pp. 189–194.

37. Taylor, "Modes of Civil Society," p. 15.

38. Anthony Giddens, *The Consequences of Modernity* (Stanford, CA: Stanford University Press, 1990), p. 97.

39. See, for example, K. Deutch, "Social Mobilization and Political Development," *American Political Science Review*, vol. 55, 1961; S. N. Eisenstadt, *Modernization, Protest and Change*, (Englewood Cliffs, NJ: Prentice Hall, 1966); S. Huntingon, *Political Order and Changing Societies* (New Haven: Yale University Press, 1968); A. Inkeles and D. Smith, *Becoming Modern: Individual Change in Six Developing Countries* (Cambridge: Harvard University Press, 1974); Talcott Parsons, *Societies: Evolutionary and Comparative Perspectives* (Englewood Cliffs, NJ: Prentice Hall, 1966).

40. In addition to his *Consequences of Modernity*, see Anthony Giddens, *Modernity and Self-Identity* (Stanford, CA: Stanford University Press, 1991).

41. Niklas Luhmann, "Familiarity, Confidence, Trust: Problems and Alternatives," in D. Gambetta (ed.), *Trust: Making and Breaking Cooperative Relations* (Oxford: Basil Blackwell, 1988), pp. 94–107.

42. S. N. Eisenstadt and L. Roniger, *Patrons, Clients and Friends* (Cambridge: Cambridge University Press, 1984), esp. pp. 1–42.

43. Edward Shils, "The Virtues of Civil Society," in manuscript, p. 35.

44. I am grateful to Elemér Hankiss for allowing me access to the as yet unpublished sources of these data and to the staff of TARKI for their technical assistance.

45. It is of some interest to note that the Hungarian responses to the 1982 questions regarding confidence in those institutions listed here were not too dissimilar from their West European neighbors. Comparative West European data for 1990 were not available, but one would assume that they did not register the same change as noted in the Hungarian case.

46. These data were originally published in Elemér Hankiss, "Between Two Worlds," *Research Review on Hungarian Social Sciences Granted by the Government: Changing Values of Hungarian Society* (Budapest, 1989), p. 43.

47. Not surprisingly this severely mediated expression of trust on the broader societal level echoes the findings of Almond and Verba's now classic data in *The Civic Culture* (New York: Sage, 1989). There, the levels of trust in the United States and Britain were higher than in Germany, Italy, and Mexico. Though Almond and Verba were studying the stability of democratic regimes and not democracy *per se* (or the preconditions for its existence), the results of both studies corroborate one another. In Germany, it should be noted, the level of social trust rose from 1948 to 1959—the year of the study—and again from 1959 to the 1970s, as the polity stabilized. See Daniel Conradt, "Changing German Political Culture," in G. Almond and S. Verba, *The Civil Culture Revisited* (New York: Sage, 1989), pp. 212–72.

48. Csepeli, "Competing Patterns" (*supra*, n. 28), pp. 334–38.

49. *Ibid.*, p. 336.

50. Andras Sajo, "Rights Awareness in Hungary," in *Changing Values in Hungarian Society* (*supra*, n. 28), pp. 27–38.

51. *Ibid.*, p. 50.

52. G. Csepeli and A. Örkeny, *The Twilight of State Socialism* (London: Pinter Press, forthcoming).

53. An ironic example of this is the recent dismissal of György Suranyi as President of the Hungarian National Bank in November 1991. Popular appraisal of the move saw it as a reaction to Suranyi's signing of the Democratic Charter—a public manifesto calling for greater real democracy in the workings of Hungarian government and society—in October 1991. The government seemed to admit as much when it explained the need for someone more "loyal" to the government in such a post. However, sources in the French Embassy knew of Suranyi's impending dismissal more than a month before the Charter was signed and released. These sources explained it as a result of Suranyi's Jewish background. There is, however, no way of knowing if this is the case or not.

54. David Stark, "Privatization in Hungary: From Plan to Market or from Plan to Clan," in *Eastern Europe Politics and Society*, vol. 4, no. 3 (1990), pp. 351–92.

55. A good example of this was to be found in the recent meeting of small entrepreneurs, trade unionists, and political advisers to discuss the political implications of the current economic situation (November 1991). The advisers presented the entrepreneurs with three "watchwords": "Quality, Solidarity, and Political Rationality." The businessmen responded by rejecting the idea of solidarity as inimical to their profession, and all attempts to explain its importance, especially in the current state of the Hungarian economy, with 25 percent of the population below the poverty line, with unemployment expected at 10 percent by the end of the year, and with another 25 percent of the population living on the edge of poverty, were met with deaf ears. We may note in passing that "political rationality" without "solidarity" is but an instance of that instrumental or strategic action discussed in the previous chapter, that is, an articulation of citizenship without its social concomitants. Source: personal communication from Professor Laszlo Boros, Faculty of State and Law Sciences, Eötvös Lórand University, Budapest.

56. The "death contract" was an arrangement whereby someone (or a couple) rented a room in an elderly person's flat, paying the owner a monthly sum with the written agreement that they would inherit the apartment upon the death of the elderly owner. Its name originates from the diametrically opposed interests of the parties to the contract and the renters' interest in the hasty demise of the owner.

57. Keith Hart, "Kinship, Contract and Trust: The Economic Organization of Migrants in an African City Slum," in Gambetta, *Trust* (*supra*, n. 41), pp. 176–93.

231

Notes

58. Insightful criticism of this position has been offered by John Dunn, "Elusive Community: The Political Theory of Charles Taylor," in John Dunn, *Interpreting Political Responsibility* (Princeton, NJ: Princeton University Press, 1990), pp.179–92.

59. Giddens, *Consequences of Modernity*, (*supra*, n. 38).

60. *Ibid.*, p. 115.

61. Jürgen Habermas, "Justice and Solidarity: On the Discussion Concerning State '6,' " in M. Kelly (ed.), *Hermeneutics and Critical Theory in Ethics and Politics* (Cambridge: MIT Press, 1990), pp. 32–51.

62. The following discussion owes much to Karl Olivercrona, *Law as Fact* (London: Steve, 1971), pp. 175–90.

63. A. I. Meldøn, *Rights and Persons* (Berkeley: University of California Press, 1980), p. 9.

64. *Ibid.*, p. 43.

65. Leo Strauss, *Natural Right and History* (Chicago: University of Chicago Press, 1973), p. 131.

66. Adam Ferguson *An Essay on the History of Civil Society*, 5th ed. (London, 1782), p. 364.

67. *Ibid.*, p. 454.

68. Claus Offe, "Challenging the Boundaries of Institutional Politics: Social Movements Since the 1960s," in Charles Maier (ed.), *Changing Boundaries of the Political* (Chicago: University of Chicago Press, 1987), p. 102, n. 3.

69. I am using the term here in its "generic" sense. The "foulard," however, can refer to anything from a complete covering of the body to a more moderate long-sleeved dress and head scarf (the "hejab" proper), to a face-revealing scarf. In France, the struggle was over schoolchildren wearing the latter. On these distinctions, see Sondra-Hale, "The Politics of Gender in the Middle East," in S. Morgan (ed.), *Gender and Anthropology* (Washington, DC: American Anthropological Association, 1989), pp. 246–67.

70. Andrew Arato, "Civil Society Against the State; Poland 1980–1981," *Telos*, vol. 47 (1981); Andrew Arato and Jean Cohen, "Social Movements, Civil Society and the Problem of Sovereignty," *Praxis International*, vol. 4, no. 3; Jean Cohen, "Strategy or Identity: New Theoretical Paradigms and Contemporary Social Movements," *Social Research*, vol. 52, no. 4 (1985), pp. 663–716; Jean Cohen and Andrw Arato, *Civil Society and Social Theory*, (Cambridge: MIT Press, 1992).

71. Cohen, "Strategy or Identity."

72. *Ibid.*, p. 100.

73. *Ibid.*, p. 92.

74. Seyla Benhabib, *Critique, Norm and Utopia* (New York: Columbia University Press, 1986), p. 279.

75. Carole Gould, "On the Conception of Common Interest: Between Procedure

232

and Substance," in Kelly, *Hermeneutics* (*supra*, no. 61), p. 264; Habermas, "Justice and Solidarity," p. 35.

76. Benhabib, *Critique*, p. 322.

77. Interestingly enough, some of the problems implied by this generalization of citizenship and solidarity are to be found in Schmitt's idea of indifferent equality noted in Chapter 3. See note 78 of that chapter.

78. Cornelius Castoriadis, "Value, Equality, Justice, Politics: From Marx to Aristotle and from Aristotle to Ourselves," in Cornelius Castoriadis, *Crossroads in the Labyrinth* (London: Harvester Press, 1984), pp. 260–340.

79. On the distinction, within the different universalist positions, between, most relevantly, Rawls and Habermas, see Seyla Benhabib, "In the Shadow of Aristotle and Hegel," In Kelly, *Hermeneutics*, pp. 1–31.

80. Habermas, "Justice and Solidarity," pp. 41–46.

81. *Ibid.*, pp. 47–48.

82. Benhabib, *Critique*, pp. 340–43.

83. Criticisms of Parsons's work are by now legion and have led to the unfortunate failure to appreciate the power and importance of his sociological vision. One of the most recent criticisms, which does not fall into this trap, is Jurgen Habermas, *The Theory of Communicative Action*, vol. 2 (Boston: Beacon Press, 1987), pp. 199–300.

84. Michael Waltzer, "The Idea of Civil Society," *Dissent*, Spring 1991, p. 303.

85. *Ibid.* These examples are taken from a longer list, which describes civil society as "more like union organizing than political mobilization, more like teaching in a school than arguing in an assembly . . . more like working in an ethnic alliance or feminist support group than canvassing for an election." However, the fundamental social and political differences (not to mention the difference in physical safety and economic security) between volunteer work in a hospital and union organizing are nowhere addressed. Moreover, working in an ethnic alliance or a feminist support group, as I understand it, would be eventually to effect changes in legislation, which in the present system of government in the United States can be achieved through only political (and party) activity. The failure of the Equal Rights Amendment should make this need for the political articulation of "civil society" clear. If they are to have any lasting meaning in the lives of men and women, these types of civic organizations must in the end be oriented toward the political implementation of their demands for (what is essentially a) greater extension of the principles of citizenship (to include minorities and women more fully). Positing them in any other terms is to relegate them to a passive rule, providing succor and comfort to those not fully protected by the reigning terms of citizenship. This is clearly not what is meant in the current demand for a return to civil society. These and similar contradictions are, however, inherent in the very idea of civil society as soon as we go beyond the polemical use of the term and attempt to give it concrete meaning.

Concluding Remarks on Civil Society

1. Robert Dahl, *Polyarchy: Participation and Opposition* (New Haven: Yale University Press, 1971); Arendt Lijphart, *Democracies: Patterns of Majoritarian and Consensual Government in Twenty-one Countries* (New Haven: Yale University Press, 1984).

2. Talcott Parsons, *The Structure of Social Action*, vol. 2. (New York: Free Press, 1968), pp. 658–72.

3. William Morris, *A Dream of John Ball* (London: Longmans, Green, 1938), pp. 39–40.

Index

Index

236

237

Index

238

Index